The Crusades

This German-to-English translation of a highly successful book is a clear, approachable, student-friendly introduction to the history of the crusades.

With a long chronological span, from the eleventh to the late fifteenth century, and with a wide geographical coverage of the whole of Europe and some of the Middle East, *The Crusades* is clear, concise and more wide-ranging than most single-volume works. Chapters on the military orders and the history of the crusader states illustrate the impact of the crusades on both sides of the Mediterranean Sea. The book takes both Christian and Islamic viewpoints into account and sets the crusades in the larger framework of European expansion in the Middle Ages.

Providing a fine overview of the crusade movement and taking recent scholarship into account, Nikolas Jaspert uses boxes, case studies, marginal directions and chronologies to make each chapter very easy to follow. Students at all university levels will find *The Crusades* to be an invaluable historical resource.

Nikolas Jaspert is a Professor of Medieval History at Ruhr-Universität Bochum. He is widely published on the crusades, on the history of the Iberian Peninsula and on religious orders in the Middle Ages.

Phyllis G. Jestice is Associate Professor of Medieval and Early Modern European History at the University of Southern Mississippi. She is a highly experienced translator and has recently completed translations of Whalen Lai and Michael von Brück's *Christianity and Buddhism* (2001) and Gerd Althoff's *Otto III* (2003).

The Crusades

Nikolas Jaspert

Translated by Phyllis G. Jestice

Routledge
Taylor & Francis Group

NEW YORK AND LONDON

'The Crusades' first published in 2003 in German as 'Die Kreuzzüge'
by Wissenschaftliche Buchgesellschaft, Hindenburgstraße 40, D-64295 Darmstadt, Germany

English translation as 'The Crusades' first published 2006 in the USA and Canada by Routledge
270 Madison Avenue, New York NY 10016

Simultaneously published in the UK
by Routledge
2 Park Square, Milton Park, Abingdon, Oxon, OX14 4RN

Routledge is an imprint of the Taylor and Francis Group, an informa business

'Die Kreuzzüge' © 2003 by Wissenschaftliche Buchgesellschaft, Darmstadt
'The Crusades' English translation © 2006 Routledge

Typeset in Sabon by
RefineCatch Limited, Bungay, Suffolk
Printed and bound in Great Britain
by Antony Rowe Ltd, Chippenham, Wiltshire

Library of Congress Cataloging in Publication Data
Jaspert, Nikolas.
[Kreuzzüge. English]
The crusades / Nikolas Jaspert; translated by Phyllis Jestice.
p. cm
Includes bibliographical references and index.
1. Crusades.   I. Title.
D157.J37   2006
909.07 – dc22
2006006741

British Library Cataloguing in Publication Data
A catalogue record for this book is available from the British Library

ISBN10: 0–415–35967–8 (hbk)
ISBN10: 0–415–35968–6 (pbk)
ISBN10: 0–203–00757–3 (ebk)

ISBN13: 978–0–415–35967–2 (hbk)
ISBN13: 978–0–415–35968–9 (pbk)
ISBN13: 978–0–203–00757–0 (ebk)

Contents

Contents

Author's foreword

The crusades—or, more properly, what has been associated with them whether justly or unjustly—have again become a central issue in recent years. The term "crusade" is threatened with loss of clear definition in public discourse, which is reason enough to issue a survey of the crusades. Not that there aren't already rigorously scholarly presentations. But for a long time there has been no short, scholarly handbook in the German language. The work that lies before you differs in approach from some earlier studies. It approaches the theme systematically as well as chronologically and also gives considerable emphasis to placing the phenomenon in the context of the history of ideas. In each chapter a primary source is showcased that elucidates the essential features of the section and invites the reader to deeper exploration of the text.

This book lays no claim to be an original contribution to the decades-long debate over what constitutes a crusade. For a long time there have been two schools of thought on this question: the first regards only expeditions to the Near East as crusades, while the second advocates a broader definition that also encompasses other regions. This volume follows a middle path. "Crusades" are understood to be all campaigns against enemies of the faith and the Church that were called by popes and included the promise of an indulgence. Thus the book includes expeditions against heretics, Muslims on the Iberian Peninsula, and the pagans of the Baltic region. But it also takes into account the fact that contemporaries regarded campaigns in the Near East as superior in importance, and it was these expeditions that had the power to mobilize people to the greatest degree. For that reason, the Near Eastern crusades receive special emphasis in this overview.

Besides the scholars whose research findings have been brought together into this synthesis, many others have contributed to the creation of this volume. Dr Nikolaus Bötcher, Professor Marie-Luise Favreau-Lilie, Matthias Maser, Dr Johannes Pahlitzsch, Dr Andreas Rüther, and Professor Dieter Weiß read all or parts of the manuscript. Their suggestions improved the work immeasurably, for which I give sincere thanks to them all. I am also indebted to Mr René Hurtienne for his help in producing the maps as well as Ms Gabriele Gumbel and Verena Artz for their painstaking editorial work. Special thanks are due to my students at Erlangen, who tested out the book's suitability for university use and, with their suggestions for cuts, helped with the most difficult task of all—staying within the prescribed bounds of 160 printed pages. The book's shortcomings remain—as always—the author's responsibility. This volume is dedicated to my wife Montse and our sons David, Lucas, and Theo.

Nikolas Jaspert
Erlangen
Fall, 2002

Author's foreword to the English edition

At first sight, it might seem surprising that a German book on the Crusades be translated into English, given the considerable amount of excellent syntheses on the subject published in the United States of America and in the United Kingdom in the course of the last two decades. Indeed, this volume is greatly indebted to these works and to British historiography of the Crusades in general. However, I hope the reader will find sufficient other academic strands and schools of thought to justify the effort that went into rendering this study into English.

My thanks go to Alan Murray for his part in bringing about this translation, to the efficient crew at Routledge, particularly to Philippa Grand and Eve Setch, and most of all to Phyllis G. Jestice for the immense work she put into converting the original version into readable and comprehensible English.

Since the first edition of this book appeared in Germany in 2003, I have received some observations and suggestions, which I have been able to incorporate into this edition; I would like to express my gratitude to Hans Eberhard Mayer as "pars pro toto" for his helpful remarks and annotations. Like all overviews, this synopsis rests on the work and toil of many men and women whose research has here been condensed into a slim volume; the concise bibliography at the end of this book can only give a vague idea how much it is indebted to them.

This English translation is dedicated to my mother, Shirley Anne Jaspert (née Benson), who has had such a major part in providing me with the cultural and linguistic background relevant to my work.

Nikolas Jaspert
Bochum
May, 2006

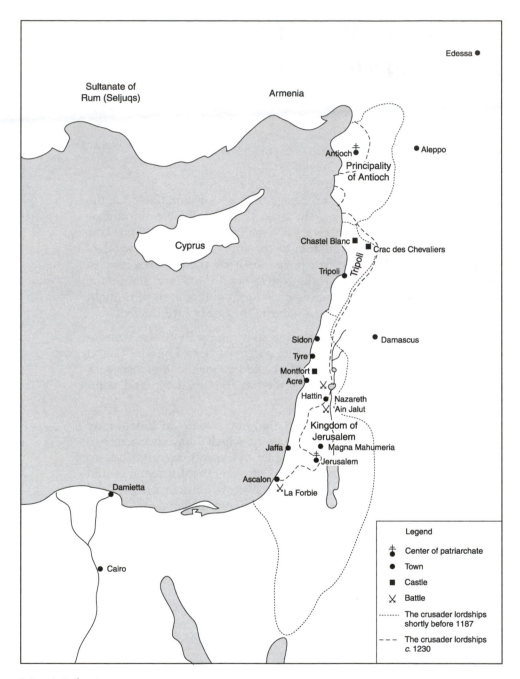

Edessa

Sultanate of
Rum (Seljuqs)

Armenia

Aleppo

Antioch

Principality
of Antioch

Cyprus

Chastel Blanc

Crac des Chevaliers

Tripoli

Damascus

Sidon

Tyre

Montfort

Acre

Hattin

Nazareth

'Ain Jalut

Kingdom of
Jerusalem

Jaffa

Magna Mahumeria

Jerusalem

Ascalon

La Forbie

Damietta

Cairo

Legend

‡ Center of patriarchate

● Town

■ Castle

✕ Battle

········· The crusader lordships
shortly before 1187

------ The crusader lordships
c. 1230

Map 1 Palestine

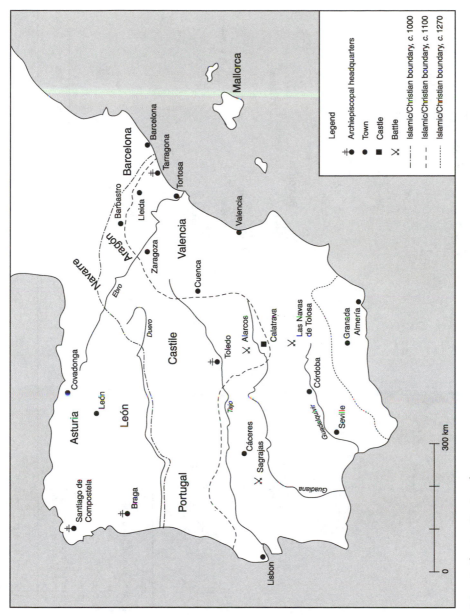

Map 2 Iberian Peninsula

Legend

⊕● Archiepiscopal headquarters
● Town
■ Castle
✕ Battle

---- Islamic/Christian boundary, *c.* 1000
--- Islamic/Christian boundary, *c.* 1100
···· Islamic/Christian boundary, *c.* 1270

Mallorca

Barcelona
Barcelona
Tarragona
Tortosa
Barbastro
Lleida
Aragón
Zaragoza
Valencia
Valencia
Cuenca
Navarre
Ebro

Covadonga
Asturia
León
León
Duero
Castile
Toledo
Alarcos
Calatrava
Las Navas
de Tolosa
Granada
Almería
Tajo
Córdoba
Guadalquivir
Seville
Santiago de
Compostela
Braga
Portugal
Cáceres
Sagrajas
Guadiana
Lisbon

300 km

0

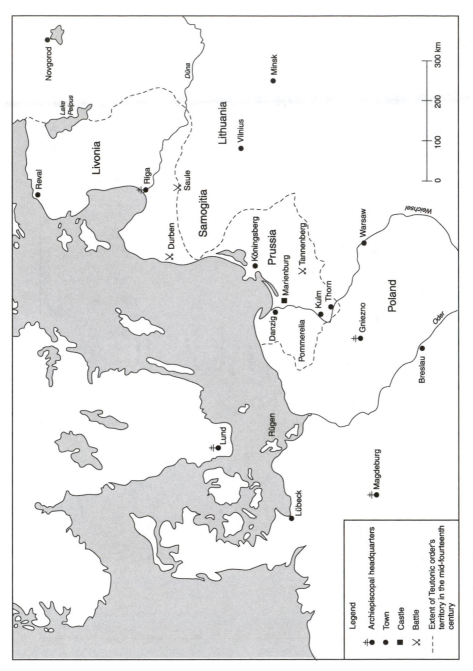

Map 3 Northern Europe

1

The background

Christendom, Islam, and the pagan lands in the late eleventh century

The Christian world in c. 1095

In the late eleventh century most people in Europe belonged to large religious groupings—Christianity, Islam, or Judaism. Their living environment was much more circumscribed, however. Among Christians, membership in a family or a parish was a much stronger tie for people than were larger organizational units. Concepts like "Europe" or "the West" were insignificant. Likewise, the geographical horizons of almost all people of the time were limited. Ancient concepts of space were only adopted in educated, clerical circles and were symbolically presented in the form of world maps (*mappae mundi*). The view of the world that appears in these maps was usually based on theology, myth, and historical understanding. Normally they took the form of the so-called T-O map, following ancient authors and Christian authorities: the continents of Europe, Asia, and Africa were divided from each other by a T created by the Mediterranean on one side and the Don, Nile, or Red Sea on the other. The ocean encircled all three land masses, forming an O. Such portrayals had little to do with political and cultural realities. For, in strong contrast to the neat world-view of these *mappae mundi*, neither Christian nor Islamic lands were unified in the late eleventh century.

Christendom consisted of two distinct regions, the Greek East and the Latin West, with their ecclesiastical centers in Constantinople and Rome. They were linguistically, culturally, and ritually divided. In the West, the old Carolingian Empire was only a distant (although frequently invoked) memory. This Frankish-ruled empire, which had reached from the Pyrenees to the Elbe, had reached its height under Charlemagne (768–814) and his son Louis the Pious (814–40). But in the course of the tenth century it had divided more or less into two realms— West Francia, from which France later developed, and East Francia, which in the tenth and eleventh centuries developed into the Roman-German Empire. The majority of the later crusaders came from regions that had been part of the Carolingian Empire, although some contingents came from non-Frankish territories such as England or Hungary. Probably those concerned were barely aware of such historical traditions. For Muslims or Greek Christians, however, the western crusaders appeared as a single community, and were identified by a single label. Thus, in Muslim and Greek sources, the Latin Christians figure as "Franks" (Arab. *Ifranǰ* or Gk. φράνγοι).

One of the elements shared by all western lands was a common liturgical language, Latin. The structure of Latin had been fixed in the course of the ninth century by the so-called Carolingian Renaissance. It was employed by the Church and served as a language for education and law, co-existing with contemporary vernaculars. Latin Europe also shared comparable political and social structures, especially what modern scholars have given the name "feudalism." This term is used to describe a legal relationship in which a vassal was granted use of a landed estate (a fief), in return for which he was obligated to perform services for the granter. Since on receiving the grant the vassal also swore an oath of loyalty (homage), feudalism developed hierarchical systems of dependence. This system had far-reaching consequences for the military class of knights, with important ramifications for the crusades. Europe was considerably more diversified when it came to economic development. After a great demographic and economic depression in the early Middle Ages there was a general increase in population that favored the development of urbanized regions along the Rhine, in Flanders, and especially in Italy. Merchants from the large port cities of Italy, like Amalfi, Pisa, Genoa, or Venice, had begun scouting out a way over the sea to the most important economic centers of the eleventh century. They made contact with Constantinople and the Muslim East, and trade brought considerable wealth both to the individual merchants and to their native regions.

In East Francia the rulers had been able to resume the Carolingian tradition of claiming the imperial title. This, along with the ability to appoint their own candidates to bishoprics and archbishoprics (a powerful element for control), had led to a strengthening of the realm under the Ottonian and Salian dynasties. However, the Salian kings also had to confront the might of regional powers, especially the dukes of Saxony, Lower Lotharingia, Bavaria, or Swabia, who enjoyed a great deal of independence. The princes of West Francia were even more independent. This region, stretching from Catalonia in the west to Flanders in the east, accepted the nominal overlordship of the Capetians who bore the title "king of the Franks." But in reality the Capetians only ruled over a small territory between Orléans and the Oise valley. The rest of the kingdom was in the hands of dukes and counts, some of whom, like the dukes of Aquitaine, Gascony, and Normandy, or the counts of Flanders, Barcelona, Toulouse, Anjou, and Champagne, disposed of far-reaching power and resources. Besides the older European kingdoms, including León in the Iberian Peninsula and England (conquered by the Normans in 1066), the rulers of several younger countries—Castile, Aragon, Denmark, Hungary, Poland, and Bohemia—had won the royal title in the course of the tenth and eleventh centuries. The rise of the Normans in Sicily was particularly spectacular. In the middle of the eleventh century, under the leadership of Robert Guiscard (d. 1085), the Normans succeeded in conquering Sicily from the Muslims and parts of southern Italy from the Byzantine Empire. Robert, who won the title of duke in 1053, established a strictly ruled kingdom that moved aggressively against the other states of the eastern Mediterranean, both Byzantine and Islamic.

The Byzantine Empire flourished particularly from the mid-ninth century to the middle of the eleventh. The reasons for this lay not only with the decline of the Muslim Abbasid caliphate but also with the evangelization and eventual subjugation of the Bulgars (completed in the 1020s). Under the rulers of the "Macedonian dynasty" (867–1056)—or their talented generals—Byzantium successfully reconquered several territories that it had lost. At the beginning of the eleventh century what is called the "Middle Byzantine Empire" reached a high point of power and magnificence under Emperor Basil II (976–1025). It was a period of great literary and artistic accomplishment, during which the Byzantine court far outshone the centers of Latin Christianity. The Greek Church was no longer torn by theological controversy, and the conversion of the Russians and Bulgars brought it to an even higher sense of its own high purpose.

The controversy of 1054

The Greek Orthodox Church was not the only one to be consolidated in the mid-eleventh century. In the course of the so-called Gregorian Reform (see "The reform papacy," p. 23) the Roman papacy developed a new, marked self-understanding that proved to be incompatible with Byzantine interests. This became clear in a conflict between the patriarch of Constantinople and a papal emissary in 1054, during which each of the two churchmen excommunicated the other. The conflict was over theological and liturgical issues, and also important questions of Church politics. One major issue was the *filioque*—whether the western addition of the phrase "and the son" to the Nicene Creed's definition of the Holy Spirit was an improper understanding of the doctrine of the Trinity. Other issues included the use of leavened or unleavened bread in the celebration of the eucharist, the Roman pope's claim to ascendancy, and the balance of power in southern Italy. It only gradually became apparent how deep the divide had become that severed East and West, so the term "schism" is misleading as a description of the confrontation of 1054. A gradual alienation in regard to liturgical and ritual practices, but especially the sack of Constantinople by western Christians in 1204, had a much greater impact on relations between the two branches of Christianity than the dispute of 1054. Still, it must be admitted that since 1054 the two Churches have never been reunited in a lasting way.

In the mid-eleventh century deep-seated weaknesses became obvious in the Byzantine Empire. The Empire's old military organization was not well-suited for the large-scale offensive wars of the Macedonian dynasty, so the emperors relied increasingly on mercenaries. This was also an ultimately unsuccessful attempt to create a counterweight to the territorial nobility's waxing power. It became clear after the death of Emperor Basil II that the great nobles were indeed a danger to the Empire, for it was rocked by a large number of attempted coups. On top of that, a new threat appeared in mid-century on its eastern border: the Muslim Seljuq Turks. At first the Byzantines had paid little attention to this Turkish dynasty, which rose to power in the first half of the eleventh century. That changed in 1071, though, when the Byzantine army was annihilated at the Battle of Manzikert in eastern Anatolia and Emperor Romanos IV (1068–71) himself was taken captive. The Byzantine state plunged into a profound crisis. The years after 1071 were punctuated by usurpations and changes of ruler until General Alexios Comnenos (1081–1118) seized power in 1081. Alexios was successful in the Aegean and the Balkans and neutralized the danger of a Norman invasion through diplomacy. But he could not break the power of either the Normans or the Seljuqs. Although he successfully won back some coastal districts of Asia Minor, southern Italy and the heartland of Anatolia had been lost forever.

The Islamic world in c. 1095

The Islamic calendar begins with the flight of Muhammad from Mecca to Medina (the Hijra) in the year 622 of the Common Era. Within a few years of that event, immediately after the Prophet's death in 632, the Arabic-Islamic expansion began. In an unparalleled series of victories the Muslims first conquered the Arabian Peninsula, and then continued expanding until by the early eighth century they had seized control of Syria, Iraq, Iran, all of North Africa, and even the Iberian Peninsula. In the process, the ruling systems of those areas were destroyed, whether they were successor states of the Roman Empire, such as the Byzantine administrations in North Africa and the Near East, or the Sassanian Empire of Persia. With the final conquest of Sicily at the beginning of the tenth century, the Mediterranean lay almost completely under Muslim control.

The Islamic expansion

Before the First Crusade began, the Islamic world, the Dar al-Islam, stretched from the Strait of Gibraltar in the west to India in the east. Trade connections criss-crossed this vast territory and extended far beyond it. Thanks to this widespread trade network, as well as Arabic acceptance and further development of ancient geographical texts, educated Muslims had a broad understanding of the world. Political realities were less coherent. In this period the old political unity under Arabic leadership was fracturing badly, not least because of Turkish incursions from Central Asia. Increasingly, Dar al-Islam had broken apart into three great political spheres. In the East the Seljuqs ruled. Their empire stretched from the Aral Sea and modern Kazakhstan to the Red Sea, with their center of power in Iran. On their western border was the region of Fatimid rule. This Arabic dynasty claimed descent from Fatima, a daughter of Muhammad; in the age of the crusades their capital was Cairo in Egypt. In the early eleventh century their territory still included the entire Maghreb, but by 1100 it was reduced to little

---

Shi'ites and Sunnis

The Muslim world was by no means united on issues of faith. Most Muslims were Sunni. For them, the Qur'an, supplemented by the good example of the Prophet was (and is) the guiding principle of conduct. The Sunnis regarded members of the Abbasid dynasty as the true caliphs—leaders of the Muslim community. Nonetheless, at the end of the eleventh century the Abbasid caliphs were completely under the political domination of the powerful Seljuq sultans. At a lower level a number of regional rulers (sultans and emirs) were nominally answerable to the caliph's central authority. The other great branch of Islam was the Shi'a. The Shi'ites regarded 'Ali, the cousin and son-in-law of Muhammad who was killed in 661, as the first legitimate caliph. They believed that 'Ali's successors (the imams), infallible and guided by God, should lead the Islamic community. The leaders of the Shi'a in the eleventh century were the Fatimids of Egypt. They had a rival caliph and claimed that by rights he should have sole control of the Islamic community (Arab. *umma*). Within the Shi'ite branch of the faith there were still further sects, whose members proclaimed different imams to be the last known successor of 'Ali and thus the highest religious authority. The division between the mutually exclusive Sunni and Shi'ite branches of Islam was of much greater importance within the Islamic world than conflict against Christians. Not only did the two branches refute each other in the pages of Muslim historians (who sometimes engaged in polemics against Muslims in the other camp); they also affected the conduct of Muslims in face of the threat of Christianity.

more than modern Egypt and Tunisia. Still further west lay the lands of the Almoravids, a Berber dynasty who in the late eleventh century had united the Islamic parts of the Iberian Peninsula, as well as the western Maghreb, under their leadership.

Political upheavals on the eve of the crusades

The years before the calling of the First Crusade were an uneasy period for the Islamic world. In 1094 the Fatimid caliph al-Mustansir (1036–94), who had ruled for nearly sixty years, died. Shortly before him the wazir Badr al-Gameli, the de facto ruler of the Fatimid caliphate, had also passed away. A struggle for the throne ensued, from which Badr al-Gameli's son, al-Afdal (d. 1121), eventually emerged victorious. A new branch of Shi'ite Islam, the sect of the Assassins, also came into existence in this time of crisis. The members of this new sect regarded the murdered son of al-Mustansir as the rightful caliph. They established a power base in northwestern Iran and also won ascendancy in northern Syria. From this latter base the Assassins became an important factor in the balance of power in the Near East. They were strictly organized under their chief and carried out assassinations against both Sunni and Christian rulers.

The Seljuq Empire also suffered upheavals. After their victory over the Byzantines at Manzikert (1071), the Seljuqs had successfully brought

Anatolia and the eastern regions of the Byzantine Empire under their control. But in the year 1092 Sultan Malik-shah (1072–92) died. Until 1105, his sons fought each other over who would succeed their father in a struggle centered on Iran, so their attention was focused away from the Syrian and Palestinian theater of war. In the western part of the Seljuq realm, in Anatolia, the local Seljuq leader Qilij Arslan (1092–1107) was able to create an independent state that soon developed into the Sultanate of Iconium (Konya), also known as the Sultanate of Rum. At the time of the First Crusade, Qilij Arslan was too deeply engaged in consolidating his rule and monitoring the power struggles in Iran to mix seriously in the events of the Levant (the eastern littoral of the Mediterranean). In that period, the nomadic Turks of Anatolia were also politically fragmented and only able to unite to take common action for short periods. Finally, in 1094 the Sunni caliph in Baghdad also died. Thus, between 1092 and 1094 *all* the major Muslim spiritual, military, and political figures of the Near East had died. Add to that the unrest among Muslims as the five-hundredth anniversary of the Hijra approached, bearing with it widespread apocalyptic prophecies, and it is clear that the Christians could not have chosen a better time to invade Palestine.

What were conditions like in Palestine on the eve of the crusades and why was Jerusalem important to Muslims? For Muslims, as for Jews and Christians, Jerusalem was and is a "holy city." This is immediately obvious in the name by which the city has been best known in Islam since the tenth century: *al-Quds* (the holy place). Jerusalem's significance for Islam rests on several grounds. One major reason for its importance is that Jesus, a major prophet of Islam, had died there. More importantly, though, al-Quds was the objective of Muhammad's "Night Journey" (Arab. *isrâ'*). In a single night the Prophet is said to have been transported to Jerusalem and back to Mecca, a testimony to his supernatural qualities and special closeness to God. Besides this, according to a folkloric Life of Muhammad that is still popular today, Muhammad is supposed to have climbed a heavenly ladder (Arab. *mi'râdsch*) whose foot rested in Jerusalem, and to have brought back from heaven the obligation for all Muslims to pray five times daily. Two major buildings were constructed in Jerusalem to commemorate these events. The Dome of the Rock on the Temple Mount (Arab. *al-Haram as-Sarif*), erected around the footprint Muhammad left embedded in rock when he ascended to heaven, was completed in 691/92. Near it stands the al-Aqsa Mosque, the goal of the Night Journey. Finally, Muslims believe that the Last Judgment will take place at Jerusalem. It is not surprising, therefore, that this holy city has a particularly intense religious meaning for Muslims, and is their third greatest pilgrimage center after Mecca and Medina.

In the early eleventh century significant religious persecution by Muslims included Christians among its victims, and in the course of the

The importance of Jerusalem for Islam

persecution the Church of the Holy Sepulcher in Jerusalem was destroyed. The political and religious environment changed rapidly, though, and the church was soon restored. Not long after this event Islamic texts, like the travel account of the Spanish scholar Ibn al-ʿArabi, reported that Palestine and especially Jerusalem was a center of Islamic, Jewish, and Christian learning. The various Christian minorities (see "Natives: Muslims, Jews, eastern Christians," p. 95) had to pay a head tax (Arab. *jizya*) and did not have legal equality with Muslims, but they enjoyed freedom of religion and were able to welcome pilgrims from both the Latin and the Greek Orthodox world. There is, however, evidence that in the years 1093/94, right before the proclamation of the crusade, the travel of pilgrims from the Levantine coastal cities to Jerusalem was obstructed.

At this time the Holy City was in the hands of the Seljuqs, who had conquered the entire inland area of Palestine, including Jerusalem, in 1071. This placed the city in a border zone between Fatimid and Seljuq rule, which had a negative impact on the region's security. The decline of a strong centralized Seljuq administration allowed the formation of smaller emirates in Syria after 1092, such as Aleppo and Damascus. On the coast, which boasted rich seaports with international trade connections (e.g., Tripoli, Acre, and Tyre), local officials took over except where the cities remained under Fatimid control. There are interesting similarities between Syria/Palestine and Italy in this period: both regions were fragmented, highly developed economically, and similarly dismissive of central authority. Only in southern Palestine did the Fatimids manage to fill the power vacuum before the coming of the crusaders: in 1098 the wazir al-Afdal took Jerusalem in a lightning strike. It is possible that he wanted to prevent the city's conquest by the crusaders in this way; he seems to have been informed about their approach. He may also have turned a blind eye on the invaders because he hoped to create a Christian buffer zone against the Seljuqs. Whatever the considerations that had led to al-Afdal's attack, Jerusalem had now become a useful advance post of Fatimid power in the interior of Palestine.

Contacts and conflicts between Christianity and other religions

Christianity's view of Islam

The historic volatility of relations between Christianity and Islam is based not on their differences but on their similarity. They are rival religions or competing cultures that developed from the same traditions and, consequently, despite some correspondences, emphasize their points of difference. Still, until the First Crusade the Latin Christians had little exposure to the teachings of Islam. The Eastern Christian author John of Damascus (d. *c.* 750) had already formulated charges against Muhammad in his Book of Heresies; they were adopted and repeated by Greek authors. These stereotypical judgments, propagated to the end of the Middle Ages, were grounded on the basic assumptions that Islam is a heretical offshoot of Christianity and that the Qur'an is not God's work. Muhammad was regarded as a charlatan of dubious life and morals, who enjoyed a godlike veneration. But the success of Islam obliged the Byzantines to reconcile these victories with this negative image. Consequently the Muslims, despite their supposedly erroneous beliefs, were seen as instruments or scourges of God, through whom the Lord was punishing the faithful for their failings. Muhammad was even seen as a forerunner of the Antichrist and thus integrated into the history of salvation. Latin Christianity's judgment of Islam was for the most part based on similar interpretations and distortions.

Co-existing with this ideological interpretation of Islam there were regular, if low-level, political and economic contacts between the Christian and Muslim cultural spheres. Charlemagne (768–814) and Otto the Great (936–73) had established diplomatic contacts with the Abbasid court in Baghdad and the Umayyad court in Córdoba respectively, and the Byzantine emperors maintained a considerably greater level of interchange with the Muslim states of the Near East. Some western merchants were also familiar with the Islamic world in the later eleventh century. Indeed, traders from the South Italian port of Amalfi visited Jerusalem so regularly that they established a hospice there to care for their fellow Christians. Ships from other Italian cities also made their way to eastern markets and goods. Christians who made a pilgrimage to the Holy Land came into direct contact with Islam and may have formed their own view of the religion. But altogether it was only a few people who established such contacts, and the sources give little evidence of personal experiences.

Views of the other

Until the end of the eleventh century, the Christian view of Islam was still for the most part characterized by ignorance, distortion, and simple disinterest. But conversely, no coherent, widespread anti-Islamic ideology existed in the Latin West before the crusade that could have won over massive support for a military conflict with the Islamic polities. The state of affairs was about the same in the Muslim world. From the latter's perspective, despite its unquestionable significance as a forerunner religion to Islam, Christianity had little to offer. Christianity had been surpassed and Islam had assumed its place; Muhammad was the last and greatest of all prophets. In terms of culture, the Christian world could not compete with the great centers of the East. In Islam's geographical world-view before the crusades, the Christian states stood very much on the periphery rather than at the center of their concerns. To be sure, Muslims had regular contact with the Greek and eastern Christians under their rule, but there was only minimal interest in or knowledge of the content of their religion.

In the Islamic world before the arrival of the crusaders, the most important sources of information about Latin Christendom were travel accounts, geographical works, and accounts by people who had spent time in the Latin West as prisoners, diplomats, merchants, or pilgrims. The most influential paradigm in creating attitudes about Europeans was a division of the world and its peoples established by Ptolemy (second century CE). Following this model, Muslims regarded the European Christians as living in damp, cold regions that affected both their temperament and their character. They thought the Christians were stupid, raw, and unwashed. This view was specific to the Latin Christians of Europe, not those of the East or indeed the Muslims' Christian subjects, with whom they were in permanent contact. In the Muslim lands, eastern Christians had played an important role in the seventh and eighth centuries in the development of Islamic culture, especially as transmitters of ancient knowledge. The various Christian churches in the Near East will be discussed later (see "The eastern Churches," p. 110); here I merely wish to emphasize that they enjoyed a special status as "religions of the Book," and were protected wards of the state (*dhimmi*). Christian subjects could practice their religion as long as they did so unpretentiously and did not try to convert Muslims, although they were certainly second-class citizens and endured both legal and tax discrimination. These disadvantages do not appear to have been so unbearable as to make many Christians leave. Only in exceptional circumstances, such as the time of Caliph al-Hakim or the period of Almohad ascendancy in Spain (1130–1269), did Christians suffer real persecution. Indeed, to those eastern Christian confessions persecuted as heretics by the Greek Church, Muslim assumption of power could appear as a significant improvement in their lot, because the Byzantine rulers had been harsher in their treatment of religious minorities— whether Christian, Jewish, or Muslim—than were the Muslims. The new Muslim rulers were therefore regarded less as enemies than as religious rivals. This attitude also became clear in Byzantine–Muslim conflicts before the crusades.

The eastern Mediterranean (the Levant) was a battleground between Muslims and Christians long before the First Crusade. This fact is easily forgotten, since traditional protagonists gave way to new ones at the time of the crusades. On one side the Turkish Seljuqs took the place of the Arabic Abbasids, while on the other Latin Christians assumed the role of the Greek Orthodox Christians. But there was in fact a long tradition of Byzantine–Muslim conflict. After over two centuries on the defensive, Byzantium had undertaken a policy of intensive expansionism under three emperors of the Macedonian dynasty—Nikephoros II Phokas (963–69), John I Tzimiskes (969–76), and Basil II (976–1025). They succeeded in reconquering considerable territory in Asia Minor in campaigns that brought the Byzantines as far as the gates of Jerusalem. These conflicts were even briefly presented in a religious context, in the reigns of Nikephoros Phokas and John Tzimiskes. But the patriarch of Constantinople refused to recognize those who fell in battle against Muslims as martyrs, for the idea of a holy war, fought with weapons and pleasing to God, was still too alien to Orthodox Christendom.

Internal problems after the death of Basil II and the rise of the Seljuqs in the mid-eleventh century put a stop to further Byzantine expansion. Even worse, the Byzantines lost Anatolia and northern Syria to Seljuq attacks, and in 1085 the major city of Antioch also fell to them. Qilij Arslan I, the semi-independent sultan from a cadet branch of the Seljuq dynasty, was able to secure his own rule after the death of Sultan Malikshah (d. 1092) and consolidated his territory into the Sultanate of Rum. Like Qilij Arslan, the Danishmendids, a Turkish dynasty whose power base lay in northern Anatolia, were able to subdue Greek-populated regions, thus putting the Byzantines under even more pressure. The nomadic Cumans, a Turkish people, also menaced the borders of the Empire.

To what extent did reports of these events reach the West? The northern Syrians, both Greek Christians and Arabic Muslims, had much to suffer under their new Seljuq masters, but the change of regime was especially harsh for the Greeks who had ruled so long. They may have carried a dark view of the situation to Constantinople. From there, reports made their way to the West, where they augmented accounts by Latin Christians from the Holy City, who were undoubtedly influenced by the volatile political relationships in Palestine.

In his attempts to counter the Seljuq offensive, Emperor Alexios I Comnenos relied on mercenaries from western Europe (Flemings, Germans, Englishmen), after conflict with the southern Italian Normans and the disloyalty of some mercenaries at the Battle of Manzikert made traditional dependence on Norman contingents appear ill-advised. In face of renewed Islamic threats, Alexios sent an embassy to the West. The Greeks arrived at Piacenza in Italy in March 1095 while a Church council was meeting. Among other matters, the Byzantines asked for military support against their Muslim enemies. Although there is no evidence of an immediate reaction by those assembled, the view that it was necessary to go to the aid of fellow Christians who were under attack was an important argument in the papal call for a crusade six months later.

> ### Help for the Byzantines: an Argument used by Urban II
> ### (according to Fulcher of Chartres)
>
> From Fulcher of Chartres, *Historia Hierosolymitana*, ed. Heinrich Hagenmeyer
> (Book 1, III.2), pp. 132–33.
>
> For it is necessary to hurry immediately to give aid to your foe-surrounded breth-
> ren in the East, as they have already often begged you to do. As has already been
> reported to most of you, the Turks, a race of Persians, have penetrated as far as
> the Mediterranean, to the so-called Arm of St. George [the Bosporus] . . . If you let
> them continue to do as they like, the faithful will be overrun still further.

Conflicts between Muslims and Latin Christians before 1095

In western Europe, too, there was a long history of conflict with Muslims. During the eighth and ninth centuries, the Muslims had conquered the Iberian Peninsula, Sicily, and parts of southern Italy. Moreover, as recently as the second half of the tenth century Muslims had raided southern France and the Alpine passes from fortified camps on the coast of Provence. In the following decades these advance posts were destroyed, but still Spain and Sicily constituted two additional regions of Christian–Muslim conflict apart from the border zone in Asia Minor. The conflicts in both areas were virulent and long-lasting.

In 711 the Muslim Berbers had defeated a Christian army near Gibraltar and in a short time had subjugated nearly the entire Iberian Peninsula. From the mid-eighth century on, though, Christians had again and again raided the Muslim-controlled south, and gradually they turned their efforts toward conquest. Long periods of peace alternated with military conflict. After the fall of the caliphate of Córdoba (1031), the conflict gained noticeably in intensity. Under King Alfonso VI of Castile (1072–1109) the Christians expanded their area of control far to the south, and in 1085 they captured Toledo, the old Visigothic capital. Almost immediately, though, the Christians suffered a severe reverse. The Almoravids, a Berber dynasty, were called to come to the assistance of the hard-pressed Iberian Muslims, and they inflicted a devastating defeat on a Christian army at Sagrajas in 1086 (see "Resistance and *Reconquista*," p. 115). In short, the eleventh century saw a serious deterioration in Muslim–Christian relations on the peninsula.

The situation of Christians in the third Christian–Muslim border region—Sicily and southern Italy—was less violent. The Normans had established their rule in this region in the second half of the eleventh century, although many Muslims still remained and attack from the south was always a looming threat. It was in part against this danger that a Pisan fleet undertook an expedition against Mahdia (al-Mahdiya), a Tunisian city, in 1087. On that occasion, the Christians who were killed in battle against the Muslims were explicitly celebrated as martyrs.

Thus in 1095 Islam was by no means advancing everywhere. It had lost ground to the Christians in western Europe, both in Spain and in Sicily, at the same time that it was on the offensive in Asia Minor under Seljuq leadership. The dividing line was in general the Mediterranean, the northern coast of which was mostly Christian, while the southern coast was largely Muslim. A nascent Christian expansion movement was also becoming apparent in other regions. The Viking invasions, which had repeatedly sowed destruction since the end of the eighth century, ended with King Harald Hardraada's failed attack on England in the year 1066. The nomadic Hungarians (Magyars) had been integrated into Latin Christendom in the second half of the tenth century. The most important religious boundary of Christendom remained northeast Europe, the home of the pagan Slavs. Even here Latin Christianity was expanding at the end of the eleventh century. Granted, the great Slav rebellion of 983 had destroyed many of the Carolingian and early Ottonian conquests and foundations. But since the mid-eleventh century lost territory east of the Elbe and Saale was reconquered and destroyed churches were rebuilt. Settlers flocked to the newly won regions, while the indigenous population was evangelized. To the east of the Roman-German Empire, Christian states and native Church hierarchies were created (Poland, Bohemia, and Hungary), although pagan peoples still remained in northeastern Europe at the turn of the century. The west Slavic Pomeranians and Wends, along with the Finno-Ugric and Baltic tribes (Prussians, Livonians, Estonians, Lithuanians, and Finns) formed a great arc of illiterate polytheistic peoples that reached from the border of Saxony to the polar circle. Their lands, just like the Iberian Peninsula and the Near East, would become an objective of crusader armies.

The European expansion

The crusades assumed particular importance in society against the backdrop of the three most important developments that have been described here—the fragmentation of political authority in Europe, the progressive confessional division of Christianity in the eleventh century, and finally the expansion movements in both East and West. They were able to surmount the barriers that stood in the way of the great expansion movement and therefore presented a clear, common goal to the warriors of Latin Europe. Contemporaries already testified to the crusades' characteristic of reaching beyond established borders. This new form of military undertaking was fundamental in giving coherence to the medieval expansion of Europe.

Holy war, knighthood, and pilgrimage

Just war—holy war

Both contemporaries and later commentators rightly regarded the First Crusade as something new. Still, it rested on a series of foundations that often reached far into the past. Many were of a political and social

The idea of crusade

nature or belonged in the realm of medieval world-view and piety. They will be presented in the next two chapters. This is all the more necessary because these basic elements of medieval life and belief are unfamiliar to most modern people. These preconditions amalgamated into what one can characterize as the "idea of the crusade"—the spiritual and ideological foundations for the expeditions. These ideas worked with varying strength on the crusading movement, affecting its intellectual leaders as well as individual crusaders. A great number of sources shed light on this issue; the extant documents and letters of crusaders do so with particular vividness.

Today, as in earlier ages, the crusades bring to the forefront the question: is it possible for a war to be just? At its most essential level, Christianity is founded on the peaceful action of Christ. Therefore, unlike Islam—whose prophet was both a spiritual and a military leader—Christianity has to resolve a great contradiction: it must reconcile the Bible's contradictory pronouncements about war. The Fifth Commandment ("Thou shalt not kill"), or Jesus' words of peace, contradicts many passages of the Old Testament especially. The official adoption of Christianity in the Roman Empire at the beginning of the fourth century had no effect on the pursuit of war. Some Christian warriors were even "raised to the honor of the altar," i.e., canonized. In the early Middle Ages bishops assumed many of the functions of city governors and as such had to guarantee the security of their domains, with armed force if necessary. The resulting theological challenge found varying responses from members of the clergy. They laid the foundations for a theology that served to legitimate war in the Middle Ages and beyond—the theory of just war. The essential components of this theory were established by St Augustine of Hippo.

The memory of Augustine's theoretical edifice was largely lost during the early Middle Ages. What became decisive in judging the justice of a war was not the warrior's inner attitude and the goal of his actions, but simply the outcome. Therefore, penances were imposed when a soldier killed, even if his victim was a violator of the peace or an aggressor, and the killer acted at the command of a legitimate ruler. The concept of the just war was not even reactivated at the time of the Muslim expansion in the seventh century, when the situation was in fact one of defense against external aggression.

Augustine (354–430) was bishop of Hippo Regius in modern Algeria. He laid out the conditions for just war in his treatise "Against Faustus the Manichaean" in the course of controversy with the Manichaean heresy, which repudiated war as a whole and also the Old Testament. In Augustine's view, four conditions must exist for a war to be just: the war must be declared by a legitimate authority, there must be a lawful reason for war, any other possible resolution must have failed, and the war must be waged with moderation. Augustine made a clear division between the inner attitude of those fighting and their deeds, so that the legitimacy of the *casus belli* became essential in judging whether a war was just or unjust. He made a further definition: the warrior acts justly who defends country, law, or customs against aggression, who enforces a judicial decision, or who fights to regain stolen property. Besides this, wars are also just that are waged by a secular power acting with God's authority (*Deo auctoritate*). But war should not serve as a means of conversion or annihilation of pagans. At its core, the Augustinian doctrine of just war (*bellum iustum*) was thus leveled against internal enemies of the faith. The restoration of disturbed peace was the most urgent goal, so the bishop understood waging war as an act of love for one's neighbor. Christian behavior was thus also guaranteed in war. Augustine had created a new ethics for warfare.

Since the ninth century Christianity had faced new threats. Attacks by pagan Vikings, Magyars, and Slavs in the north and east, as well as Muslims in the south and west, allowed Augustine's theory to reappear in both the Greek East and the Latin West. In individual cases it is possible to detect a theological discussion of the nature of war—for example in Spain, which the Muslims conquered in the early eighth century. In the mountainous north (Asturias and León) Christians defended their independence and gradually began to expand their kingdoms southward. They could point out that this was a case of recovering formerly Christian land, in which co-religionists still lived. This alone was sufficient cause to declare their war just. In Asturia and León the claim was explicitly formulated that the Christians were pursuing a just war; in other words a war with God's authority (*Deo auctoritate*) against an aggressive new religion. Chroniclers of the ninth through eleventh centuries portray the conflict not merely as a just but indeed as a holy war. Christian rulers were likened to Old Testament kings and the Spanish Christians to the people of God, contributing to the realization of God's plan for salvation.

There is no evidence that the crusaders adopted this concept directly. But for most contemporary Christians the crusades, too, were more than simply just wars, more than defense against an unjust attack. They too were sanctified, because in them warriors fought not only for the defense of Christianity but directly for God. The crusader fulfilled God's will, was God's tool. Participation in such a war was thus no longer

Holy war on the Iberian Peninsula

something that had to be repented, but an activity that would bring salvation; it was possible in this context even to speak of "meritorious warfare." The war in itself was not regarded as holy, but it had a salvific effect on the participants. This interpretation, which can be found in contemporary documents and letters, was promoted by the reawakening of interest in Augustinian writings in the late eleventh and early twelfth centuries and was an important element of the idea of crusade. Increasingly, motivation or inner intention moved to the center of interest, and the significance of actual deeds receded to the background. The crusade in itself was already justified, but it was the inner attitude of participants that made their actions meritorious before God. Pope Urban II (1088–99) specifically underscored this point by offering the crusading indulgence (see "Penance and indulgence," p. 30) only to those who "from devotion alone" (*sola devotione*) set out for the Holy Land.

War as an act of love or revenge Last but not least, war against the Muslims was especially approved because it was waged on behalf of threatened fellow Christians. This was an extension—in this case a military extension—of the concept of love for one's neighbor. Were not the Greek Christians threatened by Muslims? Did they not fear for life and limb? Emissaries from the East and the pope both presented this menace vividly before the eyes of contemporaries. Some propagators of the crusade understood the struggle (however strange this view may seem to modern people) as an act of love in the sense of the biblical commandment, even if this way of thinking may not have been central to the ordinary crusader. A different concept, derived from Augustine's idea of just war, fits contemporary values better: the idea of war to punish violators of the peace. In the eleventh century this theme was especially relevant for a sector of society that was still in its adolescence—the knightly class.

Knighthood

Without question the high Middle Ages was an era of open violence, violence that grew to even greater intensity during the eleventh century. It is not only the narrative texts that convey this impression. In the administration of justice corporal punishment in the form of mutilation and death became common instead of earlier forms of penance—both a response to and an expression of the general militarization of society. This endemic violence had much to do with the lack of an effective central power. The division and dissolution of the Carolingian Empire left a power vacuum, especially in West Francia, that was increasingly filled by local powers. These depended on the support of mounted warriors, known as *milites* (knights). This was their epoch, the period in which they rose to power. Some of these knights were rising free peasants; many others descended from officials. They carried out administrative tasks in the name of their lord and sometimes enjoyed considerable independence. A visible sign of their freedom of action was the knightly castles that had sprung up in ever-greater numbers since the beginning of the eleventh century. Scholars debate whether lesser military lords succeeded in garnering a quasi-autonomous position, whether they accomplished this transformation by force, and whether this development was connected to the subjugation of the formerly free peasantry. It cannot be contested, however, that the rise of this military elite was a major characteristic of the time and should be seen as an essential precondition to the crusades.

What differentiated the knight from other fighting men was his horse and his appropriate weapons. The primary weapon was the lance, which was clamped under the arm and gave the knight enormous penetrating power when he attacked on horseback. This effectiveness was still greater if the knights attacked in a closed formation, which also contributed to the group solidarity of the knightly class. The fundamental ideals of this warrior culture were military toughness, prowess, and honor. The young knighthood of the eleventh century had not yet acquired the heraldry, ceremonies, and courtly rules of conduct of later ages. These ideals were to affect the crusades of the late twelfth century and later undertakings. The knight's armaments—from the longsword, chain mail, and spurs, to the costliest element, the horse—were extraordinarily expensive. Such equipment could only be financed if the knight had considerable means. This usually took the form of a landed estate. It is estimated that an armored rider needed the income of twelve peasant holdings to pay for a horse and weapons.

The knight's armor

A knight in the field also required support, whether servants (who wielded weapons when needed) or infantry. Therefore a knight did not stand alone, but was the center of a small military unit. Indeed, the nobles and knights constituted only about 10–15 per cent of the larger crusade armies, because the papal call caught the imagination of men and women of all classes. But the *milites* rightly regarded themselves as the most important military element, and others concurred. It was these knights whom Urban II had in mind when he made his call for a crusade. And it was to their mental world that Urban and later popes appealed in a wide variety of ways. The only problem was how the Church was to convince this new, warlike group to enter the service of Christ and the Church.

In some parts of Europe the weakness of central, especially judicial, authorities and the power of the knights led to great abuses. Armed men carried out their feuds by military means, at the cost of defenseless clerics, women, or peasants. To counteract this abuse, the churchmen of Aquitaine, Burgundy, and northern France began to propagate the idea of the Peace of God (*pax Dei*) toward the end of the tenth century. This movement was intended to protect the defenseless groups in the population. The Peace was elaborated by establishing certain periods in which fighting was not allowed (the Truce of God, *Treuga Dei*). Whoever

The Peace of God

broke the Peace or the Truce was not merely excommunicated; in some regions secular lords also guaranteed enforcement. They swore on holy relics, with the Church's blessing, that they would take arms against peace-breakers. Although the Peace of God movement came to an end in these regions in *c.* 1030, the idea of a general or temporally specific peace and harmony league (*pax et concordia*) was adopted in other regions, such as Flanders, Lotharingia, and the Rhineland, directly before the First Crusade. At this time, too, the pope and the emperor repeatedly called for the establishment of peace.

Thus, the Peace of God and the *Treuga Dei* were attractive for a number of reasons. These movements gave local authorities a widely approved means to restrain the knights' arbitrariness. In our context, though, it is more important that the Peace and Truce movements strengthened the Church's position, because churchmen played an important role in securing peace. These initiatives also helped to condemn warfare against fellow Christians as "unchristian" in the ideological world of the knights. The solemn, religious oath taken is evidence of this development, and also points the way toward the crusades. It is noteworthy that Urban II proclaimed a Peace of God at the same time that he called the crusade, extending protection to crusaders' property. To be sure, the Peace of God was not as important for the development of the idea of the crusade as some other concepts and phenomena of the time. But, as an ecclesiastical call on knights to pledge themselves by oath to secure the well-being of fellow Christians with strength of arms, it was undoubtedly one of the steps toward the crusade movement.

Chansons de geste Some of the men who became crusaders had already fought Muslims with ecclesiastical approval before the Council of Clermont, whether in the Byzantine Empire, Sicily, or Spain. The conflict in Spain in particular had become the subject of literature. A series of epic tales, known as *chansons de geste*, developed around the figure of Charlemagne. These stories, orally transmitted at first, tell of the emperor's legendary campaign against the Spanish Muslims. Eleventh- and twelfth-century nobles, especially in France, loved these stories, and the *chansons de geste* played a role in validating and sanctioning the struggle against Islam. However, those involved saw a qualitative difference between the conflicts on the Iberian Peninsula and the expedition to the Near East. The call issued at Clermont came to the knights as something completely new and unique. Certainly this rests on the fact that Pope Urban and later crusade preachers managed to connect in a way never seen before with the fundamental values of this sector of the population. But what marked the knights' world-view? Why did they take arms on the Lord's behalf?

Economic interests Some historians have underlined economic motives for taking the cross. The financial expenditure for a participant in a crusade was enormous. It is estimated that going on a crusade could well have cost five or six times a knight's annual income. To raise the money, knights alienated land and sought loans in large quantities; the extant documents bear witness to the extreme measures they took to scrape together the necessary funds. It is modern scholars, rather than contemporaries, who have regarded this as a form of investment, made with expectation of rich future rewards. The crusaders—even the first, but more so the participants in later crusades—knew that a crusade was an extremely dangerous venture, from which a great many would never return. Indeed, contemporary crusader wills testify to a realistic evaluation of the peril, and, according to later chronicles, Urban II had already warned of this:

The call to martyrdom in Urban II's sermon at the Council of Clermont

From *Gesta francorum et aliorum Hierusolimitanorum* (I, 1), pp. 2–3.

The Lord Pope also said: "Brothers, you will have to suffer greatly for the name of Christ—pain, poverty, nakedness, persecutions, privations, sickness, hunger, thirst, and more—for Christ said to his disciples: 'You must suffer much in my name' [Acts 9:16] . . ."

Only a few of those who managed to reach Palestine and survived the fighting settled there. So it seems very unlikely that the prospect of new lands could have been a motivation for these warriors. Recent research has also presented evidence, contradicting older assumptions, that economic factors such as hope for new territory or demographic pressure were hardly important for the crusaders. Only after the establishment of the Latin lordships in Palestine was there a colonization movement worthy of mention. It should not, however, be equated with the crusades themselves. There were of course some exceptions. Several of the leaders of the First Crusade, such as Tancred (*c.* 1076–1112), Bohemund of Tarento (1050/58–1111), or Baldwin of Boulogne (1058–1118), seem to have aimed at acquiring rule over new territories. Still, the extant wills of crusaders testify that the knights in general were well aware of the danger and did not anticipate winning great riches. What inspired most knights and other fighting men to take part in a crusade was not external reward but internal motivations and ideals.

The Christianization of the knightly class had already been set into motion with the Peace of God movement. Subsequently, the idea of the *miles Christi*, which had originally referred to clerics who strove in God's service with spiritual weapons, was transferred to armed men. As such a knight of Christ, the crusader set out for the fight, perhaps to avenge his Lord and certainly to regain his Lord's inheritance, the *hereditas Christi*. These ideas were closely tied up with the knightly world. They can be pieced together from the letters and documents of

---

The knightly ethos

Three factors weighted especially heavily on knightly families: family consciousness, feudalism, and concepts of honor. It was with these issues that the papal appeals struck a deep resonance, not just Urban II's call but those of his successors. According to the chronicler Baldric of Dol, Urban described the Greek Christians under Muslim threat as blood relatives—relatives who had to be aided. Later, in the twelfth and thirteenth centuries, this argument could be understood more directly, since some knights did in fact have relatives who had emigrated to the "crusader states," or ancestors who had already won fame as crusaders. Echoes of noble feudal values can also be seen in the calls for crusades, which refer repeatedly to the loss of threatened territories. Baldric of Dol tells that Urban II made this point with reference to the eastern Christians. Later, the theologian and crusade preacher Bernard of Clairvaux (1090–1153) hammered the feudal point home much more forcefully when he characterized Palestine as the Lord's own property, the *patrimonium Christi*. Christ, he argued, had been driven from his property, and every knight of Christ is in duty bound to fight to restore his highest overlord to what is rightfully his. Such an argument appealed not only to feudal obligations but also caught knights by their sense of honor. After all, Christ himself had been dishonored by the loss of his homeland, and the living conditions of threatened or subjugated fellow Christians were also described in images that particularly invoked the dishonor involved. Members of the knightly class can have had no doubt that the crusades were vindicated on these grounds.

---

participants in the First Crusade; the chroniclers, popes, and crusade preachers of the twelfth century declared them openly. There were also further, equally strong motivations to make the decision to go on crusade, motivations that aimed both at this life and at the life to come. The most important of these was pilgrimage.

Pilgrimage

One of the reasons why pilgrimage played a special role in religious life was the saints' ability to petition God, to intervene on behalf of individuals. Concern for salvation and personal sinfulness thus relied heavily on the cult of saints and pilgrimage. The relics of some saints (bones or body parts) attracted pilgrims from far beyond local or regional borders. A net of pilgrimage centers arose in Christian Europe, with a number of major shrines. Three places above all acquired a Europe-wide significance: Rome, Santiago de Compostela on the Iberian Peninsula, and Jerusalem. Rome was appealing especially as the center of the papacy, the site where many Christians were martyred, and above all as the final resting place of the leading apostles Peter and Paul. Compostela was distinguished by the relics honored there of St James the Greater, the son of Zebedee. The pilgrimage there could also provide a special form of purification for participants, thanks to the simple fact that it was a long journey for most pilgrims—the penitential journey itself was, as it were, a substantial part of the goal. One could certainly say the same of Jerusalem. Besides, Palestine was directly linked to the Christian history of salvation like no other area. The land itself was holy, and was normally spoken of as the *loca sancta*, the holy places.

The idea of purifying and sanctifying oneself by visiting such a *locus sanctus* is older than Christianity. In Judaism, longing for Jerusalem finds its most heartfelt expression in the Passover prayer "Next year in Jerusalem," but also manifests itself in the concrete form of pilgrimages to the Holy Land. It was and still is the dream of many Jews to make this holy earth their final resting place. This idea was also strong in late antique Christianity. Many Christians not only visited Palestine but stayed there and ended their days in the Lord's land. The Church father Jerome (347/48–419/20), for example, settled in Palestine himself and also helped promote the idea. Others were content to see the holy places and then return home, bringing objects back, not as souvenirs but as venerated, salvation-bringing relics. Places as well as holy people could pass on their special power, their *virtus* or *eulogia*, to "secondary relics"—objects that touched them—which explains the spread of blessed keepsakes such as water from the Jordan or holy oil.

During the high Middle Ages the legal aspects of pilgrimage came to be regulated. The *peregrinus* swore a special oath and was placed under the particular protection of both the Church and secular officials. His goods and family were protected during his absence; debts were frozen. As evidence of their status, both male and female pilgrims wore a special badge. Not surprisingly, false pilgrims sometimes abused this special position. It is also clear that some people made pilgrimages for other reasons besides spiritual malaise and concern for their salvation. Love of adventure, curiosity, or desire to combine economic or political interests with a pilgrimage could all lead a person to set out.

Already in Late Antiquity pilgrimage traffic between Europe and Palestine was active. Egeria, a fourth-century pilgrim who probably came from Spain, wrote a detailed account of her journey. Many similar works followed, some written as tour guides for other pilgrims, others as personal accounts of experiences. Whether or not a pilgrim could make the long journey to the Near East depended fundamentally on the political conditions of the lands that had to be traversed, as well as in Palestine itself. At first the Islamic conquest put a stop to pilgrimage, but the situation was normalized in the course of the eighth and ninth centuries. The Byzantine emperors' military successes in the tenth century had a salutary effect on the Christian Jerusalem pilgrimage. True, they were not able to take the Holy City itself, but the road from Constantinople to Syria came under Byzantine supervision, and further west relations with the Fatimids were good enough to make the final stage of the journey to

Jerusalem-centered piety

21

Jerusalem quite easy. Around the middle of the eleventh century, perhaps inspired by the millennium of Christ's passion, there is evidence of record numbers of western pilgrimages to the Holy Land (see "The Great Pilgrimage of 1064," following).

Difficulties of pilgrimage

This upsurge of western pilgrimage suffered a check with the Seljuq invasion. Far-reaching Muslim control of Asia Minor and the political fragmentation of the region hindered the journey by land, and the sea route to Palestine was both dangerous and exorbitantly expensive. What's more, neither Fatimid nor Seljuq rulers were in a position to control Palestine effectively, so pilgrims were repeatedly in danger of falling prey to robbers. But despite all difficulties, the stream of pilgrims to the Holy Land continued. It is probably right to assume that if a crusader setting out for the Holy Land had had any prior contact at all with the Islamic world, it was more likely to have been as a pilgrim than as a fighter. Pope Urban II, according to the chroniclers, referred to this fact in his sermon at Clermont, when he commented that many members of the audience had themselves made a pilgrimage to the Holy Land, or knew someone who had.

The Great Pilgrimage of 1064

The Great Pilgrimage of 1064, led by Bishop Gunter of Bamberg and other high German dignitaries, is famous because of its sheer magnitude. Supposedly more than 7,000 pilgrims took part. Contemporary sources like the annals of Niederaltaich and Lampert of Hersefeld's (before 1028–after 1081) chronicle report the difficulties encountered on the long road through Hungary, the Byzantine Empire, and Syria. Robbers, swindlers, and highwaymen all preyed on the pilgrims—who ended up defending themselves. However, such instances of self-defense were most unusual and were caused by the particular circumstances of the journey. The sources explicitly stress that most of the pilgrims (as was the basic rule) traveled unarmed to the East. The 1064 pilgrimage was also exceptional in its size. Still, the chronicles and tales of this event give a good impression of the general trials a pilgrim faced on the road. They also show how conflicts could arise due to intercultural misunderstanding. Even though the number of participants in the Great Pilgrimage of 1064 may be exaggerated, they express the tendency of the age to travel—in large groups—to the Holy Land.

Urban II also emphasized Jerusalem's special dignity as a pilgrimage center. He described the desecration and defilement of the holy places in drastic terms in order to motivate his audience. As a result, many crusaders regarded the essence of their undertaking as a campaign to free the most important of all shrines, the tomb of Christ. We should not underrate the role that veneration and longing for Jerusalem played in inspiring participants, as crusaders' letters and documents eloquently testify. Independently of the question of whether or not Urban II's main goal was support for the threatened Christians in the East, for many participants in the first and later crusades their personal goal was Jerusalem. They went to "free" Jerusalem, to protect her, or to win her back again, depending on the current political situation.

The close relation between pilgrimage and crusade can be discerned in terminology. For a long time there was no clear distinction between the two journeys: both crusaders and pilgrims were called *peregrini*, and *iter* (road, march, journey), *expeditio* (expedition), or even *peregrinatio* (pilgrimage) were the standard terms used to describe the crusade. It was only in the thirteenth century that the Old French *croiserie* came into use, whereas the specific term *crucesignatus* for a crusader can be found at the end of the twelfth century; the word *cruciata* only appeared in the late Middle Ages and Renaissance. Both pilgrimage and fighting on God's behalf brought the individual salvation and purification. This affinity also becomes apparent in legal contexts and external symbolism. Both pilgrims and crusaders swore an oath, a voluntary and solemn promise to God. Through this oath they temporarily entered the clerical state, with all the moral duties this entailed, and were consequently subject to canon law. To make their special status visible, both pilgrims and crusaders wore the sign of the cross.

Pilgrimage and crusade: similarities in law and terminology

Although pilgrimage was so important for the rise of the crusades, fundamental differences between pilgrims and crusaders make it impossible to equate the two despite their similarities. The special attraction that a crusade had for laypeople, especially fighting men, was that it promised salvation through battle. The pilgrim, on the contrary, was expected to be unarmed, even though this rule was not always obeyed in the face of danger. The crusader armies, on the contrary, were *intended* for military purposes. Armed strife as an act of expiation, as a means of personal purification, as a tool of God—this was indeed something new.

Papacy, piety, and indulgence

The reform papacy

The papacy was a decisive element in the creation of the crusades, among other reasons because crusades were initiated by formal papal proclamation. The most famous of these is Urban II's sermon at Clermont on November 27, 1095. In his exhortation the pope referred to many of the "preconditions" for the crusades, which the following pages will consider from the modern historical perspective. Pope Urban's speech touched on attitudes, wishes, and fears that were already widespread in the populace. His call is reported in four very different versions, which will be examined in greater detail in the next chapter.

Urban II

Urban II (1035–99) was born to a noble family of Champagne. Before his elevation to the see of St Peter he had been prior of the famous Benedictine reform monastery of Cluny in Burgundy. As such, he was perfectly familiar with the knightly noble world to which Cluny maintained such close ties and from which he himself came. He had played an active part in the Investiture Contest, working as papal legate in France and Germany to strengthen the papal presence beyond Italy. At the time of the First Crusade he still had to face the opposition of an anti-pope, the imperial candidate Clement III (d. 1100). Even though Urban did not live to hear of the success of the undertaking he had called into life—he died on July 29, 1099, before word of Jerusalem's fall to the Christians could reach him—his name remains inextricably linked with the First Crusade. His manifold other activities are rarely remembered, such as his efforts from 1089 on to reach a settlement with Byzantium (with which he found a *modus vivendi* despite ongoing theological disagreement), and his efforts for the cause of Church reform, etc.

Papacy and war in the eleventh century

How could the pope—and through him a peace-preaching Church—advocate armed warfare? Ever since the fourth century the Christian Church had been an integral part of the Roman Empire. This had led to a certain identification between spiritual and secular rule. Later, in the Carolingian era, Christendom expanded thanks to war with and evangelization of the pagans, a process fully abetted by the clergy. The earliest testimony of popes proclaiming that those who fell in defense of the Roman Church were martyrs comes from the ninth century. Two centuries later, Christendom reached a new stage in this development.

In the first half of the eleventh century the Roman Church was still far from being the world-wide corporation it became in later times. In some regions of Latin Christendom, such as Bohemia or parts of the Iberian Peninsula, churches followed a regional liturgy instead of the Roman one. Still other regions were lukewarm in their acceptance of papal authority. The bishop of Rome himself was dependent on, and often menaced by, the political situation in Italy. The Normans were a danger to the south; to the north were the mighty Roman-German kings. In Rome itself, local noble factions posed a major security risk. In 1053 Pope Leo IX (r. 1049–54) was obliged to call together an army to fight the Normans in southern Italy. He promised his soldiers spiritual rewards for their defense of the Church—a release from performing penances. Here one can clearly see the pope presenting the idea that fighting for the well-being of the Church was a pious act.

Simultaneously, Latin Christendom was expanding in the eleventh century. Between 1061 and 1091 the Normans drove the Muslims from Sicily. Further west, Iberian Christians pushed southward and in 1085 took the city of Toledo. Popes like Nicholas II (r. 1058–61) and Alexander

II (r. 1061–73) welcomed and promoted this development. They allied themselves with the Normans and praised conflict with the Muslims as religious struggles in support of the Lord. Sometimes they went even further—for example in 1064 when Pope Alexander II specifically promised indulgences to the French knights who took part in the conquest of the Muslim city of Barbastro in Aragon. In this context, it is important that both Sicily and Spain were formerly Christian-ruled lands that the Muslims had conquered. Their return to Christendom was hailed as a liberation. Members of the papal circle saw a common element in all the varied conflicts with the Muslims. Under Gregory VII (r. 1073–85) papal support went a vital step further. After the Seljuqs defeated the Byzantines at Manzikert, Gregory even proposed in 1074 that he personally lead an army to the Byzantine Empire to support fellow Christians there—the first time the idea was broached of a papally led expedition to the eastern Mediterranean. However, he soon had to abandon the plan, when he found himself entangled in another, great conflict at home in Europe.

Paradoxically, a Church reform movement that advocated a division between secular and spiritual realms played a decisive role in the Church's changing relationship to violence in the eleventh century. The reform papacy and what is called the "Gregorian reform movement" after Gregory VII, its most famous proponent, pursued three goals in particular. The first was a turn against a tradition, reaching back to the early Middle Ages, of laymen appointing men to spiritual offices; when money or other favors were involved in their choice, this was the sin of simony. A second goal was the promotion of clerical celibacy, especially taking the form of a fight to ban the marriage of priests. As a third goal, the reformers aimed to promote the "liberty of the Church" (*libertas ecclesiae*) in general. By this, they meant the Church's freedom from lay influence, a return to a supposed earlier purity that had been lost. At the heart of the movement lay not so much a wish for independence as concern about the proper conduct of the Church's most essential duty— the transmission of salvation. The reformers argued that this central task was contaminated by entanglement with the laity.

The Church reform of the eleventh century

The reform popes became embroiled in conflict with secular rulers, above all with the Roman-German kings, over this issue of freedom to perform their role in the world properly. These rulers enjoyed a firm grip on ecclesiastical affairs; they regularly appointed bishops and sometimes even deposed popes. For example, in 1046 Emperor Henry III (r. 1039–56) had settled a papal schism by deposing three rival claimants to the papal throne and naming a new pontiff in their place. Laymen below the level of kings also meddled directly in Church matters, especially through what is called the proprietary church system, in which laypeople controlled churches and monasteries that they regarded as their own personal property. The pro-reform clergy, as well as segments of the laity, opposed this and other forms of influence on religion. A special point of contention was the rulers' right to install bishops and abbots symbolically in their office—to invest them. Thus the conflict between secular and ecclesiastical control came to be known as the "Investiture Contest." The highpoint (or perhaps "lowpoint" describes the situation better) of this development was the controversy between Pope Gregory VII and Emperor Henry IV (r. 1056–1106), which included attempts by each to depose the other, and the famous journey to Canossa (1077)—when the emperor, hard-pressed by rebellious subjects, was forced to beg for the pope's forgiveness. This is not the place to retell the story of this conflict. Three points, however, should be stressed.

The first point is that the Investiture Contest was a conflict that was waged with varying degrees of intensity and at various times in the different kingdoms of the Latin West. This means that on several occasions some ruler, engaged in one conflict or another with the popes at the time, was not included in a call to crusade. For example, at the time of the First Crusade Emperor Henry IV had been excommunicated over the investiture issue, the English king William II Rufus (r. 1087–1100) was feuding with the archbishop of Canterbury, and King Philip I of France (r. 1060–1108) was under papal interdict because of a controversy about his marriage. None of them, therefore, could take part in the crusade. Again and again similar circumstances kept rulers from joining ranks with the crusader princes. To give just one further instance, Frederick II's (r. 1212–50) crusade in the years 1227–29 was a very limited undertaking in military terms in large part because of his conflict with the pope of the time.

Strengthening of Church organization

Second, the reform movement strengthened papal influence on the ecclesiastical structure of distant regions. The reform popes invoked the principle of an active ministry. A new understanding of this duty meant that they should also visit distant Church provinces. When the popes themselves were in no position to do so, they sent officials called legates to look after papal interests. These legates furthered the reform and presided over regional synods of high churchmen. The decisions made at such assemblies (*canones*) were collected and became a fundamental part of Church (canon) law. They played a decisive role in transforming the papacy-centered Church into a stable legal corporation. Against the background of this general ecclesiastical centralization and organization, it becomes clearer why the First Crusade was invoked outside of Italy at a particularly important Church assembly, the Council of Clermont. The Church's new communication structures assured that news of the call was widely publicized, reaching many people who had not been at Clermont. Clerics preached the cross, while papal letters spread word of the call and of the Church's standpoint. The interior strengthening of Church organization was, though, not yet linked to the idea of converting other peoples. Evangelizing the Muslims was not an important consideration for either the popes or the crusaders of the First Crusade.

Finally, the papacy's greater influence was not limited merely to ecclesiastical matters. The reform popes also appealed for direct military activities or gave these their express support. Thus the popes encouraged the people of Milan to rise against "simonists," and Duke William of Normandy's attack on England in 1066 enjoyed Alexander II's explicit approval because King Harold of England had broken a sacred oath. The pope sent William a banner of St Peter (*vexillum sancti Petri*), under which the conquest took place. The Investiture Contest also marked a distancing of the papacy from the emperors, the traditional protectors of the Roman Church. The popes thus felt constrained to take military matters into their own hands and to become themselves the protectors of the Church. The vicar of St Peter himself explicitly authorized war—thus providing the Augustinian condition for a just war "with God's authority." It is clear from contemporary letters and documents that the crusaders generally accepted this new vision of papal authority. So it is understandable that the crusaders saw themselves as analogous to another group they knew of from the Bible: the people of Israel. In fact, the crusaders repeatedly invoked Abraham's departure from Ur and the Israelite exodus from Egypt by calling themselves the new people of Israel, God's army (*exercitus Dei*), led by a papal legate whom they saw as a second Moses (*alter Moses*). Thus the concept of the crusade was linked to the Bible, medieval people's basic source of religious knowledge, and it was directly defined as an element in the unfolding of salvation. The just war thus became a war for God, a holy war.

Crusaders as God's people

New orders and religious movements

Monasteries and other religious foundations that mediated divine grace had a strong influence on contemporary perceptions. For believers were driven by concern about their salvation, an attitude clearly demonstrated in extant sources, including crusader letters and the accounts of Urban II's speech at Clermont. The following will present the most important religious orders and movements of the tenth to the thirteenth century.

The oldest of these groups was the monastic confederation of Cluny. Two factors made this monastery (founded in 909 or 910) and its daughter houses particularly attractive. The Cluniac monasteries were directly subject to the pope. Thanks to this, they eluded the grasp of local bishops, which guaranteed them a relative independence. Still more importantly, the monks did not simply pursue a monastic policy of self-sanctification but dedicated themselves more intensely than other associations to intercessory prayer. As a result, the Cluniacs were exceedingly popular with the nobility of their age, who through Cluny came into especially intensive contact with spiritual centers. This popularity was expressed, among other means, in gifts and foundations. The motherhouse Cluny was able to acquire a large number of affiliated houses, especially in Italy, France, and Spain, either by taking control of existing monasteries or by founding new ones. Their close alliance with the reform papacy, and especially with the nobility, made the Cluniac monasteries the prime transmitters of two general aspects of the crusade movement—the Christianization of the knightly class and subordination to the papacy. Recent research has shown, though, that Cluny's influence on the origins of the crusade had its limits. The new religious movements of the eleventh century appear to have been more influential in this regard.

Religious reform movements

The second half of the eleventh century was marked by an upsurge of religious intensity—in Islam and Judaism as well as Christianity. The Muslim world experienced a spiritual renaissance reflected in the foundation of theological schools and in the rise of the Almoravid fundamentalist movement in the Maghreb. In the Byzantine Empire new impulses came from the monks of Mount Athos, and the clergy was again able to play a leading role in political affairs. Similarly, one can see a new self-understanding in Judaism, for example in rabbis' public defense of their faith in disputations with Christian theologians. In the Latin West, too, new forms of regular life (communal spiritual life following a rule) also emerged at the time of the First Crusade and began to change the face of Latin Christendom in a fundamental way.

Several of these new movements were influenced by eremitism; that is, they advocated a withdrawal from the world for the sake of personal salvation. The new Carthusian and Grandmontine Orders are representatives of this tendency. A new Benedictine reform movement also appeared in Burgundy in the years between the summoning of the First Crusade (1095) and the actual conquest of Jerusalem in 1099: the Cistercians. These monks turned their backs on the liturgical splendor of the Cluniacs and returned to the simple, world-denying ideals of the Rule of Benedict of Nursia (*c.* 480–*c.* 560). In 1098 Robert of Molesmes (*c.* 1028–1111) founded a monastery in the isolated valley of Cîteaux near Dijon. It soon developed into the motherhouse and gave its name to an all-encompassing order with many hundreds of affiliated houses. The Cistercians naturally did not play a role in the First Crusade, but they entered into the history of the crusades with a vengeance in the person of their most famous abbot, Bernard of Clairvaux. Bernard was not just an unusually energetic abbot, through whom the Cistercian order experienced an astonishing expansion; he was also a great theologian, mystic, and charismatic preacher who devoted himself intensively to the crusade of 1147–49 (see "The crusades to the Battle of Hattin," p. 47). In successive crusades, too, Cistercian monks frequently served as crusade preachers, even though their order played no significant role in the crusader states themselves.

By contrast, the canons regular *did* play such a role from the beginning of the First Crusade. This group consisted of clerics (rather than monks) who lived in a community following the Rule of St Augustine, so they are sometimes also called Augustinian canons. Unlike the so-called secular canons, canons regular understand the Augustinian exhortation to the "common life" (*vita communis*) to the effect that they not only eat communally in a refectory but also sleep under a single roof. Most importantly, they have no personal possessions, living in personal poverty. This form of strict clerical and communal life presented a novelty to the eleventh century, a reform movement that attracted many followers right at the time of the First Crusade. This movement also had an impact on the ecclesiastical life of the crusader kingdoms, as will be seen (see "The religious orders," p. 108). More important in our context are the spiritual and theological foundations of the regular canon movement, which had an impact on individual crusaders and can thus be seen as a precondition or motivation for the crusades. For the canonical movement rested on a general phenomenon of the age—Christocentrism—a focus of religious consciousness on the person of Christ.

The canons regular

The so-called wandering preachers also modeled their lives on that of Christ. These were men who pursued the ideal of *vita activa* in the sense of "life in the world." They preached, attracted groups of followers, and traveled around with their disciples. Church dignitaries observed their activities with a degree of skepticism, and some wandering preachers did in fact come into conflict with ecclesiastical authorities. Others, though, were integrated into the Church along with their disciples or even founded their own religious orders, such as Robert of Arbrissel (d. 1117) who founded the order of Fontevrault, or Norbert of Xanten (d. 1134), founder of the Premonstratensian Order. The wandering preacher movement was directly connected to crusading; both were profoundly motivated by the ideal of imitation of Christ. This can be seen in the events of the summer of 1096, when wandering preachers inspired entire crowds to join what are called the "People's" crusades.

Imitation of Christ (*imitatio Christi*)

The eleventh century was marked by the efforts of the faithful to follow Christ's example—what is commonly known as *imitatio Christi*. Many lay people and clerics strove to achieve an apostolic, active life (*vita activa*), lived in poverty and service to others. Imitation of Christ may have convinced some men or women to take the cross and thus follow Christ. They could point to biblical authority: "Whoever wishes to follow after me, let him deny himself and take up his cross and follow me" (Matt. 16:24). Those who took the cross, left behind their possessions, and conquered the sites of Christ's ministry on earth would have been convinced on the basis of these words that they were carrying out God's will.

Some of the preconditions and motivations behind participation in the crusade that I have discussed were part of the knightly class's world-view, such as the great significance of honor, possessions, or the fidelity of vassals. The issue of religious unrest, however, penetrated society far beyond the knights. It was a phenomenon of the age, one that gripped a broad sector of the population. This religious unrest was by no means limited to the First Crusade. The so-called Children's Crusade of 1212, initiated by wandering preachers, became a mass movement not just of the young but of the poor (see "The crusades from 1187 to the fall of Jerusalem," p. 50).

Mendicant orders The religious orders founded in the thirteenth century also played a role in the history of the crusades and of the Palestinian Church. This was without a doubt the age of the Mendicants. Many groups at the end of the twelfth through the thirteenth century adopted not only personal but also communal poverty, members vowing themselves to a life of humility, of begging for their daily needs, and thus to extreme imitation of the poverty of Christ. Only four of these groups won an accepted place in the Church. These were the Dominicans (Order of Preachers, OP), the Franciscans (Order of Friars Minor, OFM), the Augustinian Hermits (Order of Hermits of St Augustine, OESA), and the Carmelites (Order of Friars of the Blessed Virgin Mary of Mount Carmel, O.Carm). The Carmelites, who originated in the kingdom of Jerusalem, will be discussed in Chapter 3 (see "The religious orders," p. 108). Here it suffices to mention the role that especially the Dominicans and Franciscans played for the late medieval crusades and crusader kingdoms. They were crusade preachers in the West, and in the East they both gave pastoral care to existing Christians and worked as missionaries. Mendicant friars or people associated with the mendicant orders called repeatedly for reconquest of the Holy Land and drew up campaign plans for the rulers of their era (see "Attempts to win back the Holy Land," p. 58). To a considerable degree, the friars kept the idea of crusading alive in the late Middle Ages. In order to do so, their appeals must have had some resonance with the faithful; in other words, the option of going on a crusade must have satisfied some fundamental need within individuals.

Penance and indulgence

The new religious movements of the eleventh century, and to some extent the Gregorian reform movement, were at a fundamental level called into being by questions of personal guilt and sin. Misdeeds were not just punished; they led to formal performance of penance. In the handbooks of the early Middle Ages known as "penitentials," sins and the appropriate formal penances for each were specifically charted out. But in the eleventh century penances were tending to become more individual and personal. Increasingly, people's perceived need for purification did not stem from a particular deed but from a more general sense of human sinfulness. Fear of personal shortcomings and the consequence of personal failings caused many laypeople to doubt whether they would be saved. The greatest danger was not this mortal life, but possible sufferings during the much longer life after death.

There were ways of countering the menace of hellfire, for one of the fundamental principles of Christianity was and is that the relationship between this life and the life to come is one of cause and effect. In other words, the deeds of this life have an impact on the life to come. So the faithful made bequests to religious foundations, enjoining the monks or nuns to pray for their salvation. They also sought to purify themselves through their own actions. This was the purpose of penance. The later doctrine, according to which penance is only a formal act that takes place after actual reconciliation with the Church, had not yet developed at the end of the eleventh century. Instead, people believed that penances could also help win God's forgiveness for sins. The crusade, a dangerous undertaking with uncertain outcome, was a particularly rigorous form of penance. Crusaders' documents and letters testify how strong the wish was to do penance for committed sins by taking part in a crusade. From this thought sprang the idea of a spiritual privilege, the indulgence.

Crusade as penitential act

Pope Urban's original concern may have been something different. The crusade canon of Clermont speaks only of the remission of earthly penances for all those who undertook the journey solely from love of God (*sola devotione*). In the course of crusade preaching by people other than Urban and oral transmission of the proclamation, however, it soon came to be said that the pope had waived not merely penances but the *penalties* of sin in this world and the next, that he had gone so far as to promise the complete eradication of all sins. Thus the crusaders expected that if they died during the expedition they would go directly to heaven. Pope Urban II seems to have accepted this reinterpretation as a *fait accompli*, because a few months after the Council of Clermont he used the expression "remission of sins" (*remissio peccatorum*) in a propaganda text addressed to the people of Flanders.

Urban II was not the first pope to use the indulgence. In 1064 Alexander II (r. 1061–73) had offered the *remissio peccatorum*, although it only applied to some knights who were already in Spain fighting the Muslims at Barbastro, so the indulgence had little effect. Pope Urban II's initiatives in 1089 and from 1096–99 were essentially the same. In the first, he tried to motivate Christians to restore Christianity in the Catalan city of Tarragona. In the 1096–99 appeal he specifically raised expectations that participants would obtain remission of punishment for sin. Thus the link between war against Muslims and the plenary indulgence was first fully articulated on the Iberian Peninsula. But still this proclamation had much less effect than the sermon at Clermont. It is important to consider why this was the case.

Remissio peccatorum

Before the First Crusade, Church authorities had already promised partial remission of penance in return for lesser pilgrimages and donations (such as gifts to enable the construction of religious buildings). One must make a clear distinction here between the so-called temporal penance and the punishments ordained by God that await sinners after death. One could accomplish two things with penances in this life: re-admission to the Christian community and the reduction of punishment for sin. But it was not clear whether all of these punishments were indeed settled by performing penance. Fear of the life to come was strong, when mortals could expect the remainder of the punishment they had earned for their sins. Only the remission of all sins, the *remissio peccatorum*, gave certainty. It was precisely this extreme form of indulgence, what is called the plenary indulgence, that the crusaders believed the pope had offered at Clermont in 1095.

The attraction of Jerusalem Spain lacked the biblical tradition of the Holy Land. The defense or reconquest of the holy places was a cause for which many people were willing to sacrifice their possessions and their lives—unlike the conquest of Tarragona. The extant documents testify repeatedly to the powerful magnetic pull of the Holy Sepulcher and Jerusalem itself. The expedition of 1096–99 led to the Promised Land, the *terra promissionis* of the Bible. Penitential and indulgence beliefs intersected at this point with the phenomenon of mass pilgrimage and a form of piety that focused specifically on Jerusalem. It was within this larger framework that the crusades fitted—a framework that had a place not just for knights and nobles but for poor and rich, clerics and peasants, men and women.

Thus, even before the 1095 council there had already been a series of papal calls to war and even clear statements that, since the participants were putting military force to a useful purpose in the eyes of the Church, they could win spiritual grace. These developments in the Apennines and on the Iberian Peninsula took on a new dimension thanks to the Investiture Contest. This struggle put the papacy in a position in which it could exert influence on secular matters to a hitherto unprecedented degree, besides strengthening ecclesiastical organization. Other pre-existing conditions that made the crusade possible also came together in this context: the concept of war in defense of the Church was propagated as a special kind of penance, and the devotional aspects of pilgrimage were linked to the idea of just war. Without a doubt, all of these elements prepared the way for the crusade.

It was the totality of all these motivational factors that created the conditions for the vast outpouring of enthusiasm unleashed by Urban's sermon in 1095. To briefly summarize, the eight most important elements were:

1 the older understanding of just war and the newer concept of holy war as a tool of God, which made the crusade a form of meritorious use of violence;
2 emphasis on proper inner motivation and the war as service to one's neighbor;
3 the Church's appropriation of a Christianized knighthood, deeply influenced by feudal ideas of loyalty, and the diversion of its military energies to a form that was both attractive and honorable to the knights themselves;
4 the older tradition of pilgrimage, in which the Jerusalem pilgrimage took on an increased significance in the eleventh century;
5 the new, more active role of the papacy in the course of the Gregorian reform, which made the popes the recognized leaders of an expedition founded on hope of salvation and thus hallowed;
6 the religious unrest of the late eleventh century, with its manifold forms of innovative spiritual life and the Christocentrism they encouraged;
7 the growing individual concern about personal sinfulness, which came to a head right at this time;
8 the view that it was possible to find forgiveness for these sins through a special act of penance before God, and even to win remission of all temporal penalties for sin by taking part in a sanctified military expedition.

It was the collective impact of all these elements that created the explosive force of the crusades.

In the decades and centuries that followed the First Crusade, especially in the late Middle Ages, these motives were expanded and in part overshadowed by other motivations that had little to do with theology and piety. The high prestige of a crusader who returned home successfully seems to have played a more important role than before, as did longing for travel or adventure, or the wish to emulate the chivalrous ideals of late medieval noble culture. Not least, participation in a crusade could be motivated by family tradition—the presence of a crusader in the family tree could impose an obligation on later generations.

Later motivations

Nor should we forget that all of the attitudes and intentions detailed here went hand in hand with less exalted—or indeed reprehensible—actions and motivations. Crusaders presented themselves as participants in a sanctified war for the sake of God and the holy places, but their behavior was often anything but holy. Like all wars, the crusades were brutal, horrible events that brought enormous suffering to the people involved on both sides. Idealism and the sincere personal piety of many crusaders by no means precluded arrogance, ruthlessness, and grue-someness. The armies that fought for Christ consisted of warriors and civilians, poor and rich, sinners and saints, who had come together for widely differing reasons. The multiplicity of motives—specific to indi-viduals, sometimes complementary and at times contradictory—that can be seen most clearly in the crusaders' own documents, make it impossible to view the crusades as a homogeneous, monocausal phe-nomenon. Rather, in their complexity and gradual transformation they mirror the wide diversity of Latin Christendom itself. Still, we must pay heed to the many religious, spiritual, and theological motives that seem alien to modern audiences because, alongside the fundamental con-stants of all wars—issues like hatred, greed, and bloodlust—it was these motives that made the crusading phenomenon specifically a product of the European Middle Ages.

2

The crusades in the Near East

1095	November 27: Urban II proclaims the crusade (Council of Clermont)
1096	Spring/summer: pogroms against Jews along the Rhine Late summer/fall: annihilation of the "People's Crusade" in Asia Minor Late fall 1096–May 1097: armies of the second crusading wave meet at Constantinople
1097	July 1: Battle of Dorylaeum
1097–98	Siege and conquest (June 3) of Antioch
1098	Baldwin of Boulogne seizes control of Edessa
1099	July 15: conquest of Jerusalem; massacre of the populace August 12: Christian victory over a Fatimid army (Ascalon)
1101	Summer: destruction of the third crusading wave in Asia Minor
1109	Conquest of Tripoli
1123–24	Venetian crusade
1127–46	Rule of Imad ad-Din Zengi, emir of Damascus
1145–48	Crusade against Damascus ("Second Crusade")
1146–74	Rule of Nur ad-Din, emir of Damascus
1171	Saladin ends the Fatimid caliphate of Egypt
1174	Saladin assumes power in Damascus
1187	July 3/4: Battle of Hattin
1190–92	Crusade of Frederick I Barbarossa, Richard I of England, and Philip II of France ("Third Crusade")
1197	Crusade of Henry VI
1202–04	Crusade against Constantinople ("Fourth Crusade")
1204–61	Latin Empire of Constantinople
1212	Children's Crusade
1215	Fourth Lateran Council. Crusade bull *Ad liberandam*
1219–21	Crusade against Damietta ("Fifth Crusade")
1227–29	Crusade of Emperor Frederick II
1239–41	Crusades of Thibald of Champagne and Richard of Cornwall

1244	August 23: Khorezmian conquest of Jerusalem
	October 17: Battle of Forbie (Gaza)
1248–54	First Crusade of Louis IX of France
1260	September 3: Mamluks under Sultan Baibars defeat the Mongols at the Battle of ʿAin-Jalut
1270	Second Crusade of Louis IX
1291	May 18: Mamluk conquest of Acre
1332–34	First "Holy League"
1365	Crusade of King Peter I of Cyprus
1396	September 25: Battle of Nicopolis
1453	Ottoman conquest of Constantinople

The First Crusade

Proclamation, "People's Crusade," and pogroms

The historical context discussed in the previous chapter laid a foundation not just for the rise but for the longevity of the crusade movement. Factors such as medieval world-views, piety, and theology, as well as socio-political circumstances, were historical agents that worked over long periods of time. Still, the actual beginning of the "First Crusade" was a specific act that can be fixed at a particular historical moment. On November 27, 1095 Pope Urban II, speaking in an open field outside of the city of Clermont in the Auvergne, gave an impassioned speech in which he called his hearers to take part in a military expedition to the East. This event is properly regarded as the beginning of the First Crusade.

Urban II: speech at Clermont

Unfortunately, nobody copied Urban's proclamation down word for word. What we have is four later versions of his speech. These differ noticeably from one another in wording, but taken as a whole they allow us to see the nature of the pope's argument. Three of the authors were very probably at Clermont and heard the pope's speech with their own ears. These are the monk Robert of St Remi in Rheims (d. 1120), Abbot Baldric of Saint-Pierre de Bourgeueil (later archbishop of Dol, 1045–1130), and finally the canon Fulcher of Chartres (d. 1127), who actually took part in the crusade (as a chaplain). Their chronicles were composed after the crusade had been brought to a successful conclusion, a point that should be borne in mind when interpreting them. Nonetheless, despite certain differences, in general they agree in their report of Urban's address.

From the chroniclers' descriptions it is possible to infer that the pope employed every possible form of symbolic and verbal communication. To start, he described the adversities of the eastern Christians with numerous gestures, loud sighs, cries, and tears; then, acting as God's mouthpiece and supplicant, he called the faithful to take action. He made his appeal in three stages, attested by all three eyewitnesses. First was the call to take part in the crusade and fight for the good of their religion. Second came the promise of an indulgence. Finally, Urban reminded his audience of their sins and the urgent need for purification—the pope accused the gathered warriors of misusing their military prowess in warfare against one another instead of placing it at the service of their religion. This argument encouraged the hearers to undertake the crusade as an act of personal penance. As we have seen, the foundations for precisely this sort of argument had already been laid.

The response of those assembled was enormous. While the speech was still going on, as response to the appeal itself, the listeners interrupted the pope with the famous cry "Deus vult!" (God wills it). When he had finished, many threw themselves to the ground, begged forgiveness for their sins, and, as outward sign of their vow to go on the crusade, fastened cloth crosses to their chests—they "took the cross." The army's departure date was fixed for August 15, 1096.

The pope stayed in southern and western France until the summer of 1096, repeatedly preaching the crusade. But even as he was doing so, his initiative provoked very unforeseen reactions. Apparently the pope's actual goal had been to recruit a small army of knights, raised locally (in southern France), to support the Christian Church in the East and possibly to free Jerusalem. This goal can be discerned from the extant versions of the speech, as well as by three letters Urban sent to Bologna, Flanders, and the monks of Vallombrosa during the winter of 1095/96. In these letters, the pope tried to keep clerics and, under particular circumstances, also younger warriors from taking part. In the end, though, it was not the intended southern French knightly army that set out, but rather several "waves" of crusaders that headed eastward, composed of people from all social classes. It is possible to distinguish at least three of these waves: a first, unorganized one that set out before the official departure date, the expedition that successfully conquered Jerusalem, and a third wave that set out at the earliest in June 1098 and was for the most part annihilated in 1101.

The most numerous elements of the second wave came from the regions of northern France, Flanders, and the lower Rhine. They were hardly recruited directly by Urban's words, because the pope did not personally visit these areas. Instead, crusade preachers won them over in large numbers. The most famous of these was Peter the Hermit.

The "People's Crusade" of 1096

Peter of Amiens (or "the Hermit," d. *c.* 1115) was one of the wandering preachers of the late eleventh century who were discussed in Chapter 1. Peter had already gone on pilgrimage to Jerusalem before the First Crusade and there had resolved to lead an expedition to Palestine to free the holy city. He rode around from place to place on a donkey—like Christ—with a letter he claimed had been sent directly from God that urged participation in the crusade, and called the populace to take the

Sources for the First Crusade

We have excellent sources for the successful expedition of 1096–99. There are a number of crusade chronicles, some composed by actual participants in the expedition. Among these eyewitnesses was an anonymous writer, probably a Norman cleric from southern Italy. His *Gesta Francorum* (Deeds of the Franks, *c.* 1100/01), strongly partial to the Norman prince Bohemond (1050/58–1111), was widely employed as a source by other authors. Among the "crusader chroniclers" was also a chaplain named Raymond of Aguilers, who sometime between 1099 and 1105 composed a *Historia francorum qui ceperunt Hierusalem* (History of the Franks who conquered Jerusalem) completely from the perspective of Provence. The already-familiar Fulcher of Chartres should also be mentioned in this context. These one-sided eyewitness reports can be supplemented with the works of authors who did not actually take part in the expedition, but rather compiled their own impressions from written and oral sources. We have already encountered two of these, Robert of Rheims and Baldric of Dol. Other important sources of this sort are Guibert of Nogent's (d. 1124) *Dei gesta per francos*, completed in *c.* 1109, and the work of the educated Norman knight Radulfus (Raoul) of Caen, who was in the service of the Norman prince Tancred and honored his lord in the *Gesta Tancredi* of 1112. Scholars for a long time unjustly discounted the six-book crusade chronicle of Albert, probably a cleric from Aachen. Albert of Aachen's anecdote-filled account is the only one composed without reliance on the anonymous *Gesta Francorum* and gives a perspective significantly different from that of the French chroniclers. He writes favorably of Godfrey of Bouillon, within whose duchy Aachen lay, and Albert's informants for the most part were members of Godfrey's force. Besides these various texts we have about twenty letters written by participants in the crusade. These are outstanding sources that report first-hand on the crusaders' troubles, wishes, and state of mind. And finally, the crusaders produced many documents before their departure. By using all these complementary and sometimes contradictory sources it is possible to create a picture of the crusade waves of 1096 to 1101.

cross. His popularity was so great that, according to Guibert of Nogent, people collected his donkey's hairs as relics. Soon he had gathered a large and diverse army. Peter recruited participants for the successful second wave of crusaders as well as members of the first expedition. For this first wave, the so-called People's Crusade of 1096, the French noble Walter Sansavoir of Poissy and the Germans Gottschalk and Folkmar also assembled groups of varying size. They included "simple people" as well as nobles and great lords. That these forces, cobbled together from a broad sector of the populace, had little in common with the requested knightly contingents is also clear from the fact that they did not or perhaps could not adhere to the agreed departure date. Apparently the unrest in "God's army" was too great. So the first wave of the First Crusade set off southward.

Poor, undisciplined, and badly coordinated, the participants in the "People's Crusade" of 1096 had to live off the lands they passed through. The populace of the Danube region and the Balkans soon felt the brunt of this: looting and other attacks were the order of the day. The situation did not change when Peter the Hermit's and Walter Sansavoir's armies met outside Constantinople. Their plundering quickly convinced the Greek emperor Alexios I Comnenos that it was wiser to ferry the disagreeable mob over the Bosporus into Muslim territory (early August 1096). Here they paid a terrible price for their lack of military skill and coordination. Half of the People's Crusade, mostly composed of Germans and Italians, was massacred by the Seljuqs at Nicaea. The other half, mostly French, was decoyed into an ambush and also slaughtered. Peter the Hermit was absent when his army was destroyed; he had remained in Constantinople. All that he could then do was to wait for the approaching knightly armies and join them. The fate of the other forces of the People's Crusade was hardly better. The depredations of the first group on their journey through Hungary had caught the populace by surprise, but now they were prepared and repelled or killed every one of the next group of intruders to appear. Not a single contingent of the first wave of the crusade made it to the Holy Land.

The end of the "People's Crusade"

But before their destruction, parts of this group wrote a page for themselves in the annals of history that has become an inextricable part of the crusades: in the summer of 1096 they destroyed a majority of the Jewish communities along the Rhine in an unprecedented series of massacres. Since the early Middle Ages many Jews had settled in the great Rhineland episcopal cities such as Cologne, Mainz, Speyer, and Worms, as well as in other towns of the region. Under the protection of the local lords, especially the bishops, they had taken part in the economic life of these centers and helped them flourish. They developed a rich cultural life and for a long time lived with the Christians without any great disturbances. This does not imply that there was no sign of anti-Judaism (anti-Semitism is a later phenomenon) before this, but nothing compared to the scale of May 1096. Under the leadership of the preacher Folkmar and Count Emicho of Flonheim, a mob of crusaders stormed into the Jewish quarters of Mainz, Worms, and other cities in the mid-Rhine region, murdering men, women, and children. Christian chroniclers report the events, as does Albert of Aachen. But no group of sources provides as moving and shocking a description of the atrocities as the Jewish chronicles, such as the account written by Salomon bar Simson of Worms. They tell that at first those under attack sought and often received assistance from their lords, the Christian bishops. But it soon became clear that the bishops were not able or willing to protect the Jews with armed force. Many Jews died at the hands of rampaging crusaders; others, recognizing the hopelessness of their position, killed their families and themselves. After the pogroms of the middle

The Jewish pogroms of 1096

Rhineland, splinter groups of crusaders attacked the Jewish communities in Cologne, Metz, Trier, and on the lower Rhine. Attacks are also recorded in Regensburg, Prague, and southern France.

It is tempting but misguided to posit a historical connection between the massacres of the Rhineland Jews in 1096 and the Jewish genocide of the twentieth century: 1096 was not the prelude to 1933 or 1942. The anti-Jewish outrages of the Middle Ages were not based on an anti-Semitic ideology, furthered by a government annihilation program. In cases like this, one must beware of comfortable, simplistic explanations and take the effort to explain events historically, in the context of their own time and thought world.

Motives behind the pogroms   What motivated some crusaders to attack Jews? Two points must be emphasized. First is that the offenders were mobs of people without means, who were ready or compelled to live from pillage when necessary. The rich Jewish communities seemed to them to be a convenient means to provision themselves. But this is surely only a secondary issue—greed alone cannot explain the degree of violence that was unleashed. As paradoxical as it may seem, apparently the murderers saw their deeds as part of their holy war for the sake of God. One of the most important reasons for the expedition to the East was to avenge Jesus Christ and combat his enemies. Even those ignorant of theology knew that it had been Jews who crucified Jesus. Thus in contemporary understanding the new army of God met the descendants of Christ's murderers in the Rhineland. Jewish sources too report that the killers seem to have believed that they were taking vengeance for the Crucifixion and thus were accomplishing a work pleasing to God. In this context it is fitting that proselytism also played a major role—several accounts speak of forcible baptism. Finally, the internal situation of the Roman-German Empire may have encouraged the outrages. Because of his conflicts with Duke Welf II (1072–1120), Emperor Henry IV did not visit the provinces of his empire north of the Alps at all in the period 1090–97. So the Rhineland pogroms against the Jews took place during a vacuum of imperial power. However, whether Henry IV's presence would have made any difference to events is a question that can never be answered.

The expedition to Jerusalem

The armies that set out in August 1096 were very different in cohesion and level of organization from the disordered crowds of the "People's Crusades." To be sure, these forces also included women, children, peasants, and clerics, but the proportion of knights among the fighting men was higher and the troops were under the leadership of high-ranking princes with military experience. There were five distinct armies. The first and strongest contingent included people from southern and western France. They marched under the command of Count Raymond IV of Toulouse (*c.* 1041–1105). The second troop, from Lotharingia, was led by Duke Godfrey V of Lower Lotharingia (called Godfrey of Bouillon; *c.* 1060–1100) and his brother Baldwin (after 1060–1118). Normans and Flemings formed the third army, and Duke Robert II of Normandy (*c.* 1054–1134), Count Stephen of Blois (*c.* 1045–1102), and Robert II of Flanders (*c.* 1065–1111). Hugh of Vermandois, brother of Philip I of France, led a fourth contingent, while, last, the south Italian Normans were under Bohemond of Bari (later known as Bohemond of Taranto) (1050/58–1111), the eldest son of the mighty Robert Guiscard (d. 1085). Bohemond's nephew Tancred accompanied him.

Thus the leaders of the First Crusade were not kings but rather major princes and territorial lords of the high nobility, related in various degrees to the royal houses of Europe. Some of them controlled very extensive lordships, like the count of Toulouse, whose possessions were greater than those of the French king. Some of them already had experience fighting Muslims, such as Raymond of Toulouse in Spain and Bohemond in southern Italy. Whether they had fought Muslims or not, all were practiced in the arts of war. It appears that no military commander-in-chief was officially designated. Indeed, this would hardly have been possible, considering the heterogeneous affiliations of several armies, bound together in highly diverse ways by feudal hierarchies and including also some completely independent nobles. The most that can be said is that the count of Toulouse enjoyed a higher degree of authority, based on his particularly close relations with Urban II. A sign of this prestige is that Raymond appears to have been informed about plans for the crusade at a private meeting with the pope before the Council of Clermont. The selection of the campaign's spiritual leader is also a sign of Raymond's importance. The choice fell on Adhémar of Monteil, bishop of Le Puy, which lay within the count of Toulouse's domains. However, Raymond was culturally and linguistically different from many other crusade leaders, who appear in the sources as *franci* (in contrast to Raymond's western and southern French *provinciales*). Raymond's Provençal roots may have had the long-term effect of isolating him from the other princes.

The leaders of the First Crusade

In the months before their departure, the crusaders took legal and financial steps to place the expedition on a secure footing. Questions of inheritance had to be resolved, possessions sold, goods mortgaged. Many private documents still survive that shed light on these transactions and the important role that ecclesiastical institutions played in them. A great many monasteries and churches made the money "flow"—sometimes in the most literal sense of the word by melting down valuable reliquaries—to purchase goods and finance travel. In this preparation or planning phase of the crusade, a multitude of problems arose at the individual as well as the collective level, especially with logistics. Later crusaders would have to confront the same issues (see "The practical problems of a crusade," p. 61).

The journey to Antioch

In the summer of 1096 the various contingents set out, each along its own chosen route. The Lotharingians went overland through Hungary (where they had to give hostages to guarantee good behavior) and along the Danube. The southern French traveled through northern Italy and along the Adriatic coast. The northern French and Normans made their way through Italy to their kinsmen in the south and were then ferried across to Durazzo. Estimates of the total strength of these forces vary widely. Recent scholars speak of anywhere between 30,000 and 70,000 fighting men and perhaps 30,000 noncombatants. The armies met at Constantinople, reaching the city in several waves between late fall 1096 and mid-May 1097. Their gradual arrival gave Emperor Alexios I Comnenos the opportunity to deal with the leaders individually. Through diplomatic and even military pressure he won oaths of fealty from each of them. The oaths included not only a pledge to keep peace with the Byzantines during their residence but also a promise to accept imperial authority over any lands they conquered that had been part of the Eastern Roman Empire. Of the leaders, only Raymond of Toulouse succeeded in limiting his oath to a promise of respect for the emperor's person and possessions.

After all the contingents had assembled on the far side of the Bosporus in May 1097, the second wave of the First Crusade set out. Their first common military undertaking, conducted with the assistance of a Byzantine fleet, was the seizure of Nicaea. There, where the troops of the People's Crusade had failed, the second force succeeded on June 19, 1097. In the process, the Latins defeated a relief force under Sultan Qilij Arslan (1092–1107) in pitched battle for the first time. After secret negotiations the Muslims finally surrendered the city—to the Byzantines, not to the crusaders, a fact that some of the crusaders seem to have resented. Nonetheless, Emperor Alexios gave the crusaders auxiliary troops, led by the experienced general Tatikios, who accompanied and advised the expedition on its way east. The second, more important test came two weeks later, when the crusaders were able to defeat a Seljuq army commanded by the sultan near Dorylaeum (July 1, 1097). The road through Anatolia to northern Syria via Iconium, Caesarea, and Marash now lay open, although the way was long and painful. Albert of Aachen and the other chroniclers report how most of the saddle horses and beasts of burden died, while men, women, and children suffered in the sweltering heat. In late October 1097 the army, exhausted and reduced to about 40,000 people, reached the large and strongly fortified city of Antioch. After a brief discussion, the leaders decided to lay siege instead of attempting to take the place by storm.

The siege of Antioch

The siege of Antioch lasted seven long months (October 1097–June 1098), during which many crusaders fell victim to the harsh winter, food shortages, and disease. On top of their suffering, the besiegers discovered that a large relieving army was underway, under the command of Kerbogha, the governor of Mosul. The crusaders were in imminent danger of being wiped out in the open fields before Antioch's walls. Some fighters deserted, others came up with reasons for a hasty withdrawal. Among these was Stephen of Blois, who on his return journey encountered a Byzantine army personally led by Alexios Comnenos and, according to Albert of Aachen, painted the Latin situation in such dark colors that the emperor thought it was no use advancing any further. The crusaders regarded the Byzantine withdrawal as a betrayal and a breach of the oaths that had been sworn in Constantinople. Now they had no one to rely on but themselves. When their situation appeared hopeless, however, Bohemond persuaded some native Christians to open a gate in the city wall for him. On June 3, 1098 Antioch fell, except for the citadel. The conquerors' joy did not last long, though, because almost immediately Kerbogha arrived and the former besiegers were themselves besieged. Again, there seemed to be no way out. But then help arrived from an unexpected source. A certain man named Peter Bartholomew, from Raymond of Toulouse's camp, proclaimed that he had been granted a vision: St Andrew had shown him where the "Holy Lance" could be found, which, according to the gospels, had pierced Christ's side. Adhémar of Le Puy and others expressed doubt, but when powerful supporters of the visionary started digging in St Peter's Church in Antioch, a lance soon to be honored as a relic came to light. Filled with renewed courage, the crusaders under Bohemond's command attempted to break out on June 28, 1098—and were victorious. The Seljuq danger was dispelled for the moment, the conquest secured; the Lance had demonstrated its miraculous power.

Visions

Several times during the expedition participants reported miraculous occurrences or visions. The discovery of the Holy Lance is only one example of such supernatural phenomena. Also at Antioch, a priest named Stephen of Valence reported that Christ had personally promised to protect both him and the army, and Albert of Aachen tells in his chronicle of a vision of St Ambrose, the great fourth-century archbishop of Milan. In the battle itself, crusaders claimed to have seen various heavenly riders and dead comrades fighting at their side, confirming their belief that they were waging a holy, God-blessed war. Directly before the fall of Jerusalem, too, a vision is supposed to have influenced the course of events decisively in the crusaders' favor. Similar occurrences are also reported from later crusades

---

The army only continued their journey toward Jerusalem on January 13, 1099. One reason for this delay was the season—the crusaders did not want to make the long journey at the height of summer. Then an epidemic struck the city, killing many crusaders including Bishop Adhémar.

First conflicts between the crusader princes

Finally, the crusade princes occupied themselves during the winter months with smaller expeditions to conquer territory and thus secure their own positions. These are early signs that the goal for some was already to create crusader states independent of Byzantine overlordship. The departure was further delayed because many of the crusader leaders, especially Raymond of Toulouse, opposed Bohemond's demands for lordship over Antioch. Bohemond and his troops had indeed played a decisive role in the conquest and defense of the city, but by keeping Antioch he openly broke the promise he had made to Emperor Alexios. Raymond finally acceded to Bohemond's demands, but only after he had been given chief command of the expedition; Bohemond stayed behind as lord of Antioch.

The conquest of Jerusalem

The journey through Syria to Palestine was accomplished with few difficulties, because shortly before this time the holy city had fallen into the hands of the Shi'ite Fatimids; the emirs of the little states of Syria saw no reason to oppose a crusader passage through their territories, as long as the crusaders promised not to attack them. In fact, most of them provided provisions or money and therefore remained undisturbed. On June 7, 1099 the crusaders finally got their first sight of Jerusalem, from "Mount Joy" (*mons gaudii, Montjoie*). By this time, the army must have been reduced to about 20,000 men. But they were not yet done fighting: the crusaders discovered that the city was well fortified and the defenders had no thought of capitulating. All the Christians had been expelled from Jerusalem to prevent a betrayal like that of Antioch, and a long siege seemed likely. But time was slipping away rapidly, and a Fatimid army was already on the march to raise the siege. After a failed attack on June 13 the situation became critical. But Genoese and English ships, newly arrived at Jaffa, brought tools, with which the crusaders hurriedly built siege towers. Once again, a vision influenced events. The dead bishop Adhémar appeared to a cleric and urged the crusaders to perform penance. The army duly marched three times around the city, barefoot and singing, led by clerics bearing relics. Then, on the night of July 13–14, the attack began.

It took a whole day to roll the siege engines up to the walls, the attackers suffering heavy casualties the whole time. On the morning of July 15 some men of the Lotharingian contingent succeeded in getting over the northern wall, clearing the way and letting the other warriors into the city. While Raymond of Toulouse took the strategically important Tower of David in the western part of the city, a horrible massacre began. It must be acknowledged that the brutal killing of a large number of men, women, and children—both Muslims and Jews—was in accordance with the accepted military practices of the time: the defenders had not surrendered and thus could expect no mercy. We also know that the shocking, repeatedly expressed accounts of the crusaders' atrocities are based on Old Testament models, such as the conquest of

Jericho. The crusaders placed themselves in the biblical tradition by terming themselves the new people of Israel, and the chroniclers did the same in their description of the bloodshed. Here too, a balanced and analytical interpretation of the sources can keep us from overly hasty judgments and interpretations. But all the same, the massacre of July 15, 1099 was an event that provoked horror in the Jewish and especially the Islamic world, and was not forgotten. Two hundred years later it justified similar behavior by the Muslim conquerors when they destroyed the kingdom of Jerusalem in 1291.

The holy city had been taken. Now it had to be ruled and defended. In the course of the expedition Raymond of Toulouse had made a number of enemies, and many of his men wanted to return home. So he renounced any claim to rule over Jerusalem. The lordship was instead offered, with the support of the Flemish and Norman contingents, to the Lower Lotharingian Godfrey. He accepted, but refused the royal title with the words that he was unwilling to wear a golden crown in the place where Christ had borne a crown of thorns. Instead, Godfrey was called *advocatus sancti Sepulchri*, "Guardian of the Holy Sepulcher." Church leadership also went to a crusader from northwestern Europe, Robert of Normandy's chaplain Arnulf of Chocques (d. 1118), who was elected principal of the Church of Jerusalem. Almost immediately the conquered land had to be defended, because the Fatimid wazir al-Afdal (d. 1121) was already approaching with a large army. The Christians were outnumbered, but on the morning of August 12, 1099 they caught their enemies in a surprise attack near Ascalon and annihilated them. Thus crusader control of Jerusalem was assured, at least for the time being.

Securing control

The creation of the crusader lordships

After the successful Battle of Ascalon, most of the participants in the First Crusade returned to their homelands. In their eyes, Jerusalem had been brought back to Christendom, the *hereditas Christi* had returned to its rightful Lord. They could regard their mission as accomplished, and more than accomplished. Only a minority of knights remained in the Holy Land, where soon there were changes in both secular and ecclesiastical rule. Godfrey of Bouillon died in 1100, and the throne passed on to his brother Baldwin of Boulogne, who was the first to assume the title "king" of Jerusalem (Baldwin I). Patriarch Arnulf, for his part, had to abdicate his office under ecclesiastical/political pressure.

The crusaders' return

For the time being, those who remained in the East could hope for speedy reinforcement, since the third wave of the First Crusade set itself into motion in 1100/01. But only a few of the crusaders of this third wave made it to the Holy Land; the troops of this so-called "Crusade of 1101" were slaughtered in several battles.

The crusade of 1101

In the period after the conquest of Antioch, a third great wave of crusaders had been recruited. It consisted of Italian contingents from Lombardy, Frenchmen from Burgundy, Nevers, and Poitou, and Germans under Duke Welf I of Bavaria (d. 1102). There were at least as many fighters in this army as in that of the second wave, but their undertaking had a completely different outcome. The Seljuqs now decided on a "burnt earth" tactic. Disagreements and tactical errors did the rest, so that in the course of several battles the troops were almost completely destroyed. The horrible fiasco of the crusade of 1101 led to it being almost completely forgotten in the Christian world.

The creation of the crusader states

Jerusalem was the most important crusader state, but it was not the only one or even the first. A total of four independent territories were formed (see Map 1): besides the kingdom of Jerusalem were the principality of Antioch, the county of Edessa, and the county of Tripoli. Bohemond of Taranto had stayed behind in Antioch in the summer of 1098. Here he created a state that was designated the principality of Antioch. Despite its exposed position on the border of the powerful emirate of Aleppo and the deaths of several princes in battle, this state remained in existence until the second half of the thirteenth century. Shorter-lived was the county of Edessa, the oldest of the crusader states. Baldwin of Boulogne, Godfrey of Bouillon's brother, had created it early in 1098, even before the conquest of Antioch. He had left the main army in Armenia with a force of knights and took advantage of the inner turmoil of the mostly Armenian Christian population to drive out Turkish garrisons, eliminate local magnates, and take over the lordship of Edessa for himself. But already in 1144 the city fell to 'Imad ad-Din Zengi (r. 1127–46), the lord of Mosul. The rest of the county was soon lost.

The region between the principality of Antioch and the kingdom of Jerusalem was the last area the crusaders conquered. The territory had been left undisturbed during the advance, and the Christians only succeeded in subjecting it after 1102, when they took the major port of Tortosa. After his political defeat at the hands of Godfrey of Bouillon, Raymond of Toulouse set out to establish his own state here. The count himself died in 1105, but his troops, led by other members of the comital house, were able to conquer Tripoli in 1109 and secure their rule. The enterprising Norman Tancred tried to establish another principality in the Galilee, but it was unable to hold out as an independent state. The four independent crusader states—Jerusalem, Antioch, Edessa, and Tripoli—were often called "Outremer" (the Latin territories "on the far side of the [Mediterranean] Sea"). Crusaders continued to flow to these regions, although Outremer's inner development was only indirectly shaped by the crusades. The history, institutions, structure, and composition of these "crusader states" will therefore be discussed elsewhere from an internal perspective (Chapter 3). In the following, we will trace the course of the crusades themselves.

The crusades of the twelfth to fifteenth centuries

The crusades to the Battle of Hattin, 1187

The First Crusade has assumed a preeminent position both in medieval texts and historical research. It created the crusader states of the Near East, and it was marked by motivations, political alignments, and military problems that would also affect later crusaders. The expedition of 1096 to 1099 was the spectacular prelude to a long series of military undertakings to defend or win back the Holy Land. The practice of numbering some of these crusades is not medieval but rather a modern device; the Second Crusade, and the Third, etc. have by now become accepted terms. These numbers, however, are problematic. They were not necessarily applied to the largest or the most successful expeditions, but often to those led by kings or that ended in the creation of new polities. To blame is a modern fascination for medieval rulers. This numbering system has placed a few of the expeditions in the limelight and thus disguised the fact that there were in reality a great many crusades in the high and late Middle Ages. It is for that reason that these numbers will not be used in this book. Nonetheless, due to space constraints, it is necessary to be selective. The following is only a rough sketch of the most important ventures undertaken by Christians in the Near East.

There were periods of greater and lesser fascination with crusading. At first, interest was high: there were several expeditions in the first twenty-five years after the conquest of Jerusalem. For example, from 1107 to 1110 the Norwegian king Sigurd (r. 1103–30) crusaded, taking part with his fleet in the conquest of the port city of Sidon. Similarly, there was a Venetian crusade in 1123/24, which destroyed a Fatimid fleet and conquered Tyre. After that, the crusader states were fully established and relatively stabilized. Perhaps this comparative security explains why there was a pause of nearly a generation before the next really significant undertaking, the crusade of 1145–48.

The cause for this crusade was the fall of Edessa on December 23, 1144. The loss of the oldest crusader state and an appeal for help from Palestine persuaded Pope Eugenius III (r. 1145–53) to proclaim a crusade on December 1, 1145 with the bull *Quantum praedecessores*. But what the pope had in mind was not merely support for the threatened crusader states of the Levant: he planned a broadly conceived offensive for the defense and spread of Christendom on several fronts. Besides an

Counting the crusades

The crusade of 1145–48

expedition to the Holy Land, Eugenius also had preachers proclaim campaigns on the Iberian Peninsula and on the Baltic. The Danish chronicler Saxo Grammaticus (*c.* 1150–*c.* 1220) wrote: "Every province . . . received the command to attack whichever part of the barbarian world was closest to it." Nobody recruited crusaders more urgently and effectively than Bernard of Clairvaux, the greatest theologian and most influential churchman of this time.

Bernard of Clairvaux (1090–1153) came from a noble Burgundian family. In 1112 he—along with thirty companions—entered the reform monastery of Cîteaux, founded barely a decade before. Three years later he became abbot of Clairvaux, one of Cîteaux's first daughter houses. Bernard's charismatic personality is an important reason for the meteoric rise of the Cistercian Order. Bernard composed sermons, theological and mystical texts, and treatises—including a work in support of the young order of Knights Templars. He placed all his rhetorical skills in the service of the idea of crusade. On March 31, 1146 Bernard made an ardent call for the crusade at Vézelay, upon which King Louis VII of France (r. 1137–80), his wife Eleanor of Aquitaine (*c.* 1122–1204), and many nobles took the cross. At the Cistercian's urging, the Hohenstaufen Roman-German king Conrad III (r. 1138–52) also joined the expedition on Christmas 1146. Bishop Otto of Freising, the king's half-brother (*c.* 1112–58) accompanied him and described the crusade in his *Deeds of Emperor Frederick I*. Bernard recruited further contingents, presenting the crusade as a once-in-a-lifetime opportunity to assure salvation. Whoever calculated like a "clever merchant" could not let the chance go by. Not surprisingly, the rush of the faithful was great—as was their criticism after the crusade came to its inglorious end. Bernard blamed the failure on the Christians' sinfulness.

In some respects, Cistercian monks like Bernard of Clairvaux played the same role for later crusades of the twelfth century that wandering preachers like Peter the Hermit had played in the years 1096 to 1099. According to Otto of Freising, it was also a Cistercian, a man named Rudolf, who incited a new series of pogroms against the Rhineland Jews. But Bernard of Clairvaux asserted his authority against the outrages, so that the violence did not reach the horrific proportions of 1096.

The failure of the crusade

The German army followed Godfrey of Bouillon's route and made it past the Bosporus without any great difficulties. The first reverse came soon after, though—several days after the army had divided into two parts for logistical reasons. At Dorylaeum, Conrad III's contingent suffered a heavy defeat at the hands of the Seljuqs; the second column, under Otto of Freising, fared no better. The king, his half-brother, and some companions barely escaped with their lives. They returned to Constantinople and took the sea route to Palestine with the remnants of their force.

Louis VII's army, too, followed Godfrey's route as far as Adalia on the Mediterranean coast. Heavy casualties in skirmishes and the lack of Byzantine support had weakened the army during its march through Asia Minor. So the king decided to go the rest of the way by sea. There was not enough shipping available for the entire army, though. Louis therefore ordered the infantry to make its way to Antioch on foot, along with the remainder of the force. The troops were attacked not far from Adalia at the beginning of 1148 and practically destroyed. The king, meanwhile, made the voyage to Antioch with his churchmen and knights. Louis's sojourn in Antioch has excited the fantasies of both contemporaries and posterity mostly because of rumors of an incestuous relationship between his wife, Eleanor of Aquitaine, and her uncle Raymond of Antioch (r. 1136–49). Whether out of a sense of injured honor, antipathy toward the Antioch-allied Byzantines, or for other reasons, King Louis refused to let his army fight to the advantage of the Antiochene prince. Instead the crusaders carried on toward Jerusalem.

Once in Jerusalem, Louis united with the remaining German crusaders and more troops that had arrived from Provence. Eventually a contingent from England, Flanders, and the lower Rhine also joined him; it had sailed to the Holy Land via Portugal. Despite these reinforcements, the army was not large enough to attempt the reconquest of Edessa. So instead they decided to attack the emirate of Damascus—a long-time ally of the Christians. The expedition of July 1148 was an utter failure. After a few days the crusaders raised the siege and departed, completely humiliated. In every sense the crusade of 1147/48 was a fiasco: it angered an important ally of the Christians (Damascus), deepened tensions with the Byzantine Empire, and damaged the prestige of the crusades in the Latin West. Despite repeated appeals, until 1187 no noteworthy expeditions were assembled to go to the Holy Land, with the exception of a few smaller initiatives like that of Count Philip of Flanders (d. 1191) in 1177/78.

Moreover, the fiasco of 1147/48 revealed the military limitations of the Christian knightly army. Their driving force rested entirely on the massed charge of heavily armed horsemen. Muslim armies had little they could set against such a force, so their battle tactic was very different: they wore down the resistance of the less mobile, armored knights with a steady hail of arrows shot by mounted archers, and tried to encourage the breakup of tight lines with pretended flights. Only then did the riders go over to the attack. In the course of the twelfth century both sides gradually changed their weaponry. The Christians fell back on so-called *turcopoli*, a light cavalry composed of native allies or mercenaries (also Muslims). The Muslims too began to resemble their opponents. This was especially apparent in the second half of the twelfth century, when the Christians of Outremer found their most dangerous opponent yet in Saladin (Salah ad-Din ibn Ayyub, r. 1169–93). His army

Military tactics and armament

consisted in the first line of professional Turcoman and Kurdish fighters, supplemented with slave soldiers (called Mamluks) and mercenaries. Bedouin and Turcoman contingents also joined, in hope of loot. Among the Muslims, the only ones armed with the highly effective compound bow were the professional elite units of mounted archers. The majority of warriors used lighter, less-powerful bows or light lances and swords. The officers and the Mamluks, though, wore heavy armor, comparable to that of the Christian knights. It was such an army that destroyed the Christian army of Outremer at Hattin on July 3/4, 1187.

The crusades from 1187 to the fall of Jerusalem, 1244

The lead-up and course of the Battle of Hattin belong less in the context of the crusades than in the more general history of the crusader states (see "Establishment and fluctuation of borders," p. 83). Reports of the defeat hit the Latin West like a hammer. The destruction of the Christian army, the Muslim conquest of much of Outremer, but above all the fall of Jerusalem on October 2, 1187 and the loss of its most important relic, the Holy Cross—these events sent shock waves to the farthest reaches of Christendom. The crusade movement as a whole got an extraordinary boost—during the following century hardly a year passed without a crusade somewhere in Europe, Asia Minor, or the Near East.

The Crusade of 1190–92 Immediately after news of the defeat had spread, Pope Gregory VIII (d. 1187) called for a crusade, with the bull *Audita tremendi* of October 29, 1187. Emperor Frederick I Barbarossa (r. 1152–90), Richard I "the Lionheart" of England (r. 1189–98), and Philip II Augustus of France (r. 1180–1223) all labored to assemble the greatest crusader army of the Middle Ages. The German force was the first to set out. The Germans won an impressive victory over Seljuq troops at Iconium on May 18 and soon reached Armenia. But, without warning, the emperor died on June 10, 1190. Frederick I, the most powerful ruler and thus the "natural leader" of the great crusade to win back Jerusalem, drowned while crossing the river Saleph. His army disintegrated, most of the crusaders turning around and going back home. Only a small remnant under the emperor's son Duke Frederick of Swabia (1167–91) continued and took part in Richard I and Philip II's crusade.

The conquest of Cyprus While making his way to Palestine by sea, Richard unexpectedly conquered the island of Cyprus. The *Itinerarium regis Ricardi*, a revealing if partisan source on the English king's crusade by an anonymous London canon and based on Ambrose's *Estoire de la Guerre Sainte*, tells of this sudden coup. The unplanned conquest—Richard attacked the island because the Byzantine governor had arrested some crusaders—was extraordinarily momentous. Cyprus remained under Latin rule for four centuries and played an essential role in the survival of the crusader states in the thirteenth century.

The armies of the two kings arrived before Acre in April and June 1191. The crusaders found a city that had already been under siege by Christian troops for two years. With their reinforcement, it finally fell on July 12, 1191. Shortly thereafter the French king returned home. Certainly a reason for this was his rivalry with Richard I, which cast its shadow on the entire Anglo-French crusade of 1191/92. Their disagreement had its roots in disputes over possessions in France and was apparently sharpened by personal animosity. They quarreled repeatedly over political and military decisions as well as the division of loot. After Philip's departure, Richard was able to justify his reputation as a brilliant knight through several impressive successes, such as the successful Battle of Arsuf on September 7, 1191. At the same time he destroyed Saladin's aura of invincibility. However, on account of his limited military resources and the danger that threatened his European possessions, Richard was forced to make a three-year truce with Saladin in September of 1192: the Christians reclaimed the coast from Tyre to Jaffa, and pilgrim access to Jerusalem was guaranteed. The survival of the crusader states was not assured by the 1191/92 expedition, but their danger was considerably eased, particularly after Saladin's empire fell apart upon his death in 1193.

There was one more crusade in the last years of the twelfth century, when Frederick I's son and successor, Henry VI (r. 1190–97), sought to link his wide-reaching plans in the eastern Mediterranean to an expedition to the Levant. German and southern Italian troops had already been shipped to Acre when the totally unexpected news of the emperor's sudden death (September 28, 1197) reached them. But the crusade of 1197 had its successes nonetheless: the reduced number of crusaders who set sail in spite of the bad news conquered Sidon and Beirut and thus reestablished the militarily and economically important land link between the kingdom of Jerusalem and the county of Tripoli. Henry VI's crusade was the last of the twelfth century, but already in August 1198 a new crusade proclamation by Pope Innocent III (r. 1198–1216) announced that the crusading movement had by no means come to an end.

The crusade of Henry VI

In the thirteenth century the number of crusades did indeed swell, but on the whole these were smaller expeditions, less often provoked by particular events (such as the lost Battle of Forbie, 1244) than they were by the general plight of the crusader states. The crusade developed into the *passagium particulare*.

Smaller crusades of the thirteenth century

Worthy of mention are the 1239–41 expeditions of Count Thibald of Champagne (d. 1253) and Richard of Cornwall (d. 1272), of Count Odo of Nevers (d. 1266) in 1265, the Aragonese crusade of 1269, and the

---

Passagium

The term *passagium* comes from the world of trade, and in our context means a "crossing" that individual knights or contingents could undertake at any time of the year. This steady stream of battle-ready strangers played an important role in the survival of the crusader states. When noteworthy expeditions were undertaken that did not take the form of a general, great crusade (the *passagium generale*), they were designated as a *passagium particulare*, a specific expedition with a limited goal.

---

expeditions of French and English forces in 1288 and 1290. These smaller ventures, led by great nobles, could register only limited successes, such as the conquest of particular castles or towns. Large armies came together only in exceptional circumstances. Four crusades fall in this class—that of 1202–04, which ended with the conquest and sack of Constantinople, that of 1217–21 against Egypt, and the two crusades of King Louis IX of France in the years 1248–54 and 1270. Less for the number of its participants than for its results, the crusade of Frederick II (1226–29) is also significant.

The crusade of 1202–04   Judgments of the great crusade of 1202–04 have been particularly harsh. Its outcome—the conquest and sack of Constantinople—indeed produced fundamentally negative results: it decisively deepened a rift between Greek and Latin Christians that has still not been completely healed today. Besides, during the nearly sixty years that Latins ruled Byzantium, energies were diverted from support of the Levantine crusader states. Paradoxically, the undertaking had been planned as an expedition for the reconquest of Jerusalem. Pope Innocent III made the proclamation; preachers like Fulk of Neuilly publicized it effectively. Its most important leaders—Margrave Boniface of Montferrat (d. 1207), Count Louis of Blois (d. 1205), and Count Baldwin IX of Flanders (1171–1206)—had made careful preparations. Godfrey of Villehardouin (d. *c.* 1212/18), marshal of Champagne, who wrote one of the most important histories of the campaign from the Latin perspective, tells of their plans. In 1201 he himself negotiated a treaty with the doge of Venice whereby the Venetians would transport 33,500 fighting men to Acre. But only 11,000 men turned up in Venice in the summer of 1202. The Venetians, who had made enormous efforts and assembled the largest fleet in their history, demanded that the conditions of the agreement be carried out. To meet their debts and keep the crusade from disbanding, the crusade leaders agreed to conquer Zara (modern Zadar), a formerly Venetian-held city on the Dalmatian coast that had been seized by the Hungarians. The leaders set aside their misgivings and a papal prohibition (Zara's people were Latin Christians and the king of Hungary had even taken the cross himself). They conquered the city in November 1202.

Since turning Zara over to the Venetians still did not solve their financial problems, the crusaders then agreed to a Venetian-sponsored proposal the exiled Byzantine prince Alexios Angelos made to them: to sail to Constantinople and put him back in power. In return, the prince promised to give the crusade financial and military support. The crusaders did indeed succeed in overthrowing Emperor Alexios III (r. 1195–1203) in July 1203, but then had to wait until early 1204 to continue their venture. In the meantime, in part because of increasingly strained relations with the crusaders, the new emperor Alexios IV was himself deposed and murdered. The crusaders thereupon felt justified in proceeding against the new emperor and besieging Constantinople. On April 12 they were unexpectedly able to take one of the gates of the well-fortified and defended city wall and thus seize the greatest and richest city of Christendom. Constantinople was systematically looted. The crusaders stole countless works of art, raped women, and desecrated holy places. Niketas Choniates (d. 1217), a Byzantine senator and chronicler, paints shocking images of the sack, which, especially because of the systematic desecration of Christian holy places, left deep wounds. Constantinople never completely recovered from the catastrophe of 1204. Pope Innocent III, who had excommunicated the crusaders after they departed from their original goal and attacked fellow Christians, nonetheless accepted the *fait accompli*. The crusaders, loaded down with their loot, returned home, where some built churches to house their purloined relics. Even today the bronze horses on the Venetian church of San Marco, and other artworks, testify to the greatest art theft of the Middle Ages.

The sack of Constantinople

The crusaders put Baldwin of Flanders on the throne as the new ruler (r. 1204–06) of the newly created Latin Empire of Constantinople. This entity existed until 1261, but from its very beginning was barely able to survive. The number of Latins was limited, and their rule was hated. In addition, the rulers had to content themselves with a mere quarter of the conquest; the remainder was divided up as fiefs for crusader knights who settled permanently or was handed over to Venice, the true victor of 1204. The Latin Empire was economically and, in part, also politically dependent on Venice. Militarily, the state had been weakened ever since its defeat by the Bulgars at Adrianople (1205). On its eastern border the Greek successor states of Trebizond, Epiros, and Nicaea came into being, all of which claimed the imperial title and longed for a reconquest. Although their disunity delayed the fall of Latin rule for several decades, the Greek Empire of Nicaea progressively expanded its sphere of power and territory. Under the former general Emperor Michael VIII Paleologos (r. 1259–82) the Greeks finally succeeded in winning back Constantinople (July 25, 1261).

The Latin Empire of Constantinople

It was not greed, like the sack of 1204, that stood behind the venture known as the "Children's Crusade," but rather its opposite—the poverty movement, the call to follow the poor Christ.

The children's crusades

The term is misleading, since the "children's crusades" were neither papally sanctioned nor coherently planned and organized, and they didn't consist solely of children. The phenomenon consisted of several groups that included the poor, lower clergy, the elderly, women, and the young, who attached themselves to leaders vowed to poverty. One of these, Nicholas of Cologne, traveled through the Rhineland preaching in 1212 and collected a growing mob of followers, assuring them that the sea would part for Christ's followers so they could walk across the seabed to Palestine. In July/August 1212 they crossed the Alps. When the prophesied miracle did not occur and Pope Innocent III also failed to sanction the enterprise, the group broke up. Most returned home or settled in Italy. Shortly before this, another crowd under the young shepherd Stephen had experienced a similar fate in the Orléans region. They delivered a letter to King Philip II, supposedly written by God, that demanded a crusade, but then disbanded soon afterward. According to an unverifiable legend, some who still sought a passage to Palestine were betrayed by shipowners and sold in the Levant as slaves.

The so-called children's crusades were in part a reaction to the miscarried expedition of 1202–04, the poverty movement, and contemporary eschatological currents. They were also a result of papal crusade initiatives. Papal efforts encouraged increased devotion for the cross and fascination with the crusade. Later popular movements have similar characteristics, such as the *pastoureaux* (shepherds') movement active in northern France in 1251 or the flagellants who first appeared in about 1260. Although these movements always included other, partly sociopolitical concerns, they all had a recognizable crusade element, which led some of the *pastoureaux* and flagellants to embark for Palestine. But they had much less effect on the defense of the crusader states than did the papal and princely initiatives of the thirteenth century.

The crusade of 1217–21
In April 1213 Pope Innocent III called yet again for a crusade in the important bull *Quia maior* and two years later arrangements for the journey were further elaborated by a crusade decretal issued during the Fourth Lateran Council (1215). In 1217 Christian armies under Duke Leopold VI of Austria and King Andrew II of Hungary (r. 1205–35) sailed to Acre. From there they marched out on various ultimately unsuccessful expeditions against the Muslims. After King Andrew had departed in 1218 because of quarrels with the other princes, the

crusaders settled on a plan that had already been considered several times before, including by Richard the Lionheart: an attack on Egypt, home of Saladin's successors, the Ayyubids. The crusaders believed that if they could conquer Egypt the occupation and defense of Jerusalem would be a comparatively easy undertaking. In May 1218 the army set out against Damietta on the Nile Delta. There they were reinforced by crusaders from Frisia and the lower Rhine, who had already fought Muslims in Portugal while on their way to Palestine. The united army besieged the city for eighteen months, reducing the citizens to starvation and widespread sickness. The master of the Cologne cathedral school, Oliver of Paderborn, reports that people were paying eleven gold pieces for a single fig. The city finally fell on November 5, 1219. The Ayyubid sultan al-Kamil (r. 1218–38) had offered generous peace terms that even included ceding the city of Jerusalem, but the crusaders had refused. The leader of the crusade at this stage, the papal legate Pelagius, wanted the conquest of Egypt. Matters turned out very differently, though: in late August 1221 the army was trapped at al-Mansurah on the Nile and forced to surrender. The crusade came to a shameful end; its main effect was to sanction the conquest of Egypt as a legitimate goal for future crusaders.

The papacy had directed the failed crusade of Damietta more closely than any of its predecessors. By contrast, the next major initiative to win back the holy places would be led by a ruler who was in open conflict with the pope. Some might contest that this was a crusade at all, because it did not have papal authorization. Nonetheless, the expedition had its origins in a papally welcomed and approved plan that only ended in dispute at the last minute. This papal turn against its own crusade only makes sense against the background of growing tensions between Emperor Frederick II Hohenstaufen and the papacy over Italy. Already at the time of his imperial coronation in 1220 Frederick had renewed an earlier crusade vow. But political circumstances kept him from fulfilling his promise. When papal pressure on the emperor became intolerable, he swore in the Treaty of San Germano (July 1225) to undertake the journey—on pain of excommunication. Frederick's marriage in November 1225 to Queen Isabella II of Jerusalem bound the Hohenstaufen still more firmly to the fate of Outremer. In 1227 a first contingent of the army set out by sea, but the emperor himself was unable to depart because of illness. Consequently, Pope Gregory IX (r. 1227–41) excommunicated him.

The crusade of Emperor Frederick II

The emperor set out on his crusade despite the papal excommunication, landing at Acre in September 1228. There he surveyed the military and political situation and decided to employ diplomatic means to achieve his goal. Modern scholars, influenced by contemporary papal criticisms, have overemphasized how exceptional this step was. In fact, however, by this time a long history of diplomatic contacts between crusaders and Muslims could be traced; one need only consider Richard I's treaties with Saladin. What was new in Frederick's case was his almost exclusive recourse to diplomatic means; Frederick's army saw hardly any military action at all. At any rate, success proved the emperor right. He was able to win control over Jerusalem and several other cities (including Bethlehem and Nazareth) in a treaty signed with the Ayyubid sultan al-Kamil on February 18, 1229 at Jaffa. The agreement was limited to ten years, however, and specifically excluded Christian control of the Temple Mount with the Dome of the Rock and the al-Aqsa Mosque. Besides, the bizarre spectacle of an excommunicated crusader who entered the Church of the Holy Sepulcher in full imperial regalia, thereby expressing his claims to the throne of Jerusalem, damaged the prestige of both the crusades and the papacy.

These years gave the threatened city its last breathing space. The 1239–41 expeditions of Thibald of Champagne and Richard of Cornwall did nothing to alter the military situation. To be sure, regions of northern Palestine could be won by conquest and others in southern Palestine were acquired by treaty, but all the while a new threat was growing against the crusader states—the Khorezmians. This central Asian Muslim tribe of nomads had been driven from its homeland by the Mongols, and the Ayyubids had settled them in Syria as confederates. A Khorezmian army launched a sudden assault on Jerusalem and sacked the holy city on August 23, 1244. The Christian inhabitants were slaughtered, the churches destroyed, and with a single blow Christian rule of Jerusalem was brought to an end.

The crusades between 1244 and the fall of Acre, 1291

As if the fall of Jerusalem were not enough, two months later the Christian army of Outremer suffered its worst defeat since Hattin at the Battle of Forbie (Gaza) on October 17, 1244, against an Egyptian-Khorezmian army. Most of the fighters, including many members of the military orders, were left dead on the field. The only reason the catastrophe did not lead directly to the destruction of the crusader states was because a new and unexpected threat turned Muslim attention away from the Christians of the Levant: the Mongols.

The Mongols (Tatars)

"Mongols" is the collective term used for tribes of nomadic horsemen from the regions of western and northern China. Under the leadership of Chinggis Khan (1155–1227) and his grandson Batu (d. 1242) they had enjoyed an unparalleled expansion that led them westward as far as the gates of the Roman-German Empire and eastward to the Pacific Ocean. A number of ancient Central Asian civilizations fell victim to their brutal conquests. Among others, the Khorezmians gave ground to Mongol pressure (thus their appearance in the Levant). In 1258 Baghdad, the Abbasid capital, fell to Hulagu, another grandson of Chinggis Khan. In January 1260 Hulagu's troops invaded Syria and took both Aleppo and Damascus. The Christians in the Latin West regarded this as the approach of a potential ally and equated the Mongol khans with the legendary Prester John, a Christian ruler who was expected to come to the aid of his co-religionists. But on September 3, 1260 the Muslims defeated the Mongols decisively at the Battle of 'Ain-Jalut near Nazareth. To be sure, for centuries the Mongol Empire remained decisive in Asia and repeatedly established diplomatic contacts with the Christians that proposed common action against the Muslims. But these plans were never put into effect on a large scale.

The French king Louis IX (r. 1226–70) also maintained good relations with the Mongols. The honored, deeply pious king had taken the cross when he heard of the defeat at Forbie; the first Council of Lyons in 1245 approved his campaign and provided it with financial support. Louis's army traveled via Cyprus to Damietta, site of the ultimately failed campaign of 1219–21. Louis succeeded in taking the city on June 6, 1249, but as the crusaders marched on Cairo in the winter of 1249/50 they were defeated at al-Mansurah on February 8. Jean de Joinville (d. 1317), who took part in the expedition, tells in moving terms of the privations the army had to suffer as it retreated. Decimated by disease and further attacks, the crusaders, including their king, surrendered on April 6. Louis won their freedom in exchange for Damietta and a large ransom, but stayed in the Holy Land until 1254, where he took steps to buttress the crusader states. The crusade was over; a military success was no longer possible.

In 1270, the French king, then aged 56, undertook a second crusade, intended to counter the gradual advance of the Mamluks, Islam's new military power. Under Sultan Baibars (r. 1260–77) the Mamluks conquered Jaffa and Antioch in 1268 and posed an increasing threat to Acre. Louis IX received support from the English prince Edward (later King Edward I). The Sicilian king Charles I, on the other hand, pursued his own political interests in the Mediterranean basin and convinced his brother Louis to attack Tunis. But the pious French king—he was

The first crusade of King Louis IX (1248–54)

canonized as a saint in 1297—died in an epidemic soon after his arrival at Carthage (August 25, 1270), and his expedition came to a premature end.

The fall of the crusader states

At this time the crusader states needed outside help more than ever. A powerful opponent, dedicated to their destruction, had appeared in the person of Baibars, who closed the ring ever tighter around Acre. After Antioch, he took the important castles Crac de Chevaliers, Chastel Blanc, and Gibelacar (1271). Although a truce between Prince Edward and Baibars in 1272 gave a breathing space, the threat was by no means averted. But the Latin rulers were too busy with other matters to listen to appeals for help coming from the East. The German kingdom found itself in a period of upheaval after the fall of the Hohenstaufen dynasty, the great Italian sea powers were at war with each other, and the dispute between the kingdoms of Aragon and Sicily over possession of Sicily developed into a major conflict that drained western military energies beyond those of the direct participants. All the while, the noose drew tighter around Acre. On April 2, 1289 the Mamluks took Tripoli, massacring the male population.

Appeals for a crusade went out repeatedly to the western rulers; plans were laid and funds raised. But only a few small fighting units made it to Outremer to support King Henry II of Cyprus (r. 1285–1324), the defender of Acre. When an enormous Mamluk army under Sultan al-Asraf Halil (r. 1290–93) moved against the city early in 1291, all possible resources were pulled together for defense. The siege of Acre lasted several weeks, but the undermined walls crumbled on May 18 and the conquerors flowed in. Just as at Tripoli, all the men who could not save themselves by ship were killed, along with many women and children. Those who remained were sold into slavery. The last bastion of the crusader states of the East had fallen. Many survivors found a new home on Cyprus. There, a flourishing court life developed around the kings of the Lusignan dynasty, keeping alive the memory of the lost kingdom and crafting ever-new plans to win it back.

Attempts to win back the Holy Land

News of the fall of Acre hit the West like a bomb. There had been widespread fear that such an event could occur—now the worst had actually befallen. In Palestine, the Mamluks immediately set about the complete destruction of the formerly Christian port cities of Acre, Sidon, Tripoli, and others, to prevent an eventual crusader return. All the same, in the last decade of the thirteenth century efforts were made to establish bridgeheads at Nephin (near Tripoli) and at Ruad. Their failure quickly made it plain that a large general crusade would be needed for any long-term success.

Against this backdrop a series of memoranda and treatises on the *recu-peratio Terrae Sanctae*, the recovery of the Holy Land, were written. Some were produced by rulers like King Charles II of Sicily (r. 1285–1309; treatise 1291), the Armenian prince Hethum (1307), or King Henry II of Cyprus (1321), some by men with military training, like Jacques de Molay (d. 1314; treatise 1305/06) or Foulques de Villaret (d. 1319; treatises 1305, 1306/07), the masters of the Templars and the Hospitallers. Others were composed by political advisors like the French Pierre Dubois (d. *c.* 1321) or merchants like the Venetian Marino Sanudo the Elder (d. 1343). Most of the authors, though, were churchmen. Worthy of mention here are the Catalan theologian Ramón Llull (d. 1316), the Franciscan Fidenzio of Padua, and the anonymous Dominican author of the *Directorium ad passagium faciendum* of 1332.

Treatises on the recovery of Palestine

In part, these texts outlined very precise tactical–strategic proposals. Many recommended assaults on Armenia, Egypt, or Tunisia. Repeatedly the plan was mooted to unite the military orders or to dissolve them out of hand and found a new one. Naturally, there was also much talk of far-reaching political alliances between rulers. And in fact various rulers did take the cross, such as the French kings Philip IV (r. 1285–1314) in 1313 and Philip VI (r. 1328–50) in 1331. The 1320s in particular saw the birth of intensive preparations and plans. But the power struggles between the kings of Europe and the growing mistrust between them stood in the way of such wide-ranging plans. For example, the question had to be answered to whom the new military orders should be subject. The heart of the problem was the struggle for preeminence in the Mediterranean. The papacy for its part had entered a period of weakness since 1303, when Pope Boniface VIII (r. 1294–1303) was humiliated by order of the French king. The curia's move to a new papal residence at Avignon only strengthened its dependency on the French crown. Under these circumstances, the many treatises that continued to urge the recovery of the Holy Land were only so much paper. On the diplomatic front, however, there was some progress. For example, the Franciscan Order won permission to found the *custodia Terrae Sanctae*.

In the fourteenth century, too, Christians and Muslims fought repeatedly in the Levant. Quite in the tradition of earlier crusades was King Peter I of Cyprus's (r. 1359–69) campaign in 1365. His chancellor, Philippe de Mézières (*c.* 1327–1407), and the French poet and musician Guillaume de Machaut (d. 1377) have left reports of it. Despite limited support from the West, the king and his small fleet succeeded against all expectation in conquering Alexandria through a surprise attack (October 9, 1365). Many of the city's people were killed. As a Muslim relief fleet approached, most of the crusaders left with their plunder, and King Peter, against his will, had to follow. Similarly lacking in success was a large-scale assault against Mahdia (al-Mahdiya) in modern Tunisia, conducted by a Genoese fleet with the support of French, English, and Spanish knights in 1390.

The *custodia Terrae Sanctae*

The kings of Aragon had already established diplomatic relations with the Mamluk sultans before the fall of Acre. These ties benefited the trade of Catalan merchants in the Mediterranean basin and North Africa. At the same time the rulers repeatedly interceded with the sultans on behalf of Christian pilgrims and prisoners. In this way they came to establish a sort of protectorate over the affairs of their co-religionists in Mamluk territories. This position also had a political dimension, because in the western Mediterranean the rulers of Aragon were in competition with the Angevin kings of Sicily. These, too, made contacts with the sultan on behalf of Christians and in the mid-1330s won permission to send some Franciscan friars to Jerusalem. They were soon allowed to establish themselves at the tomb of Christ. The Franciscans took over the guardianship of the Holy Sepulcher, the *custodia Terrae Sanctae* (or *custodia di Terra Santa*), looked after the Christian pilgrims, and continued the tradition of dubbing noble or wealthy travelers as "knights of the Holy Sepulcher." Today, the Franciscans still maintain the *custodia* at Christ's tomb in Jerusalem.

Late medieval crusades in the Balkans

Crusading took on a new character in the Balkans. The Mongols had destroyed the Seljuq sultanate in Asia Minor, but from the ruins rose a new power, the sultanate of the Ottoman Turks. In the course of the fourteenth century the Ottomans united the emirates of Anatolia under their rule and crossed the Bosporus. With this move, they applied pressure not just to the eastern Mediterranean but to central Europe. Latin Christendom found its heartland threatened by Muslims for the first time in centuries. The conflict with the Ottomans is the most distinctive feature of the late medieval crusades. To ward off the danger in the Aegean, various alliances, called "holy leagues," were formed between Christian sea powers (1332–34, 1344, 1359, etc.), that made common cause against the Turks and thus earned crusading indulgences. The members of these leagues were mostly local powers (such as Venice and the Hospitallers on Rhodes). Only exceptionally did troops from central and western Europe join them.

The fall of the Byzantine Empire

The most important exception to this local character of the wars in the Balkans was in 1396 when a large army of crusader knights under the Hungarian king, and later emperor, Sigismund (r. 1387–1437) launched an expedition against the Ottomans. Many nobles of France and Burgundy, imbued with chivalric ideals, joined in. They had a rude awakening on the battlefield of Nicopolis on September 25, 1396, where they were completely annihilated by an Ottoman army under Sultan Bayazid I (r. 1389–1402). Hungary, Bohemia, and all of Central Europe were placed in danger of attack. But the Ottoman army and its sultan soon themselves fell victim to a powerful enemy: on July 20, 1402 the Mongols under Timur the Lame (Tamerlane, r. 1370–1405) defeated them in a great battle. Only the khan's interest in another front (China) and his death in 1405 saved the Ottoman Empire. The Turkish catastrophe of 1402 gave the Byzantine Empire a grace period of half a century. In 1422 it successfully warded off an Ottoman attack, but slowly the danger increased once again. Appeals for help were sent to the West; the Byzantine emperor even agreed to reunification with the Roman Church (1437). But the Greek Orthodox Christians of Constantinople ignored the ecclesiastical union, and a Polish-Hungarian crusader army suffered a horrible defeat at Varna in 1444. The event that had been evaded so many times by fate or good fortune finally came to pass on May 29, 1453: Muslim troops under Sultan Mehmed II (r. 1444–46, 1451–81) conquered Constantinople. The Byzantine Empire, for whose help the First Crusade had been called in 1095, had ceased to exist.

Practice, theory, and critique of crusading

The practical problems of a crusade

The organization and conduct of a crusade brought many challenges, both for its leaders and for individual participants. The crusaders had to spend a great deal of money, especially when, like the knights, they not only had to purchase expensive war gear but had to pay attendants (squires, etc.), too. Property often had to change hands. Already the First Crusade had caused a considerable reshuffling of real estate, many monasteries buying land from financially strapped crusaders. More often, landowners mortgaged their estates, because the land could be used and revenue earned from it as long as the crusader was away. If he came back, the land returned to its proprietor once the mortgage was paid; if he died, it was transferred to his heir under the same conditions. Crusaders also had to take steps for their souls' well-being during the journey and in the afterlife. So they donated considerable funds to religious institutions in return for prayers. Finally, the estate, the castle, or the kingdom had to be put in the hands of competent and trustworthy deputies. For kings, this was normally a relative; sometimes the pope also took a role as advisor to the regent.

Before their departure, the crusaders had to buy durable food supplies like cheese, salt meat, and beans. The purchases posed major logistical challenges when it was necessary to provision entire armies. Still more complicated was the question of transport. From the end of the twelfth century, most crusaders traveled by sea. The potentate, like King Richard I the Lionheart of England, who had his own fleet, was in an enviable position. In such cases, not only the passage but military and logistical support were assured. Normally, however, the fleets of Mediterranean trade cities like Genoa, Venice, or Marseille, already

Logistical and financial problems

experienced in pilgrim transport, were hired for the task. The shippers charged a graduated tariff, according to comfort level and equipment. The solution of organizational and financial problems was made easier by institutions in Outremer. Besides the territorial lords, this meant above all the military religious orders, which, thanks to their presence on both sides of the Mediterranean, offered the best means for carrying out financial transactions. But what was needed above all was the organizational ability and authority of the army's commander. Crusade armies usually consisted of diverse contingents of troops. The command structure had to be agreed on and unified to ensure the undertaking's success. It also served to keep discipline during the journey. After the pillaging of the first undertakings, draconian punishments were imposed to keep the peace both within the army and toward the inhabitants of lands they marched through.

Financial problems also often remained dire while the campaign was underway. As far as they had any means left, crusaders exchanged money in foreign lands and bought food from local merchants. Crusader poems and other sources tell of the decisive moment in a crusader's life when the money he had brought along finally ran out. For the great as well as for the lesser men, this often meant changes in their original plans. For example, the decision the crusaders of 1202–4 made to detour to Zara and later to Constantinople was imposed by financial pressure. In general, it seems certain that most crusaders returned home impoverished—if they ever got home again at all. The situation was even worse for those taken captive. Great Muslim victories flooded eastern markets with Christian slaves and made the prices plummet. Only the wealthy could hope for ransom from captivity, and this financial burden reduced some noble families to penury. When even the well-to-do often encountered financial problems, it is not surprising that the burdens placed on the poorer crusaders were often much worse. "Living from the land" was only possible to a limited degree, and besides was only officially allowed in enemy territory; often people had to help themselves as best they could. A crusader in the service of a powerful lord had fewer difficulties, since the latter had to provide subsistence (for which he could in turn demand taxes and dues). This, however, by no means applied to all simple crusaders, for many people who were not warriors accompanied the expeditions, although in the normative texts they are rarely or never mentioned. Among them were churchmen, physicians, and women.

Clerics and physicians as crusaders

Officially, monks were forbidden to participate in a crusade, because the journey was a breach of their vow of stability of place (*stabilitas loci*). Already in the first crusades, though, it appears that this prohibition was frequently ignored. Many secular clerics also journeyed to Outremer, some as chaplains to a magnate, others on their own initiative. Among the laity, there were groups like the physicians, who mostly took part in the crusade to practice their healing arts—which does not mean that they did not take up arms at need. And finally there was a group whose presence was repeatedly, and unsuccessfully, forbidden in the crusade bulls—the women. In the medieval crusades, women played highly diverse roles: as serving women and wives traveling with their husbands, as prostitutes, and as fighters.

Women on crusades

From the first expedition of 1096–99, many female crusaders traveled to the East. Albert of Aachen and other authors report that on the one hand the women supported the army, but on the other hand could be a hindrance on the long marches. The pattern repeated itself on later expeditions. The *Itinerarium regis Ricardi* tells that before Acre in 1191 the women helped with the earthworks, and the Anglo-Norman poet Ambrose reports in his *Estoire de la Guerre Sainte* that there were women fighters among the crusaders. Some of these tales became part of the edifying literature of the age as *exempla* of moral behavior—such as the story of the wounded crusader woman who asked to be thrown into the ditch at Acre so that in death she could help fill it and thus aid in the city's conquest. But it was not only fighting women who accompanied the expedition. Prostitutes, too, took part, and were sometimes blamed for military failures: God's army, moralists declared, had sinned and therefore justly suffered defeats. This was an important reason for the prohibitions against women taking part in crusades. But they had little effect, and there is evidence that many nobles and princes took their wives along to the East. Some of them, like the French queen Eleanor of Aquitaine (d. 1204), also had an active influence on political relations in Outremer.

The sources speak repeatedly of gambling, falconry, and other pastimes of the wealthier knights. Blatant licentiousness, though, was certainly exceptional; crusaders pledged personal purification in their crusade vow. But such occurrences are an indication of the practical problems of the crusade. They called for action; in the course of the twelfth century the crusade expeditions were established on firm principles that will be discussed in the following chapter.

Creating an institutional framework for the crusades

The First Crusade was something new, and fixed rules for it did not really exist. It brought many legal and organizational challenges to the Church, secular rulers, and the crusaders themselves. Solutions only gradually emerged, starting in the second half of the twelfth century. This "institutionalization of the crusades" was completed in its essentials by the end of Innocent III's pontificate (1216), after which only details still needed to be refined. In this context, it is possible to

Legal and organizational challenges

distinguish five task or problem areas that required the establishment of firm rules. First was the question of protection: these newfangled expeditions took men from their families and possessions for far longer periods than previous campaigns. In their absence, how could the security of those who stayed at home and the economic survival of the estate be assured? Second was the financial problem: crusades were for the most part undertaken voluntarily and thus should be privately financed. But here, too, solutions had to be found. The difficulties encountered depended on the organization of crusade financing by secular and religious institutions. Third was the commitment by oath: the first crusaders had sworn an oath. But how binding was this crusade vow—was it possible to fulfill it without personally making the journey to Palestine? Fourth was the unclearly defined scope of the crusade indulgence. It was not obvious how far the privilege extended at Clermont reached. In 1095/96 this issue had not remained completely under the Church's surveillance, an important consequence of which was the "People's Crusades." To prevent similar unforeseen consequences, control of the channels of information (crusade preaching and publicity) had to be organized more strictly. A series of answers were found to these five pressing questions.

Perhaps the most urgent issue was clarification of the crusaders' legal position, and thus their worldly privileges. The already-mentioned bull *Quantum praedecessores* of December 14, 1145 settled this point: the Church took the crusader, his possessions, and his dependants under its protection. In other words, it removed the crusader from secular jurisdiction. Debts and interest payments were frozen while he was gone, mortgaging of possessions was expressly permitted. During the pontificate of Innocent III (r. 1198–1216) crusader privileges were expanded still further to include freedom from taxation and special services, as well as permission for clerics, during a crusade, to enjoy the income from benefices or to mortgage them. These rights were attractive, and some were quick to take the cross but slow to carry out their oaths. In reaction, in 1286 the papacy decreed that a crusader's privileges only came into force when he actually set out. These and other legal definitions of crusader status were essentially a matter for the canon lawyers.

Crusade taxes
After the legal issue, the second problem, the financial aspect of a crusade, was particularly important. The crusaders took their vows of their own free will and thus had to finance themselves. But crusading devoured enormous sums. A system that relied solely on the initiative of individuals put these to too great a strain: families could be deprived of the fundamentals of life, and whole lineages collapse. So in the course of the twelfth century financing passed considerably, although never exclusively, into the hands of the Church and kings. As early as 1166 Louis VII of France (r. 1137–80) levied a crusade tax, a measure taken again in 1185. This form of crusade finance reached a new level with the

---

Canon law

Canon law is the law of the Catholic Church. It is based on the Bible, the works of the Church fathers, the prescriptions (*canones*) of synods (assemblies of bishops), and papal declarations. In the eleventh century several collections of such *canones* were created, but canon law first really flourished in the twelfth century. In 1140 the most famous canon law collection, the *Decretum Gratiani* (Gratian's Decretum) was completed. Along with later collections it formed the *Corpus iuris canonici*, which regulated not just churchmen's lives but many areas of lay behavior. In terms of canon law, the crusaders belonged to the prior group, because their crusader vows temporarily transplanted them to the clerical state; thus, their rights could be regulated through the laws of the Church. The importance of canon law in the twelfth century can be seen in the fact that several canonists were elected pope during this period. The most famous of them was Innocent III (r. 1198–1216), under whom the legal status of crusaders was finally clarified. Canon law also assured that the papacy's leading role in the call and organization of a crusade remained unquestioned. The canonists also established the theoretical foundation for expanding the idea of crusade to include attacks on heretic and schismatics in the thirteenth century (see "Enemies within," p. 134).

---

crusade tax of 1188, called the "Saladin Tithe," that both the English king Henry II (r. 1154–89) and the French king Philip II Augustus (r. 1180–1223) raised. It was levied on both lay and clerical income and paved the way for the English and French kings' demanding a fortieth part of all income in 1201. Still, the expenses remained enormous. For his first crusade, Louis IX had to raise six times the regular annual income of the crown, a total of 1.5 million livres tournois. To bring together such a massive sum of money, the crusade organization had to expand both administratively and logistically. Thus the thirteenth-century expeditions were usually fundamentally better planned than their predecessors. Above all, in the second half of the century, official powers took the matter of the *passagium* into their own hands, and individual initiative took second place.

The papacy played a vital role in this sort of institutionalization. The Church had access to three major sources of income—taxation of the clergy, general contributions, and subsidies. In 1199 Innocent III levied a tax of one-fortieth of all ecclesiastical incomes, although admittedly the clerics affected were slow to pay. A demand for a twentieth, to be paid over the course of three years, followed in 1215 to finance the Damietta crusade. The papacy found itself—not least because of the clergy's general unwillingness—compelled to create a more comprehensive system. It established collectors, who were put in charge of specific districts. Their records form an important source of information on ecclesiastical wealth in the Middle Ages. Collection boxes were also placed in churches and monasteries and the faithful were exhorted to give generously. The subsidies called for on specific occasions also provided welcome financial boosts, which however had to be defended against the covetousness of secular rulers.

Dispensation and commutation

Finally, the Church received payments in return for freeing crusaders from their vows (dispensation). This measure not only brought financial gain but also helped solve a legal difficulty of the crusade. Through dispensation, those Christians for whom direct military activity was impossible received an opportunity to contribute their share to the crusade. Dispensation also solved the problem of hastily made vows, for it now became possible to substitute something else for the vow; in other words to "commute" it. This could be done in three ways: first, instead of going to the Holy Land, one could fight the enemies of the Church on another front (e.g., in Spain or against heretics); second, it was also possible to send a warrior to the East as a substitute; or third, one could give the cost of the crusade to the Church. The person involved received the status and privileges of a crusader despite the dispensation or commutation. Freeing from vows through monetary payment increasingly developed into a special form of purchasing indulgences. At the same time, commutation gave the papacy a useful tool for political power: crusade armies could now be used for other, eventually papal goals. In 1236 Gregory IX commuted the crusade vows of several hundred French knights so he could use them to defend the Latin Empire against the Greeks. Similarly, in 1264/65 knights were "diverted" from fighting the Mamluk sultan Baibars to wage a campaign against the Hohenstaufen in southern Italy. This practice did not win universal acceptance and encouraged criticism of the crusades.

As far as the actual crusade indulgences are concerned—the fourth problem—they came to be broadly defined in general thought and the sermons of crusade propagandists; already in Urban II's time popular belief held that an indulgence was a complete cancellation of actual sins. This point of view became well established despite the efforts of individual theologians, who at the beginning of the thirteenth century still attempted to distinguish between cancellation of the *guilt* of sin and its *punishment*. The crusade proclamations of 1145 and 1198, for example, explicitly stated that those who fulfilled their vows and went on crusade would win complete *remissio peccatorum* (see "Penance and indulgence," p. 30). Early in the thirteenth century Innocent III simplified the conditions by offering the indulgence for forty days of active service in the Albigensian Crusade. Besides the full (plenary) indulgence, graduated partial indulgences were also offered—by the late Middle Ages even for merely listening to a crusade sermon. As well as dispensations, the new indulgence regulations made it easier to participate in the crusades without taking any military part; the crusades more and more became a special, often nonviolent form of religious devotion. This transformation can be seen in crusade sermons.

Crusade sermons

Many such sermons from the high and late Middle Ages, including handbooks of crusade sermons like that compiled by the Dominican Humbert of Romans (*De praedicatione Sanctae Crucis contra Sarracenos, c.* 1266), are extant. These texts are important sources of information on medieval views, images, and modes of communication. The preachers told anecdotes and *exempla* (short instructive tales), drew attention to the unique opportunity to win the indulgence, and called for defense or reconquest of the Holy Land.

These sermons and other speeches were fundamental components of crusade propaganda, organized primarily by the Church. Popes, archbishops, bishops, and even parish priests are known to have preached the cross as part of their offices. However, there were also clerics who received special commissions to devote themselves full-time to the task. In the twelfth century, many of these special preachers were Cistercians and secular clerics; afterward friars of the mendicant orders were preferred. Famous preachers like Bernard of Clairvaux (see "The crusades to the Battle of Hattin, 1187," p. 47), the head of the Cologne cathedral school Oliver of Paderborn, or the later bishop of Acre Jacques de Vitry (see "The Latin Church," p. 104) were enlisted for this task. Normally crusade preachers were authorized by the pope, whose most effective means for advertising the crusade was the crusade bull. The bulls *Quantum praedecessores* (1145) and *Ad liberandam* (1215) became the models for later such documents. *Quantum praedecessores* was the first to introduce the repeatedly copied sequence of narrative—exhortation—privilege (*narratio—exhortatio—privilegia*). Transmission of crusade bulls was regulated, at the latest by the beginning of the thirteenth century, thanks to the growing comprehensiveness of the papal bureaucracy. First archbishops and then suffragan bishops had copies of the document prepared that were then sent out to the parish clergy. Crusade sermons, often given in an atmosphere of festive processions and public prayers, then spread the word to the faithful. This process very often culminated in the listeners swearing crusade vows and taking the cross.

Crusade advertising

A secular form of propaganda—songs and poems that exhorted people to take the cross—supplemented ecclesiastical initiatives. Fame and amorous success served in these works as inducements for taking the cross. The poets aimed especially at a type of crusader that became more significant in the fourteenth and fifteenth centuries: the chivalrous noble, who sought out foreign courts in the so-called late medieval grand tour, motivated by a characteristic blend of longing for adventure, crusade ideology, and wanderlust. This development forms part of a general tendency. On the one hand, for broad sectors of the populace the crusades had become a special form of devotion. At the

The crusade as knightly "grand tour"

same time, though, on the other hand the social and geographical recruiting ground for actual fighters became narrower—among other reasons because of the financial, logistical, and organizational changes that have been described. The crusades increasingly became a noble venture undertaken for the most part by the groups that were under the most direct threat. Mostly Germans participated in the Hussite crusades, mostly Spaniards fought in the Iberian expeditions, Hungarians concerned themselves with fighting the Ottomans, etc. The practice of the crusade had become significantly different from its origins. This fact led to criticism, not only from churchmen. Narrative sources, treatises, and poems testify that these and other reproaches were also known in wide sections of the population. A chorus of critical voices rose that rejected specific crusade practices or the expeditions as a whole.

Criticism of crusading

Ever since the first failed crusade undertakings (1096, 1101, 1147/48), some people demanded an explanation: how could it have come to pass that an expedition called on the Lord's behalf had failed? The oft-repeated answer to this question was that human sinfulness had cost the crusaders God's support. Pope Eugenius III already provided this explanation in the bull *Quantum praedecessores* of December 1, 1145. It also served to exculpate the fiasco of 1147/48, as well as other reverses. Reports of loose living on the crusade journey, of pride, greed, and other failings, only appeared to substantiate the charge. Prior Gerhoh of Reichersberg (1093–1169) gives a further explanation for the crusaders' defeat. In his *De investigatione Antichristi* of 1160/62 he identified two other guilty parties besides the crusaders: the Byzantines for their half-hearted support and especially the Latins of the crusader states, who through their greed had supposedly brought about the unhappy end of the expedition. Earlier reservations about journeys to the Holy Land supplemented this form of crusade—or more accurately, crusader—criticism.

General criticism of pilgrimage and of war

Objections had been raised to pilgrimage since long before the First Crusade. Above all, two complaints had been brought up repeatedly: first, that it was simply not necessary to travel to distant places for sanctification, and second that pilgrimage brings direct dangers to both body and soul. St Jerome had admonished, in a letter to Paulinus, that living well was more salutary than leaving one's home. From the ascetic-monastic perspective the pilgrim's mobility appeared to be downright negative, because it broke the command to maintain *stabilitas loci* (remaining in the same place). As for the inner danger to the pilgrim, this was especially reduced to sexual offenses. As the late medieval popular theologian Thomas à Kempis (1379/80–1471) put it: *Qui multum peregrinantur, raro sanctificantur* (he who travels much on pilgrimage is rarely sanctified). Well beyond the Middle Ages these and similar objections were still a recurrent theme. One need only think of Luther's biting critique of pilgrimage: that it was nothing but adventure, and that besides, the showing and veneration of relics was dangerously close to worshiping idols.

Still more fundamental was the objection against military strife itself: that wars against the Muslims were sinful, since they were contradictory to Christ's words and deeds of peace, the pacifistic passages of the Old Testament such as Ezekiel 33:11, or the voluntary martyrdom of the saints. We know that such voices existed because theologians argued against them. The canonist Gratian (d. *c.* 1150) did so in his *Decretum*, as did the author of a letter written sometime in the period 1128–36 to the young community of Templars, who argued the question of whether it was wrong and depraved to kill enemies. Admittedly, these voices were apparently not particularly loud, and barely a single advocate of this line of argument is known by name. Fundamental criticism of pilgrimage or war, although ongoing, is not very well attested.

More familiar by contrast were concrete reproaches against participation in a crusade. Some of these objections were completely practical in nature, such as the complaint that a man's absence would place his family in danger. Reports of encroachments against crusaders' possessions and dependants testify that such warnings were justified. Despite that sort of complaint, contemporary criticism usually did not focus on the practice of crusading in itself. The objections about negative corollary phenomena were addressed mostly against those who exploited the situation, rather than against the crusade as such.

The majority of objections were leveled against three features of the crusades, all consequences of the thirteenth-century institutionalization described above. First was the expansion of the idea of crusade beyond its original Palestinian goal, second was the delay of crusades to the Holy Land, and third was the use of crusades by secular or ecclesiastical potentates to serve their own political, financial, or military objectives. Very often these complaints were treated as related to each other, such as by the southern French troubadour Guilhem de Figueira (active 1215–40) in the period *c.* 1227–29. He accused the popes of acting against Greeks and Latins from greed, but sparing the Muslims. The Albigensian crusades of the early thirteenth century, and the calling of a crusade against Emperor Frederick II, received particularly harsh censure from poets and singers.

Concrete criticisms of the crusade

Further events of the thirteenth century, especially the gradual Mamluk advance, gave greater impetus to crusade criticism. The failure of many undertakings and the difficulty in organizing more expeditions led some contemporaries, like the Italian chronicler Salimbene de Adam (or of Parma, 1221–88) to the conclusion that winning back the

---

The troubadours

At the end of the eleventh century singers in the Midi (southern France) began to compose songs in their own language, the *langue d'oc*. Soon afterward, troubadours also started to create poems in eastern Spain and Italy. This genre had a deep influence on the German-speaking minnesingers. At the heart of their works were love and the "service of ladies," but they also expressed their opinions on the crusades. Often they furthered the work of crusade preachers; in other cases they linked the crusades to the subjects dear to them. *Militia amoris* (chivalrous knighthood) was linked to the *militia Dei*, service of love became service of God and vice versa. In this genre, participation in a crusade often became a journey through which one won the love of a lady. Troubadours and minnesingers played an important role in the crusade movement, both by composing calls for the defense or conquest of the holy places and by idealizing true or fictional experiences. However, they also seized on contemporary criticism and strengthened it. The disillusioning end of the 1202–4 expedition, but especially the Albigensian war and the condemnation of Frederick II, had a negative impact. In the early thirteenth century southern France was both a theater of war and the heartland of troubadour poetry, and some minnesingers recited their pieces at the Hohenstaufen court. Walther von der Vogelweide (d. *c.* 1230), the most famous of the minnesingers, composed both exhortations to take the cross (*ouwê waz êren sich ellendet von tiuschen landen*, 1227/28) and poems against the pope's presumed greed (*The Irritated Song*, 1213) and his trespasses against the emperor (*Emperor Frederick's Tune*, 1224/27).

---

holy places was not God's will. At the second Council of Lyons in 1274, the Dominican theologian Humbert of Romans (*c.* 1200–77) compiled at Pope Gregory IX's (r. 1271–76) request possible objections to crusading in an assessment (the *Opusculum tripartitum*) under seven headings. These ranged from practical considerations about the numerical imbalance between Christians and Muslims in the Near East to the charge that crusading kept Muslims from the possibility of conversion, to doubts about whether crusading was pleasing to God at all.

Criticism of the papacy — New reverses came in the fourteenth century, and with them emerged new grounds for complaint. A special target was the papacy's lust for power, which found expression in the curia's move to Avignon and the papacy's resulting dependence on the French kings, as the dissolution of the Knights Templars at the urging of the French king Philip IV demonstrates. All these factors undermined papal prestige and thus indirectly also that of the crusades, because the canonists had juridically linked the papacy with crusading. The expansion of the bureaucracy that dealt with papal finance, which had served the thirteenth-century crusades well, quickly became the object of further attacks, when funds were collected but no expeditions set out. Crusade criticism was in this case to a large degree criticism of the papacy, especially when directed against the popes' political crusades, undertaken to secure papal power in Italy (see "The Church's secular enemies," p. 141). Occasionally this anti-papal criticism of the crusades made common cause with contemporary spiritual trends like Joachimism (named after Joachim of Fiore, d. *c.* 1202/5) and other millenarian movements. These movements advocated the peaceful conversion of the Muslims as a sign of a new, emerging age of humankind and consequently relegated the crusades to an older age soon to be overcome. But despite their growing numbers and various charges, the effectiveness of the diverse critiques, here given in broad outline, was limited. Certainly the idea of crusade did not collapse in the late Middle Ages. In the fifteenth century, too, plans were made and campaigns carried out. The only difference is that such initiatives could no longer hope for a massive resonance that reached beyond political boundaries. They usually remained a matter for individual princes.

The crusades from the Muslim perspective

The crusader lordships in Islamic power structures

Conflict with the Christian invaders was merely one element, and not the most important one, in the complex history of the medieval Islamic world, the Dar al-Islam (see "The Islamic world in *c.* 1095," p. 5). Therefore, in the following section I intend to place the presence of Latins in Outremer into the larger context of events in the Near East. The crusades appear here solely in the form they were usually perceived by the Muslims: as campaigns to provide military support for the Christian states of the Levant. The question must also be investigated how demarcation from the Christians helped foster the idea of jihad and to which political use this concept was put in the course of the twelfth century. Finally, I will move from military and political history and the history of ideas to the field of perception of the Other, to consider how the Muslims visualized their new neighbors or lords. Muslim historians like the lord of Saizar, Usama ibn Munqid, are important sources for many of these issues.

Usama ibn Munqid (1095–1188) came from the Shi'ite clan of the Banu Munqid and ruled over the town and region of Shaizar (Caesarea on the Orontes) in northern Syria. He fought the Latins on various occasions, but also frequently had diplomatic contacts with them. Among those with whom he dealt was King Fulk of Jerusalem (r. 1131–43), whom he visited in the course of one of his diplomatic missions. In his chief work, *Kitab al-i'tibar*, Usama describes how divine providence determines human life. To prove his point, Usama presented a wide variety of anecdotes, in part stemming from his encounters with the Christians of Outremer. The work is not an autobiography, an important point to bear in mind when interpreting it. Usama expresses contempt for Christians in stereotypical fashion, but also mentions positive experiences with particular individuals. He sketches a valuable picture of the common Muslim attitudes and prejudices toward Christians as well as the various sorts of interaction between the two faiths in the crusader states.

Muslim reactions to the First Crusade

In the Muslim world, the First Crusade and the fall of Jerusalem at first had little impact, at least as far as we can see from the modern perspective. It was in fact hard to imagine that the invading northern barbarians—some authors, like the Seljuq poet al-Abiwardi, confuse them with Byzantine troops—would not only hang onto the narrow strip of conquered land on the Levantine coast but would also be able to expand it. Only over time did the annoyance come to be recognized as a real problem. Not a single Arabic text can properly be called a "Muslim crusade chronicle," and within Islam even the neighbors of those attacked took little notice; in Egypt, Iran, or the Maghreb, sources for the most part pass over crusade events in silence.

It was not, however, these distant areas that were decisive for the survival of the crusader states but rather the attitude of the great powers of the region, the Fatimids and the Seljuqs. Both were slow to react in the area the crusaders directly targeted. The Fatimids under Wazir al-Afdal doubtless held the crusaders' intentions too lightly, offering at first limited, but then suddenly sharper opposition. After the defeat at Ascalon on August 12, 1099 the wazir returned to Egypt, and after further unsuccessful attacks in 1104/05, 1105/06, and 1111/12 he left the conquered territory in crusader hands—perhaps partly from desire to use them as a buffer against the aggressive Seljuqs. After the death of Sultan Malik-Shah the Seljuqs became embroiled in conflict over the succession; their attention was focused on their heartland around Baghdad and Isfahan, not on the little Christian enclave on their western border. To be sure, in the period 1110–15 the Seljuq sultan Muhammad sent some troops to Syria, but they failed—not least due to the distrust of the local emirs, who appear to have feared a restoration of Seljuq central rule. Basically, the Seljuqs never seriously threatened the crusader states, although they were in the best position to destroy the Christian states while they were still being established.

It was left to the emirates of Palestine and Syria to make agreements with or to oppose the Latins. After the death of Malik-Shah most of these small states had gained *de facto* freedom from Seljuq control or were under loose Fatimid overlordship. They were ready to make alliances with each other—and when necessary with the Christians—to stabilize their precarious position. Usama ibn Munqid is an example of these local rulers who had dealings with Christians. This readiness to accommodate the newcomers was an important precondition for the crusader states to be able to establish and consolidate themselves in the Muslim environment. Among Syria's regional powers Aleppo was especially important, since it was one of the area's great towns and lay on the inland route between the Red Sea and the Black Sea. Local Seljuq governors, called atabegs, established their own rule there. The most significant were Il Ghazi (d. 1122), the lord of Mardin, 'Imad al-Din Zengi, the ruler of Mosul, and his son and successor Nur ad-Din (r. 1146–74).

'Imad ad-Din Zengi succeeded in building Aleppo into a state that was *de facto* independent of the Seljuqs; in 1144 he recovered Edessa from the Christians. His son Nur ad-Din made Damascus, already nominally ruled under his father, into his new power center, and pursued the conquest of Egypt from there. For that goal he commissioned an army that consisted for the most part of Turcomans and Kurds under the command of his general Shirkuh and Shirkuh's nephew Saladin of the Ayyub family. Saladin succeeded not only in taking all real power in Egypt as wazir in 1169, but in ending the Fatimid caliphate in 1171 in favor of the caliphate of Baghdad. Although Saladin took pains to acknowledge his nominal master's overlordship, this did not prevent him from returning to Damascus after Nur ad-Din's death in 1174, where he deposed Nur ad-Din's son and united the two states. After he had subjugated Aleppo in 1183, the rule of all Syria and Egypt was in his hands. Only the crusader states appeared as a foreign body intruding into this newly established realm. Their almost complete destruction after the Battle of Hattin also served to justify Saladin's usurpations in Syria and Egypt.

Saladin's empire, called the Ayyubid sultanate after Saladin's father Ayyub, was ruled in the style of a dynastic federation by members of the founding family. This system brought continuous problems in its wake, since the rulers of the core lands—Egypt, Syria, and upper Mesopotamia—repeatedly fought each other. Only the Egyptian branch of the family—sultans al-Malik al-'Adil (Saladin's brother, r. 1200–18), his son al-Kamil (r. 1218–38), and al-Kamil's son as-Salih (r. 1240–49) succeeded in maintaining a limited hegemony. They also made alliances with the Latins of the crusader states. As early as 1107 Christian Antioch and

The Muslim rulers in Syria

The Ayyubids

Muslim Mosul had formed an alliance, and a treaty between Jerusalem and Damascus defined relations in Palestine for a long time. The Ayyubids continued this policy in the thirteenth century. Thus from the Muslim perspective the crusader states were actually integrated into the system of Syrian local powers. The Ayyubids profited from the economic vitality of Christian harbors and cooperated sporadically with the Latins in the administration of cultivated areas. They wanted peaceful relations with the Latins; confrontation in the form of a new crusade was not in their interest. Al-Kamil, for example, signed a trade treaty with Emperor Frederick II in 1229 that even gave up Muslim control of Jerusalem, while in 1240 Sultan as-Salih handed over a series of castles to the Latins to protect his back during a conflict with his nephew.

The Mamluks   The same internal considerations led as-Salih to purchase hundreds of slave soldiers (Mamluks) from southern Russia, who soon came to form their own elite corps. But after as-Salih's death, in 1250 these Mamluks launched a coup and seized power in Egypt. Their ascendancy was based above all on their military potential, which continued to rest fundamentally on slave soldiers. Even after the Mamluks had taken power, to rise in the ruling caste a man had to have been born outside of Dar al-Islam, to have converted to Islam after enslavement, to have received training as a Mamluk, and finally to have been freed. Members of this warrior elite occupied all the military as well as many of the key administrative positions in the strictly ruled Mamluk sultanate.

Thanks to their military proficiency, the Mamluks succeeded in warding off the greatest danger that had ever confronted Islam—the Mongols (see "The crusades from 1187 to the fall of Jerusalem, 1244," p. 50). On September 3, 1260 they decisively defeated a large Mongol army in the Battle of 'Ain-Jalut not far from Nazareth. This victory, extraordinarily important for the history of the Near East, not only gave the hitherto rather disjointed Mamluk military rule a new legitimacy and a special prestige, it also created an *esprit de corps* that played an essential role in their survival. Sultan Baibars, the true founder of the Mamluk sultanate, created and consolidated a large empire that provided a counterbalance to the Mongol Empire east of the Euphrates. It brought centuries of security, prosperity, and opportunities for cultural development to Egypt and Syria and, until its destruction by the Ottomans in 1517, determined Islam's fate in the Near East. As usurpers, the Mamluks emphasized their Sunni orthodoxy by establishing a new caliphate (dependent on them) in Cairo. Baibars and his successor Qalawun (r. 1279–90) turned away from the later Ayyubids' lax posture toward the Latin states of the Levant—probably also for fear of a Mongol–Christian alliance—and proceeded against them with unremitting harshness, until they drove the Latins from Palestine in 1291.

Crusade and jihad

It was not merely the geographical origin of the crusaders that many on the Muslim side misunderstood: observers in Cairo, Damascus, or Baghdad were also at first ignorant of the specific character of their expedition, the religious foundation of the undertaking. There were, however, exceptions. For example, in the early twelfth century the Damascus jurist and preacher ʿAli ibn Tahir al-Sulami (d. 1106) called for resistance against the invaders, whose advance he saw as linked to Christian successes in Sicily and Spain. The author thus recognized the overarching dimensions of the crusade movement and understood that it was a phenomenon not just limited to Palestine. Soon other Muslims, too, came to discern the religious core of the crusade movement— not least due to crusader desecration of Islamic religious and cultural sites, including the frequent conversion of mosques into churches or the destruction of libraries like the one in Tripoli. They reacted by resuscitating an old Islamic concept—jihad.

Strengthening the concept of jihad in the twelfth century

Greater and lesser jihad

From the beginning of Islam, Muslims regarded the inner struggle waged against one's own weaknesses, similar to the contemporary concept of the *militia Christi* in Christendom, as the most important (or "greater") jihad. But the Qur'an (e.g., in Suras 2:216, 9:14, and 9:36) and the transmitted sayings of the Prophet also already spoke of "struggle" (jihad) to spread Islam. This "little jihad," the collective conflict between the Islamic world, the Dar al-Islam, and all other regions—the House of War (*Dar al-Harb*)—was a basic principle of the Islamic movement from its beginning. The two forms of "struggle" were joined inextricably, so one cannot simply translate the term "jihad" as "holy war." Under the pressure of the new threat, in the twelfth century Muslims defined the concept more precisely. Jurists made a distinction between the two forms of jihad. Among other elements, they divided between an offensive jihad that all supported but that only volunteers undertook, and a defensive jihad. This latter struggle to drive out an oppressor who had conquered Muslim territory was the premier duty of every able-bodied Muslim, with an emphasis on individual obligations. Such warfare was not only directed against Christians but also against enemies of the faith within Islam. Voluntary warriors of the faith, called *gazi* in Arabic, had existed long before the crusades. These were individuals who fought predominantly or exclusively for religious reasons. They could form corps of volunteers to take part in expeditions, or they could also live in communities that adhered to strict religious-military rules. These monastic centers, defended by volunteers, were called *ribat*.

The concept of jihad, weakly applied hitherto, was revived in the Levant in the time of ʿImad ad-Din Zengi. The conquest of the crusader state of Edessa was especially responsible for this development. The high point of jihad propaganda followed under Zengi's successors, his son Nur ad-Din (r. 1146–74) and Saladin. Nur ad-Din's efforts to subdue the Christians of Outremer were, in actuality, limited; he was more concerned to secure his power in Syria and win control of Egypt. Still, he portrayed himself, for example in his building projects, as a champion of Islam; the authors of his time also celebrated him as such. To this context belong works like the *Sea of Precious Virtues* (*Bahr al-Fava'id*), composed by an anonymous Persian scholar at Nur ad-Din's court. This work described detailed preparation and pursuit of voluntary strife against enemies of the faith.

When Saladin took power in Egypt and Syria he too concentrated at first on winning overlordship over Aleppo and Mosul rather than on subduing the Christian regions, with which he made treaties meanwhile. Only after this goal was reached in 1183 did he begin to threaten the crusader states. Internal politics were also responsible for his ever-increasing focus on jihad. Saladin, the Kurdish usurper of Egypt and Syria, was able to use the concept of jihad and conflict with the Christians to give cohesion to the fragile political structure he had created. The schism within Dar al-Islam between Shi'ites and Sunnis also made itself felt in the question of jihad, which was of little importance in Shi'ism for theological reasons. But now, after centuries of divided rule, Syria and the formerly Shi'ite-ruled Egypt were again united, and jihad took on a more central role than ever before.

Saladin's public image

Saladin had gold coins minted on which he was celebrated as "Sultan of Islam and all Muslims"; an inscription with the same words was erected in Jerusalem in 1191. Courtiers and administrators in the sultan's chancellery, like al-Qadi al-Fadil (d. 1200), helped to present an image of their lord in their writings as deadly enemy of the Christians in the Islamic world. Advisors close to the sultan, such as 'Imad al-Din al-Isfahani (d. 1201) and Baha' ad-Din ibn Saddad (d. 1234), who wrote biographies of Saladin, as well as authors like Usama ibn Munqid, strengthened this prestigious image. It filled Saladin's image as foremost fighter of Islam that he even asked the Almohad ruler Abu Yusuf Ya'qub al-Mansur (r. 1184–99) in Spain for help against the Christians. The struggle was for the defense of all Islam. Poets revived forms of Bedouin lyric from pre-Islamic times that sang of characteristics like courage, manliness, and magnanimity. Saladin especially valued these poems. There is evidence that the Ayyubid was indeed filled with a sense of mission to defeat the Christians and bring Jerusalem back to Islam. It is thus hard to weigh between political and personal-religious motivations for his actions.

Jerusalem played an important role in this renewal of jihad thought. Nur ad-Din and his successors stressed the excellence and special position of al-Quds (Jerusalem) for the Islamic world. For this purpose, propagandists could look back to older collections about the "excellences" (Arab. *fada'il*, sing. *fadila*) of Jerusalem, which now attained a new importance. For example, before the campaign against the Christians in April 1187, Saladin had such works read publicly; in the same year the early eleventh-century text of the Jerusalem preacher al-Wasiti was employed for the same purpose. The reconquest of the holy city, accomplished with an eye for effect on October 2, 1187, the anniversary of Muhammad's night journey, was then also celebrated throughout the Islamic world as the Ayyubid's most important achievement.

Saladin's successors pursued a laxer policy toward the Christians, and jihad lost in significance. But under the pressure of Mongol danger, the Mamluks again took a less forbearing stand on religious questions. They regarded the struggle against the invaders as the most pressing form of jihad, put increased pressure on their religious opponents within Islam (the Shi'ites), and turned their military power resolutely against the crusader states. The Mamluks, like Saladin before them, had usurped power, and just like their famed predecessor the Mamluk sultans Baibars and Qalawun celebrated themselves as true wariors of jihad in inscriptions, poems, and chronicles. The conqueror of Acre, Sultan al-Asraf Halil, even assumed the honorary title Salah ad-Din (savior of the faith). After these military successes the Mamluks proceeded against heretics and enemies of the faith within the Islamic world. The Ottomans, too, pursued this course. For centuries they waged war under the banner of jihad—not just against Christians but also against the Mamluks of Egypt and the Safavids in Iran.

The war for the faith under the Mamluks

What are the differences between Christian holy war (see "Just war—holy war," p. 13) and Islamic jihad? To start, the latter is more broadly conceived. Since its inception, it has always included inner struggle, not just military endeavor. Second, jihad only developed in Islam to win back formerly Muslim regions and reestablish holy places after the establishment of the crusaders in the Holy Land. This was not yet the case in the expansion period of Islam. Third, the crusade as holy war also included the idea of punishing evildoers in God's name, a concept alien to jihad. Fourth, Christianity had, in the papacy, a generally accepted religious authority that again and again called for war in the name of God. These differences keep us from equating jihad and holy war, despite certain similarities between the two.

Muslim images of Christians

During the crusade era new geographical works like those of al-Idrisi (d. 1165) and al-Qazwini (d. 1283) supplemented preexisting concepts of Christian Europe. The Muslims already had stereotyped images of its inhabitants before the crusades, which served as foundations for later assessments. In the eyes of most Muslim authors, European Christians were slow-witted, uncultivated, foul, and immoral, but were also strong and brave. Did these views change through direct encounter with the foreign invaders?

Muslim
anecdotes
from the
crusader states

Even though some Muslim texts that apparently dealt with the Christians and their faith are no longer extant, we have other works, such as the travel account of the Spanish Muslim Ibn Jubair (1145–1217) or contemporary Arabic epics and poetry, sources that present a many-layered picture. The already-mentioned Usama ibn Munqid also often dwells on the Latins and their customs in his *Kitab al-i'tibar*. Most surviving works cater to the traditional Muslim image of Christians, underscoring in particular three deficiencies: the Christians' lack of wisdom, morals, and cleanliness.

Purity and pollution

The defect of insufficient hygiene also had implications in the religious sphere, because the invaders' pollution of sanctified places and objects played an important role in the Muslim image of Christendom. Islam prescribes, as everyone knows, strict purity rituals on all believers. Wine, pigs, and excrement were and are regarded as particularly unclean. In the Middle Ages all three articles were directly connected to the Christians and made them appear especially impure. Only this background can explain the Hispanic Muslim Ibn Jubair's description of Agnes of Courtenay as "the sow, who is called queen, mother of the swine that rules Acre." To be sure, the Muslims had long known the religious practices of the Christians who lived in their territories, but with the formation of the crusader states the situation changed dramatically. Now the Christians occupied Muslim holy places and marked them with their signs—especially the cross, but also with bells, statues, images, and so on. Outstanding religious structures like the al-Aqsa Mosque and the Dome of the Rock on Jerusalem's Haram as-Sarif possess an extraordinary value in Islam; their occupation by enemies of the faith who were perceived as unclean hit particularly hard. Muslim sources are also consistent in reporting that the prayer niches of the al-Aqsa Mosque were used as pigsties and thus desecrated in a particularly horrible fashion. We have no way of knowing if these are factual reports or fears and expectations that were literarily fulfilled. It cannot be doubted, though, that the Muslims regarded their holy places as desecrated and polluted; for example, after Saladin's conquest of Jerusalem in 1187 they had them ritually purified and reconsecrated, as 1mad ad-Din al-Isfahani reports.

At one point Usama ibn Munqid reports the ignorance of a Christian doctor who without hesitation amputated a knight's abscessed leg, upon which the man died. The author also gives his opinion of Christian permissiveness: men even allowed their women to talk to other men on the street and in general neither the women's morals nor the men's jealousy seemed to him very strongly marked. This judgment by no means excludes the fact that various Arabic authors allude with praise to the special beauty of the Christian women, their light skins, blue eyes, and slim figures. There are many references to lack of hygiene—Ibn Jubair for example tells of the filth and stench of Christian cities. Usama ibn Munqid's anecdote of a Christian knight in a bathhouse is particularly famous: the knight misunderstood the elementary rules of a Muslim bathhouse in multiple ways, first by not wearing a loincloth, second by tearing off a Muslim attendant's loincloth, only to be reduced to wonderment at his shaved pubic area, whereupon the knight not only had himself shaved publicly by the attendant but had the man shave his wife, too—on a day that the bath was only open to men. In this account no fewer than three prejudices against the Christians are interwoven: crude manners, lack of manly pride toward their own women, and ignorance of the most basic accepted rules of hygiene and morals.

Familiar images of the Christians were supplemented by a negative judgment of Christianity as a religion. In the already-mentioned *Sea of Precious Virtues* (*Bahr al-Fava'id*), its anonymous author collected in broad strokes the standard judgments of the Christian religion: the Christians' belief in the Trinity amounted to polytheism, and that God's son could have been born of a woman in a natural manner was a view that only a lunatic could hold. Similar reproofs and mockeries appeared repeatedly. These general reproaches, known before the crusades, were integrated and propagated, in face of direct Christian threat, in calls to jihad or texts in praise of Jerusalem. Before the crusades the cross had seldom provoked animosity. But now it became the target of Muslim aggression because it was rightly interpreted as a sign of victory and symbol of the secular rule of the crusaders, who desecrated mosques and religious centers like the Dome of the Rock with it.

Religious calumnies

In general it can be observed that at least some educated Muslims gained an understanding of their opponents' religious values and motivations over time. The sources especially make frequent reference to the Christians' religious fervor. Texts from Saladin's circle testify that his scholars were well-informed in this regard. The courtier and historian 'Imad ad-Din al-Isfahani, for example, gives an accurate depiction of the significance that the relic of the True Cross or the defense of Jerusalem possessed for the crusaders. It was people like him who argued for the complete destruction of Acre or the Church of the Holy Sepulcher, since otherwise the Christians would not rest until they had again established a foothold in the Holy Land. They assessed the crusade movement correctly, and the Mamluks put part of this plan into effect a century later with their destruction of the Levantine port cities. While Christian authors apparently knew next to nothing about jihad—William of Tyre thought the Muslims fought for their families, their freedom, and their homeland (*patria*)—for their part some Muslim authors used the term "jihad" to describe the Christians' struggle in the East.

This is by no means to suggest that understanding of their enemies' religious motivations led to greater acceptance or sympathy for them. Reports of the Christians' religious ardor in general only strengthened the Muslims' own fervor against their religious enemies, and the descriptions of Christians in the Muslim sources are rarely unbiased. Although they were often called *Ifranji* or *franj* (Franks) when they arrived in Outremer, just as often one finds disparaging terms like "swine," "dogs," "devils," or religious insults like "polytheists," "enemies of God," "Trinitarians," and so on. From the middle of the twelfth century on, stereotyped curses also gained vogue; for example, in 1158 we first see what became a standard addendum: "God punish them." By comparison, the commentators hardly mentioned crusaders' physical appearance—the crusaders only rarely figured as "the blond-haired," or, as 'Imad ad-Din al-Isfahani called them, as the "blue-eyed enemy."

Positive assessments

Still, some contemporary Muslim authors also spoke positively of the Christians. Usama, for example, gives high praise to individual Christians, although he specifically declares them to be exceptions. Some physicians, in his opinion, stood out from the ignorant masses, and he himself used their prescriptions and healing methods successfully. The Christians' fear of God was also repeatedly underscored, as in Usama's description of the churchmen at the tomb of St John in Sebasteia near Nablus, or in the work of Saladin's advisor 'Imad ad-Din al-Isfahani.

Christian piety from the Muslim perspective

From Gabrieli, *Arab Historians of the Crusades*, pp. 83–84 and 148.

Usama ibn Munqid: "I paid a visit to the tomb of John the son of Zechariah—God's blessing on both of them!—in the village of Sebastea in the province of Nablus. After saying my prayers, I came out into the square that was bounded on one side by the Holy Precinct. I found a half-closed gate, opened it and entered a church. Inside were about ten old men, their bare heads as white as combed cotton. . . . The sight of their piety touched my heart, but at the same time it displeased and saddened me, for I had never seen such zeal and devotion among the Muslims."

'Imad ad-Din al-Isfahani: "The Franks said: 'Here our heads will fall, we will pour forth our souls, spill our blood, give up our lives; we shall endure blows and wounds, we shall be prodigal of our spirits in defence of the place where the Spirit dwells. This is our Church of the Resurrection, here we shall take up our position and from here make our sorties, here our cry goes up, here our penitence is performed, our banners float, our cloud spreads. We love this place, we are bound to it, our honour lies in honouring it, its salvation is ours, its safety is ours, its survival is ours.' "

Of course, one must bear in mind first that the author asserts in the same passage that Muslim sufis are still more pious and second that in this description he is trying to call people to jihad. By contrast, praise of Christian military proficiency was unstinting. Especially members of the military orders were attested as having extraordinary abilities, which in Muslim eyes made them particularly dangerous enemies.

These passages should not blind us to the fact that only in a few exceptional cases did the Muslims of the Near East develop a real interest in the beliefs and culture of Latin Christendom. It was only with the eastern Christians under their rule that they held theological disputations, sometimes in public. Saladin alone sought this sort of content-based interchange with Latins—and he did it in secret. Despite some similarities, in Muslim eyes Christians were misguided and morally reprehensible; an intellectual disputation about the weaknesses and errors of their religion would be unrewarding. Knowledge of certain capacities and organizational forms of the crusaders were usually employed to gain the upper hand politically or militarily over the enemy, or to imitate certain features that had proven effective. In their dealings with the alien belief, the Christians and Muslims of Outremer resembled each other to a striking degree.

3

The crusader lordships

Secular rule

The third chapter of this book is not concerned with the crusades in the East, but rather with the states to which they gave birth. These are often called "crusader states," although the term suggests a higher degree of administrative coherence, political autonomy, and legal self-understanding than these creations really possessed. So I will only use the term in quotes in the following discussion, instead for the most part substituting the term "crusader lordships." In the following three sections I will present their constitutional and economic, ecclesiastical, and socio-historical aspects. The first subsection will begin by providing a broad outline of the crusader lordships' political development, after which we will examine the ruling houses of the various crusader territories and their connections to the monarchical world of Europe. The theme of the third subsection is state-building and the role of the aristocracy. This section on secular rule will close with an overview of the economic significance of the crusader lordships, the rights of Italian traders in them, and the political weight of the Levantine states.

Establishment and fluctuation of borders

Between 1098 and 1109 the first crusaders founded the four lordships that constituted Outremer: the county of Edessa, the principality of Antioch, the kingdom of Jerusalem, and the county of Tripoli (see Map 1). Even after their initial conquest, the new rulers faced considerable difficulties. Above all they had to accomplish three tasks: first, they had to secure the Christian territories in the interior; second, they needed to conquer the coastal cities with their harbors; and third, they had to fortify natural, defensible borders. It was possible to achieve the first task without great difficulty, since there was no longer any organized opposition. By contrast, conquest of the coastal cities was a major challenge. It could only be accomplished with naval support, so the Latins had to rely on outside help. This assistance came in the form of several fleets from the Italian merchant cities—but not without a price. The sailors from Genoa, Venice, and Pisa were keenly aware of their home cities' interests and bartered for economic and political advantages before they supported the crusaders. However, once agreements had been reached, the fleets played a decisive role, conquering all of the coast cities except Ascalon (which only fell in 1153) in the first three decades of the crusader lordships. The third task—securing the frontiers—was for the most part accomplished in the reign of King Baldwin I (r. 1100–18). He succeeded in extending Christian rule to the Transjordan region and conquered the Golan Heights. With these advances the Christians controlled the land link between the two most important Muslim centers of the region, the Seljuq emirate of Damascus and the Fatimid caliphate of Egypt. In a few years, under

Consolidation of the crusader lordships

Godfrey of Bouillon's successor, the kingdom of Jerusalem had nearly reached its maximum expansion.

These gains of the early twelfth century were held and stabilized in large part thanks to the aid provided by a series of further crusades. Another important condition for success was an alliance made with the emirate of Damascus against the expanding power of Zengi, the lord of Mosul. This alliance was still in effect when Zengi conquered Edessa in 1144, but broke up three years later. A crusade was called in reaction to the fall of Edessa, advancing in 1148—not against Zengi, but against Damascus, which so recently had been an ally. The decision to take such a step presumably rested on the advice of the resident Christians. It was a major mistake: the alliance between the Christians and Damascenes was suspended, but Damascus was not taken. Instead, the person who accomplished this task in 1154 was Zengi's son Nur ad-Din (r. 1146–74). Nur ad-Din's success placed the strategically vital city in the hands of an opponent who was intent on expansion and war against the Christians, who had moreover set out to establish his rule over the Fatimid caliphate of Egypt. The Latins faced the threat of being hemmed in on two sides. Despite this menace, they succeeded in conquering the important port city of Ascalon as a counter-measure to the fall of Damascus and after that even launched attacks against Egypt. It was not the crusaders, though, who conquered Cairo in 1171, but rather Shirkuh, a Kurdish general in Nur ad-Din's service. This event brought the epoch of the crusader states' consolidation to an end. We have an outstanding source for this phase of stabilization and the era of external threat and internal strife that succeeded it—the chronicle of William of Tyre. Its value is the greater because only three chronicles from Outremer from the twelfth and thirteenth centuries, hardly any diplomatic correspondence, and only a limited number of not very revealing documents have survived. Except for these fragments, the sources for the crusader lordships have all been lost.

William of Tyre (c. 1130–86) was born in the kingdom of Jerusalem and is one of the few educated locals whose works have come down to us. After his education in Europe, he returned to the "crusader states" in 1166, where he rose to be archdeacon of the Tyrian church. In 1170 he became tutor to the future king Baldwin IV (r. 1174–85) of Jerusalem, and after Baldwin came to the throne William served as royal chancellor. Elevated one year later to the archbishopric of Tyre, he held office until his death. Besides a lesser work, William composed a "History of the Eastern Princes" (*Historia Principum Orientalium*), which is no longer extant. His chief work, however, was a chronicle of the kingdom of Jerusalem in twenty-three books, composed between 1170 and 1184. It is rightly regarded as an outstanding work of high medieval historiography and as a fundamental source for the history of the "crusader states."

William also tells of the rise of Saladin, Shirkuh's nephew, who succeeded in establishing his rule over Egypt and Damascus (1174) as well as over Aleppo (1183) and Mosul (1186). Then he proceeded against the kingdom of Jerusalem. In Jerusalem, Baldwin IV and Baldwin V died in rapid succession (1185/86). Noble factions fought over the throne, which was finally won by the up-and-coming French noble Guy of Lusignan (r. 1186–92, d. 1194). While influential, long-settled barons counseled caution, reckless newcomers like Reynald of Châtillon (d. 1187) convinced the king to commit the kingdom's entire army to open battle. On July 4, 1187, the army was slaughtered at the "Horns of Hattin" in one of the most famous battles of the Middle Ages, and the kingdom, stripped of its defenses, lay at the mercy of Saladin's troops. Between Hattin and 1190 the victorious sultan was able to conquer the entire kingdom, except for Tyre. The county of Tripoli, more so than the principality of Antioch, forfeited extensive regions, but their core areas survived.

Internal crises and the Battle of Hattin

The Battle of Hattin called into being a series of far-reaching changes in the eastern Mediterranean. The conquest of Cyprus in 1191 created a new Latin kingdom off the Levantine coast. In Cilicia, bordering the principality of Antioch, the kingdom of Armenia was founded (1198). The conquest and sack of Constantinople in 1204 replaced Greek rule with the Latin Empire. Finally, in Palestine and Syria the lost coastal cities were regained between 1191 and 1197. The crusade of Richard I the Lionheart (r. 1189–99) in 1191/92 affected not just the conquest of Acre but also secured other important cities, like Arsuf and Jaffa. The expedition of German crusaders in 1197 led to the reconquest of Beirut and parts of Sidon. By ten years after the catastrophe of Hattin a narrow, roughly 300-kilometer-long strip of land had been conquered. In the following forty-five years it was possible to expand this region considerably to the south and east. This was accomplished less by direct military campaigning than through a series of treaties. For the Christians made use of the arrival of new crusader forces and internal strife among the Muslims to gain diplomatic concessions. In this manner, Frederick II's crusade (1228/29), like those of Count Thibald of Champagne and Duke Richard of Cornwall (1239–41) brought territorial gains, so that by 1241 the kingdom of Jerusalem had effectively regained many of the losses of 1187. However, the conflicts within the Muslim world eventually had a negative impact on the "crusader states": the tribe of the Khorezmians, who originated in the region north of Iraq, were summoned to aid one faction, invaded Palestine, and in 1244 plundered Jerusalem. On October 17, 1244 they annihilated the Latin army at La Forbie. The consequences of Mamluk seizure of power in Cairo in 1250 were even harsher: after they settled internal quarrels and defeated the Mongols in 1260, the Mamluks set about the gradual reconquest of Palestine. In a number of thrusts, interrupted by truces, they reconquered the Christian territories one by one, until finally Acre fell on May 18, 1291.

Reconquest and loss of the crusader lordships

The dynasties of Outremer

The four crusader princes who succeeded in forming their own lord-ships in Outremer founded their own dynasties. Jerusalem was ruled by the successors of Baldwin, brother of Godfrey of Bouillon from the house of Bolougne. In Tripoli the Saint-Gilles lineage, descended from Raymond of Toulouse, held power. In Antioch the Hauteville descend-ants of Bohemond and in Edessa the Courtenay family ruled, des-cended from Joscelin I (r. 1119–31). But frequent military conflicts and disease meant that several ruling families died out in the male line. One result of this was to heighten the importance of female members of the family. Queens of Jerusalem like Melisende (r. 1131–50), Sibylla (r. 1186–90), and Isabella I (r. 1190–1205), or princesses like Constance of Antioch (r. 1131–63) pursued an independent political course. In the whole Middle Ages, there is hardly another region in which women played a comparably influential political role. Another consequence of this lack of male heirs to the throne, though, was that foreign dynas-ties married into the ruling families, so it is only possible to speak of a continuity in the ruling houses in relative terms. Thus, for example, in Antioch the house of Poitiers came to power through the marriage of the count's son Raymond (r. 1136–49) to the heiress Constance in 1136, and the Angevins obtained the throne of Jerusalem the same way in 1131. The list of outsiders who married into the crusader dyn-asties can easily be extended. Usually these foreigners came from the French-speaking parts of Europe. The "crusader states" were also a recruiting ground for dynastic alliances, because the ruling families of Outremer frequently made marriage agreements with each other. Finally, the Armenian-Byzantine region provided a third source for the marriage market: various members of the comital house of Edessa married Armenians, while the ruling houses of Antioch and Jerusalem formed alliances with the Byzantines. These marriages testify that the dynasties of Outremer operated at the highest levels of the European nobility.

Byzantine interests But which interests led the great European dynasties to ally themselves with the crusader lordships and their rulers? The Byzantine emperors sought by this means to restore their influence over a region that they saw as a usurped part of their empire. Alexios Comnenos and his son John II (r. 1118–43) had already made their claims—although unsuccess-fully; but under Emperor Manuel I Comnenos (r. 1143–80) the Byzantine presence in the Levant became stronger. Through a campaign to north-ern Syria in 1158 the emperor won a role as protector of the "crusader states," dynastic alliances were made, and in 1171 the Latins and Byzantines launched a joint attack (unsuccessfully) against Egypt. However, after the Byzantines' serious defeat in battle against the Seljuqs at Myriokephalon on September 17, 1176 and the brutal mas-sacres committed against the Pisans and Genoese in Constantinople (1182), relations cooled.

None of the Latin kingdoms of Europe succeeded in forging a comparably close link to the "crusader states." When considering which European rulers bound themselves to the crusader lordships through crusades or dynastic relations, it is possible to discern four constants or focal points. First, rule over Sicily appears to have led naturally to political interest in the Levant. All rulers of the island—whether Norman, Hohenstaufen, or Angevin—sought to rule the eastern Mediterranean and thus reached out to Outremer. Second, the imperial dignity apparently evoked a heightened interest in the fate of the Holy Land. Charlemagne, the prototype of the Christian emperor, was regarded as the first Latin protector of Jerusalem, and eschatological views strengthened the belief that the head of Christendom should rule the holy places. Three emperors and a Roman-German king took the cross—Conrad III, Frederick I, Henry VI, and Frederick II. Third, new marriage alliances created durable dynastic interests. The alliance of Jerusalem's royal house with the Angevin lineage in 1131 forged a lasting connection, which resulted in support at the political level in the case of King Henry II of England (r. 1154–89) and military aid from his son Richard the Lionheart (r. 1189–99). Fourth, Outremer acted as a springboard for upwardly mobile nobles hoping to win themselves a lordship. This can be seen in the cases of several kings by marriage who came from significant lineages, such as Conrad of Montferrat (d. 1192), Guy of Lusignan (d. 1194), Henry of Champagne (d. 1197), and John of Brienne (d. 1237).

The changes in the eastern Mediterranean world at the turn to the thirteenth century—the defeat of Hattin, the conquest of Cyprus and Constantinople, as well as the foundation of the kingdom of Armenia—of course had consequences for the dynastic framework of Outremer. For a long time the king of Jerusalem had enjoyed a certain preeminence among the Latin rulers of the Levant, which for example enabled him to intervene occasionally in the internal conflicts of Tripoli or Antioch. The situation now changed: from the Battle of Hattin on, the fates of the three lordships became much more independent from each other.

The rulers of Outremer in the thirteenth century

In the county of Tripoli the Saint-Gilles line died out in 1187. The heir was a prince from Antioch (Bohemond IV, d. 1231), whose successors ruled until Tripoli's fall in 1289. In Antioch, on the other hand, a protracted contest for the throne was waged between members of the Antiochene ruling house and the kings of Armenia, a struggle eventually won by the former. All the same, Antioch remained dynastically oriented toward the north and therefore followed its own unique path of development. In the kingdom of Jerusalem, after 1187 the rule passed through two heiresses, since the queens did not bear sons. Queen Isabella I (r. 1190–1205) and Conrad of Montferrat produced a daughter (Maria, d. 1212), who in 1210 married the French count's son John of Brienne (d. 1237). Their daughter Isabella II then married Emperor

Frederick II in 1225, but died in childbirth in 1228. The emperor became regent for Conrad (1228–54), the son born of this union, and soon assumed the title "king of Jerusalem," which the Hohenstaufen retained until their line ended in 1268. While the husbands of Queens Isabella I and Maria ruled personally and for the most part effectively, with the Hohenstaufen the kingship of Jerusalem went into a decline. The rulers no longer lived in the country, and their deputies could not enforce their will against the kingdom's powerful barons. Among these were members of the Lusignan line, who attempted, although ultimately unsuccessfully, to win the kingship during the second half of the thirteenth century.

The age of the *seigneurs* and *baillis*

The lords (*seigneurs*) or regents (*baillis*) exercised lordship in place of royal officials. Many of them were members of the Lusignan clan. Their power base was Cyprus and some of them even ruled as kings of the island. As a result, they were rarely present on the mainland. So they in turn appointed officials to represent them, further weakening the kings' authority. The nadir was reached after the death of the last Hohenstaufen in 1268, when an heiress to the throne sold her rights to the Sicilian king Charles I of Anjou (r. 1266–85) in 1277. But he, too, proved unable to assert his authority. For the few years remaining until the fall of the kingdom, rule returned to Lusignan hands.

Even this brief overview allows us to discern some basic tendencies. While Tripoli and Antioch oriented themselves dynastically toward the north and were thus able to maintain their power structures largely intact, the kingdom of Jerusalem was reduced to a bone fought over by foreign interests. Neither the Hohenstaufen nor the Angevins could or wanted to take personal control of their nominal lordship. For their part, the Cypriot Lusignans strove earnestly to add authority to their power on the mainland. They came into conflict, though, with the real power-holders of the kingdom, the barons. These were the true beneficiaries of the kingdom of Jerusalem's various crises in the thirteenth century.

The barons and feudalism

Feudalism in the crusader lordships

For the most part, it was Latin knights who conquered Outremer. These knights brought their government system east with them: feudalism. The basis of this system was the personal legal relationship between the so-called feudal lord and his vassals. It gradually took a form in which the lord gave a fief and in return received services, including military aid, advice, and loyalty. The vassal could in turn install subvassals, becoming *their* feudal lord. The majority of the kingdom of Jerusalem was given in this manner to "crown vassals" by the king; he only excercised direct authority in the royal domains. It was also from the domains that he received his revenue, which was greater than that of the royal vassals and gave the monarch an economic preeminence. The holders of court offices assisted the king in ruling his kingdom. These included the seneschal, who represented the king at need, and the constable, who was responsible for military affairs. The core of the knightly army came together through the feudal duty to perform military service. All of these points corresponded with the system practiced in the Latin West. Peculiar to the Levant, though, was the so-called "money fief": the scarcity of available land to grant to vassals made it necessary to pay vassals with regular revenue rather than an estate. This practice was employed especially because no other option was available after the loss of so much territory in 1187; it weakened the rulers' financial power.

The noble leadership class of Outremer can be distinguished in two manners: by their position within the feudal system and by the date they had come to the East. Within the first criterion, one can distinguish between the baronial ruling class and the subvassals. The leadership group of barons or magnates of the kingdom of Jerusalem, for example, was formed by about ten families, which ruled as royal vassals over large, heritable lordships called *seigneuries*. The princes of Galilee or the lords of Caesarea belonged to this group of largely independent magnates. They in turn commanded large numbers of subordinates, including lower-ranking knights. These knights, unlike their counterparts in Europe, rarely lived in their own castles; instead they usually resided in their lords' fortresses.

The barons

If one focuses on the second criterion and considers the date of emigration to Outremer, one can further divide the group of magnates between the families that came to the Holy Land with the conquest of 1099 or shortly thereafter, and those who settled only in the mid-twelfth century or later. Families like the Ibelins belonged to the first category; the Lusignans or men like Reynald of Châtillon were in the second group. It is possible to see in William of Tyre's chronicle that contemporaries, too, considered a family's age important. In his descriptions of individuals, the archbishop repeatedly distinguishes between older and newer families. And the nobles themselves contributed to this phenomenon by creating their own legends of origin, claiming to be as long-established and high-ranking as possible. The Ibelins, for example, who apparently came from a family of northern Italian townsmen, created a false genealogy that linked them to the viscounts of Chartres. This further strengthened their baronial standing and self-perception.

Since the second third of the twelfth century at the latest, these magnates had claimed a say in Outremer's politics. It was the easier to fulfill this goal in the kingdom of Jerusalem thanks to the numerous regencies (such as for Baldwin III, d. 1163), some rulers' inability to carry out their

Weakness of royal rule

office (at times Baldwin IV), and the multiple breaks in the male line— all of these events gave the territorial nobles opportunities to interfere. While in the period up to *c.* 1130 the king could grant and confiscate fiefs from his vassals, the situation changed radically in the course of the twelfth century. Rulers were now repeatedly forced to give up parts of the royal domain as heritable lordships (*seigneuries*) to crown vassals, which significantly weakened royal power. For the region the king actually ruled was in reality limited to this territory, the royal domains. Only there did the king issue documents, from there he drew his income, there he had control over his officials, and only there did he have full powers over the legal system. In the royal domains he established his own administration, resting primarily on his five viscounts and his income from the major ports of Acre and Tyre. One can say that the king only really ruled in his domain lands. This point became particularly clear in legal matters.

The Haute Cour

The highest court in the kingdom was the Haute Cour, in which the barons also were represented. In the course of the twelfth century the Haute Cour developed into a feudal court that determined relations between king and magnates, as well as the locale for the most important political decisions. The ruler's freedom of action was circumscribed since he had to win the barons' agreement for major decisions. King Amalric I's (r. 1163–74) law known as the *Assise sur la ligece*, introduced shortly after 1163, should be seen as a reaction to this development. Through this edict, the Haute Cour was opened to the lower nobility. Besides, these subvassals were allowed to appeal to the monarch in conflicts with their feudal overlords if all judicial options had been exhausted. With this action, King Amalric was trying to link the lower nobility directly to himself again. His policy found striking expression in the fact that the lesser nobles were now expected to swear loyalty directly to him. But in truth, the decision did not bring the king the results he had hoped for. The lesser nobles slowed down decisions, and in the long term they could not leave their fiefs to take part in the Haute Cour regularly. For their part, the barons used elements of the *Assise sur la ligece* to assert their rights successfully against the king. Besides this, collections of customary law were made, also called "assizes," that substantially reduced royal rights in favor of the barons.

This stripping of royal power was facilitated by two factors: first the monarchs of the thirteenth century were foreign rulers by marriage who lacked a personal power base in Outremer, and second they were hardly ever present in Palestine after the first third of the century. In this vacuum various powers moved to the fore, leading to a fragmentation of rule in the kingdom of Jerusalem. Five groups assumed wide-reaching power. Three of them—the barons, the Italian communes, and the cities—will be treated in this section; the other two—the patriarchs and the military orders—will appear in the following one. These five "*de*

The assizes

The late twelfth century saw the composition of French-language collections of customary law, called "assizes" (*assises*). A group of assizes, the *coutumes* of the Haute Cour, laid out the crown's feudal rights. Some of these collections were even personally compiled by members of the baronial class, who developed into excellent feudal jurists. The assizes of John of Ibelin, lord of Jaffa (d. 1266) are the best example. Apparently the major crusader lordships sometimes enacted their own assizes, but that of Jerusalem took on the character of prototype and was adopted in other regions, such as Cyprus. Unlike Roman law, which strengthens the ruler's position, the customary law of the assizes propagated the image of the monarch as first among equals (*primus inter pares*), and minimized the ruler's rights. Relying on these texts, the barons were able to establish their right to a say in important areas. Even in the naming of high officials like the *bailli* they had a voice in the decision.

---

facto powers" were rivals; sometimes they followed different policies and even made separate and independent treaties with the Muslims. This fragmentation of power is most evident in two conflicts. From 1229 to 1243 some barons, in alliance with some cities (such as Acre), fought against Hohenstaufen rule. From 1256 on, the entire kingdom was embroiled in the so-called War of St Sabas (see p. 94). By contrast, the rulers of the principality of Antioch and the county of Tripoli succeeded for the most part in retaining power in their own hands.

Trade and cities

The Christian Levantine trade was already underway before the crusades; in the eleventh century merchants from Naples, Amalfi, Venice, and other cities journeyed to the East. An important source for this trade, and other subjects, is the "geniza" documents, documents from the tenth to fourteenth centuries that were discovered in a Cairo synagogue. The crusades did not prevent Muslims and Christians from trading with each other; at the worst they caused short-term interruptions of economic contacts. The Muslim traveler Ibn Jubair commented that even during periods of open war Christian–Muslim trade continued. Only starting in the late twelfth century did popes place embargoes on war materiel, which were often quietly traded anyway.

Outremer enjoyed an internal trade between the crusader states as well as long-distance trade with other regions. One can distinguish between three types of mercantile activity: first the high-sea trade over long distances, second the coast trade with the closer port cities, and third the land trade. The crusader lordships' most important trade centers were Tyre and Acre. Smaller harbors like Laodicia, Tripoli, or Beirut concentrated on the internal and overland trade and on the coastal sea

Types of trade

trade. In the thirteenth century, in terms of high-sea trade they merely played a limited role as transshipment centers for the trade between Asia Minor, Cyprus, and Egypt. The important ports of Acre and Tyre, by contrast, had great harbors at their disposal, at which the Italian trading fleets touched. These cities were in ongoing rivalry with each other, although Acre enjoyed a preeminence, not least because of its relatively good route to the Syrian hinterland with its great trade center, Damascus. Alexandria—the economic gateway to the Red Sea and India—was the second Muslim economic and trade metropolis of the Near East; many Christian traders settled there, too.

Trade goods   What did the merchants trade? A customs list from Acre gives insight into the goods exchanged in the city in *c.* 1245. From the West, above all, came raw materials—hides, wood, dried fruits, grain, and so on. Some finished products, too, were highly regarded in the East, most notably weapons and luxury textiles. Most important for military purposes were horses, weapons, and the wood necessary to build ships. These were the goods put under papal boycott in the twelfth century; the list was expanded at times. From the East the merchants received spices, dyes, perfumes, ivory, slaves, cotton, alum (important in dyeing cloth), and other goods. The items were stored in *funduqs* (Arab.) or *fondaci* (Ital.). These were warehouses, in which the traders also had to reside during their stay in a city. From there, the goods were either sold on the local market or traded on.

Pilgrims constituted a special, economically important cargo. Venice in particular, but also Marseille and other cities, specialized in transporting pilgrims to the Holy Land for cash. Transportation contracts minutely regulated how much space each pilgrim could use, how many and where the stops would be en route, and what duties the passengers had to perform as crew. Impoverished pilgrims constituted a significant drain on the crusader lordships, since they had to be fed and sheltered; but at the same time pilgrimage brought income, because in general the rulers levied a pilgrim tax of one-third of the pilgrims' transport cost. Well-to-do visitors also brought the land important supplemental income, and many pilgrims made donations to Outremer's religious institutions in return for prayer.

The crusader lordships did not merely serve as exchange places for foreign goods; they themselves represented a native market that was based on goods from both Christian- and Muslim-ruled regions. They also produced both raw materials and finished products for the overseas market: cane sugar, soap, raw silk, and cotton, as well as silk fabrics, cloths, and gold brocade. It is evident from all this how very dependent the crusader lordships were economically on long-distance trade. Commerce had a regular, cyclical character, due to sailing conditions. The simple open-sea ships of the high and late Middle Ages could only operate easily in the eastern Mediterranean in the spring and summer, because of prevailing winds. Every year the trade fleets set out for the Levant in this season, and returned home in late summer or early fall. The safest route was via southern Greece, Crete, Rhodes, southern Turkey, Cyprus, and Syria.

The regular arrival of the high-sea ships was essential for the survival of the crusader lordships. Their failure to appear was a catastrophe. But it was not these moments of crisis that demanded a smoothly functioning finance and credit system. Bankers from the major Italian banking houses lived in the trade cities in the thirteenth century. They operated in a money market that provided letters of credit and could change currencies, thus simplifying long-distance trade. Besides these groups, one of the religious foundations of the crusader lordships won a special position in this business: the military orders. Thanks to their many-branched network of filiations they were particularly well-suited for the system of letters of credit; money received in Palestine could be paid out in another house of the order at home, or vice versa.

Mercantile practices

Most of the eastern Mediterranean trade did indeed lie in the hands of Italian merchants, but there were also other traders. Nomads sold saddle horses and beasts of burden, native farmers and small traders offered their wares in the markets, and Provençal and Catalan long-distance traders also emigrated to Palestine. There is even evidence of Muslim long-distance traders: Damascene merchants led whole caravans through the deserts on the Levantine coast, and traders from Mosul had their own confraternity in Acre. Neither the sea trade between Egypt and the crusader lordships nor the border-crossing land trade to the Muslim hinterland lay in the hands of a single group, but the Italians enjoyed a notable preeminence.

Many Italian merchants possessed economic or legal privileges due to their place of origin. As early as 1098 the Genoese were granted a church and a trade settlement (*fondaco*) in return for their support in the conquest of Antioch, and later the Italians often negotiated a third of the conquered city, a church, and a *fondaco* before they put their fleet to the service of fellow Christians. The Venetians were still more successful in 1124. In return for their help in the conquest of Tyre, they won—in a famous treaty, the *pactum Warmundi*—not only substantial rights in the city but also free trade for their citizens in the entire kingdom of Jerusalem. In the course of the crusader lordships' reestablishment after the loss of Jerusalem in 1187, the trade cities again had the upper hand and put the rulers under strong pressure. And where no privileges were issued, they knew how to help themselves: up to the mid-thirteenth century a forgery studio in Marseille prepared a series of documents claiming special rights in Outremer. One could not pass up any chance, because competition was brutal. The rivalries between the Italian mercantile cities in the West had their effect upon their branches in the East.

The Italian trade quarters

By the end of the twelfth century there were already tensions between the various groups, but they climaxed in the thirteenth century with the War of St Sabas.

The War of St Sabas

In 1256 a conflict broke out between the Genoese and the Venetians. The fighting started over some houses that had belonged to the monastery of St Sabas in Acre, to which both parties believed they had a claim. The controversy escalated between 1257 and 1259, drawing in other groups, among them the Pisans, non-Italian communes, local barons, and the military orders. A Venetian fleet occupied the harbor of Acre and destroyed the Genoese ships there, quarters were burned, watchtowers seized. Barons used the opportunity to fight each other and carried the conflict to the hinterland. The war appeared to be at an end after the defeat of a Genoese fleet in July 1259, but flared up repeatedly until Acre's fall in 1291.

These rivalries and fights contributed to the fall of the crusader lordships. They were only possible because many merchants remained citizens (in legal terms) of their home cities. They swore loyalty to their Italian commune and were not subject to local laws. Their own officials, often called consuls or viscounts, functioned as judges and watched over the maintenance of the group's special privileges. The merchants were also set apart spatially, living in their own quarter of the city. These legal enclaves, defined by their inhabitants' special rights, were called "trading quarters." It is tempting to designate them as extraterritorial in the modern legal sense, but the Italians only rarely succeeded in freeing themselves completely from their obligations. Weights and measures, taxes on purchases and sales, remained in place for the most part, and the princes often reneged on their promises.

Fraternities and commune formation

In the course of the thirteenth century, though, the major cities freed themselves more and more from lordly control. In cases when they did not live in their own quarters, the inhabitants organized themselves into what are called confraternities. Often people from the same state who found themselves in a foreign land gathered in such organizations. Their premier function was religious, but they also offered members financial or legal support at need. Besides these social functions, they sometimes formed their own military corporation, which did its part in the city's defense. The confraternities evolved into independently operating foundations that established their own policies and could also fight each other. Their role was notable in the conflicts over the rule of the kingdom of Jerusalem, when for example the communes of Acre or Tyre decided on their own policies and joined one party or the other. The cities thus also bore their share of the blame for the fragmentation of government and joined the other *de facto* powers of the kingdom. The division of power in the thirteenth century between the nominal rulers, the barons, the military orders, the Church, the Italian quarters, and finally the urban communes and confraternities substantially weakened the "crusader states."

Christians, Muslims, and Jews

Natives: Muslims, Jews, eastern Christians

The crusader lordships were noteworthy for their extraordinary ethnic and confessional variety. In this section I will classify the inhabitants according to the time of their arrival and the duration of their presences in the Levant, distinguishing between natives, newcomers, and visitors. The native population was in turn divided between Christians, Muslims, and Jews, and still further differences existed within these groups. The Latin Christians were only one of many communities and were a minority in their own land. All estimates must be approximate, but it appears that in the flourishing period before the defeat at Hattin a total of about 100,000 to 120,000 Latins lived in the crusader lordships, of whom about half dwelt in cities. There were considerably more Muslims. In the first decade after the seizure of Jerusalem, the Latins staged massacres of Muslims several times, but by the time of Sidon's conquest in 1110 at the latest they knew that it was to their advantage to spare the natives after they had capitulated.

Ethnic and confessional multiplicity

The Latin conquerors adopted old Muslim traditions in their relations with other confessions. They took over in its essence the *dhimmi* system, which accepted adherents of subject foreign-belief communities as their legal wards (Arab. *dhimmi*). The subjected peoples were allowed to practice their religion, but did not enjoy legal equality with the Muslim population.

The Muslim system of *dhimma*

The non-Islamic faith communities that received the status of "wards" enjoyed religious freedom and far-reaching autonomy, especially in the realm of marriage and inheritance law. In return for protection, they were obligated to pay a head tax, the *jizya*. Leadership and judicial powers were left in the hands of the religious leaders—they were responsible for both secular and religious affairs.

In the same way, the Latin Christians, the other Christian confessions, and the non-Christian population were far from equal in the crusader lordships. Much more, the crusaders created a "second-class society" based on confessional criteria rather than nationality or ethnicity. This consisted of the Latins on one side and the rest of the population on the other, although in the second, subject group there was a further hierarchy between the Christians and the non-Christian groups. This hierarchical ordering should not come as a surprise, because there was neither a theological nor a legal foundation in the Middle Ages for the legal equality of other religions. With these provisions, the non-Latin religious communities found themselves in about the same situation as the Christians and Jews had been in the period of Muslim rule.

Few sources speak of the living conditions of the subject populace. The most detailed are the collections of customary law, the assizes, of the kingdom of Jerusalem dating from the thirteenth century. We have already considered these collections in terms of the crown's feudal rights (see "The barons and feudalism," p. 88). The second large group of assizes, the *coutumes* of the *cour des bourgeois*, encompasses the legal rights of non-nobles. The most famous works of this group, like the *Livre des Assises de la Cour des bourgeois*, which was written *c.* 1240–44, give information about the legal standing of subject Christians, Muslims, and Jews, among other material.

The subject Muslims

The Muslims were the largest sector of the population in the "crusader states." Some were enslaved and some were free. In the whole Mediterranean world prisoners of war or slaves bought in regional markets were used as laborers, and the "crusader states" were no exception. Only in rare cases were the Christians interested in freeing the slaves; they were just as little interested in converting the Muslims to Christianity. The economic consequences of evangelization were simply too great, because a Christian could not be held as a slave.

The majority of Muslims in Outremer were not slaves. These were above all Arabic-Syrian farmers and, more rarely, bedouin nomads. By contrast, the Turkish or Kurdish Muslims who had ruled parts of the Levant before 1099 appear to have left after the conquest or to have been killed. This means that the subject Muslims were ethnically different from the leaders of neighboring powers. They had little in common with the Turkish Seljuqs, the Kurdish Ayyubids, or the southern Russian Mamluks. One can say, ironically, that the Arabs of the Near East were subjugated outside as well as within the crusader lordships. For the Muslim population the differences may have been blurred: from their perspective, the Latins may have been just another ruling elite.

The subject Muslims retained a certain measure of autonomy. They could deal with issues of low justice in their own court, the Cour du Raïs, at which the Qur'an was accepted as the binding text on which the Muslims took their oaths. A Muslim local official, the *ra'is*, presided over the Cour du Raïs. Besides him, the *shaykh*, as a sort of spiritual leader, had an authoritative position within the village community.

Hardly any sources exist to show us the daily life of these Muslim villages. The work of the Muslim author Diya' ad-Din al-Maqdisi (d. 1245), "The Miracles of the Shaykhs of the Holy Land" (*Karamat mashayih al-ard al-muqaddasa*) is an exception. It describes how the Muslims of the Nablus area had their own mosques in which they could worship, a situation also attested by other sources. There were, to be sure, limitations. Many mosques were converted into churches, in Jerusalem Muslims were prohibited from settling after the conquest, and al-Maqdisi reports in another work that in the mid-twelfth century entire communities emigrated from Christian-ruled Samaria to Damascus, because they had been kept from practicing their religion.

It is hard to judge whether the specific cases mentioned here were typical or how much the Muslims' lives in general were affected by the arbitrariness of their lords. Even though various sources report that native Muslims collaborated in attacks by invaders who were co-religionists, their fate was not so unbearable that they risked open, large-scale rebellions. Ibn Jubair in 1184 was of the opinion that Muslim agricultural laborers paid fewer taxes than their fellow Muslims in neighboring parts of the Islamic world. Usama ibn Munqid tells of Templars who let him pray in their Jerusalem headquarters, the al-Aqsa Mosque, or of a Christian knight who protected him from an attack by fellow Christians. But Usama ibn Munqid and other Muslim authors did not live in the crusader lordships; they were foreigners. One must take care not to present the "crusader states" as a haven of religious tolerance on the basis of isolated text passages. *Reliability of the sources*

The paucity of sources is in itself a powerful statement: the Muslim agricultural communities were, in Christian eyes, not worth mentioning. The Muslim farmers were, it is true, obliged to pay taxes and thus economically significant, but they usually lived in conditions where contact possibilities were limited. On the Muslim side, too, there appears to have been little readiness to forge connections with the foreigners. Levantine authors like Usama ibn Munqid show us that they did not want to learn the Latins' language. Still, one can presume that in the cities, where Muslims worked as physicians, traders, and so on, this must have occurred and there was much more interchange. In a few cities in the north there is even evidence of Muslims in upper administrative positions.

The Jews of Palestine also lived by preference in the urban centers. At the time of the Christian conquest these Jews were above all Syrians and Yemenites. They were deeply Arabicized; in other words, influenced by Arabic culture and language without adopting Islam. Among other sources, one can see this in the already-mentioned *geniza* documents from the Cairo synagogue (see "Trade and cities," p. 91). During the 200-year Christian presence in the Near East the Palestinian Jews were exposed to western influences in two ways: first through their *The Jews* co-religionists who came from Latin Europe to the Holy Land and settled there, and second through the crusaders and their culture. This "westernization" or "de-Arabization" is an important element in the history of Jews in the "crusader states." The process is illustrated by the fact that, in the course of the thirteenth century, ever more Jewish texts were composed in Hebrew rather than Arabic.

The Jewish inhabitants of the crusader lordships did not have a common, supervisory institution that could represent their interests either externally or internally. The strongest influences on the Levantine communities were exercised by recognized religious authorities in Damascus or Cairo. This explains why there are few sources from the first century of Latin rule. Still, some Jewish pilgrims, like Benjamin of Tudela, composed valuable travel reports.

Benjamin of Tudela was from Navarre, in modern Spain. Sometime between 1166 and 1168 he made a pilgrimage to Palestine, about which he composed a travel narrative. This text offers us a graphic image of the Jewish communities that Benjamin visited along his route. The author paid special attention to the situation in Palestine. From his account, we learn that in this period about 500 Jews lived in Tyre and about 200 in Acre. There was also a flourishing community in Ascalon. He reports that in some cities the Jews had their own synagogues, schools, and bathhouses, and played an active role in economic life as traders, bankers, and artisans (dyers, glassblowers). Benjamin is one of the few Jewish authors who also speaks (in passing) of the Christians in the "crusader states"; most other Hebrew sources barely mention the crusaders and settlers from the West.

The conquest and sack of Jerusalem in July 1099 counted a great many Jewish inhabitants among its victims. After this, Jews as well as Muslims were forbidden to set foot in the city. But in the second half of the twelfth century restrictions were eased for Jewish pilgrims, and Benjamin of Tudela speaks of Jewish artisans in the city: "And there is a dyeworks there, which the Jews buy every year from the king, so that none but the Jews can work as dyers. There are about four of them. They live beneath the Tower of David on the edge of the city." After Saladin's destruction of Ascalon in 1191, the families of many Jews who had taken refuge there in 1099 returned to Jerusalem. In the parts of Palestine that remained in Christian hands, Acre developed into the undisputed spiritual center of Jewish life. Christian pilgrimage apparently served as a model for the Jewish communities in Europe, because an ever-increasing stream of Jewish pilgrims came to the Levant from modern Spain, Germany, and France. Some of them settled permanently. Among these was a large number of important scholars at the beginning of the thirteenth century—the texts speak of the "migration of the three hundred rabbis." Their offspring as well as the other Jews of Acre were killed alongside the Christians when the Mamluks conquered the city in 1291.

Already before the conquest of Jerusalem a variety of Christian confessional groups lived in Palestine. John of Würzburg, who made a pilgrimage to the Holy Land in 1165, was the first westerner to give a detailed list of the Latin and eastern Christians he encountered in Jerusalem: "There are Greeks, Latins, Germans, Hungarians, Scots, Navarrese, English, Ukrainians, Bohemians, Georgians, Armenians, Surians [i.e., Arab-speaking members of the Byzantine Church], Jacobites, Syrians, Nestorians, Indians, Egyptians, Nubians, . . . Maronites, and many others whom it would take too long to enumerate. . . ."

The Christians

The eastern Christians were by no means the legal equals of the Latins, although their position was also different from that of the Jews and Muslims. Some of them gained responsible positions in the Latin administration, and in some cases there is also evidence of military contingents composed of eastern Christians. No Christian could be sold into slavery, and in the market court (the Cour de la Fonde) in Acre, four easterners served along with two Latins as jurors, as the *Livre des Assises de la Cour des Bourgeois* reports. Outside of Acre the native Christians enjoyed judicial autonomy in what were called the Cours des Suriens. When the Latins took power, the Greek Orthodox Christians—who had enjoyed a privileged position under Muslim rule as the largest Christian minority—lost much of their influence and power. For this very reason other religious communities, like the Syrian-Orthodox Christians, may have welcomed the Latins' arrival. The Greeks appear to have reacted by agitating against the Syrian-Orthodox in places like Antioch, where the proportion of Greek-Orthodox inhabitants (and thus their influence) was particularly high. Still, relatively few conflicts between the Christian communities appear in the sources.

The legal position of eastern Christians

It is difficult to characterize the highly varied ethnic and confessional structures of the "crusader states." This society has been assessed very differently by various scholars. While some interpret it as concerned about integration or even as a model of multiculturalism, others label the crusader lordships as an "apartheid system" or as an oppressive society. In Outremer one can certainly not speak of the equality of all inhabitants, but all free people possessed legal security. This can be explained especially from the rulers' self-interest, whose material and political safety dictated their dealings. In cities, the lot of the subjects appears to have been lighter than in the countryside, but in neither place was there a real mingling of the various groups of inhabitants. Much more, they appear to have lived next to each other rather than *with* each other. The term used in Iberia for the peaceful coexistence of different confessions—*convivencia*—should be supplemented or even replaced both there and in the Near East by *conveniencia*—expediency. On this rationale rested the Latins' decision to continue the Muslim system of *dhimma*, just as it had been in Muslim interests to put it into operation in the first place.

Newcomers: the settlers

The Latin settlement of Palestine and Syria belongs in the larger context of European expansion, because in this period Christian settlers were also establishing themselves in newly conquered territories in other border regions, such as on the Baltic or on the Iberian Peninsula. There, too, it is possible to observe many of the characteristics of the crusader lordships: the invasion of a feudal knightly elite, the immigration of farmers, the development of legally privileged cities. But still the crusader lordships had their own peculiarities within this larger movement. To begin, the original desire of most participants in the First Crusade was *not* to lay claim to territory and settle there. Another important distinction was that the territory to which they came was much better known than other Christian border regions: for this was the Promised Land of the Bible. By taking the cross and the crusade oath they had entered a new religious position; now they were *hierosolimitani* (Jerusalemites). In a sense they were returning as heirs of Christ's, and thus their own, homeland—they did not found a new lordship but restored an older one. All these points made the Christian seizure of land in the Near East something unique within the larger expansion movement.

Geographical and class origins of the crusaders

After the unexpected success of the First Crusade, some crusaders remained in the Holy Land. The new inhabitants followed their military leaders for the most part; in other words, south Italian Normans tended to establish themselves in Antioch, Provençals in Tripoli. In the kingdom of Jerusalem, however, the pattern is less clear. Soon Latin settlers joined the crusaders. They came from all social classes: merchants and artisans, farmers and nobles sought new homes on the far side of the sea, and they settled both in the cities and in the countryside. In this section I will consider the life of these settlers under four perspectives: first, their living conditions; second, legal regulation; third, whether they developed their own self-identity; and finally, how special a role the cities played in this society.

Recent archaeological excavations have shown that the Latins settled in the countryside, not just in the cities. But for the most part they established themselves in locales where eastern Christians were already living. This means that strongly Muslim-imprinted regions like northern Samaria and eastern Galilee remained untouched by the settlement activity. In some cases new settlement villages were also founded on a large scale, as was the case at Magna Mahumeria near Jerusalem.

Magna Mahumeria

The canons of the Church of the Holy Sepulcher were among the greatest landholders in the kingdom of Jerusalem. In 1120 at the latest they founded the settlement of Magna Mahumeria north of Jerusalem. They attracted settlers from the areas of modern France, Italy, and Spain with especially favorable conditions. A community developed here with division of labor among farmers and artisans. They had their own church, their own storehouses, and so on. An administrator, who collected the settlers' dues, lived there. The settlers also owed military service. In 1155 Magna Mahumeria already had about 450 inhabitants; in the period up to its fall in 1187 the population rose to about 700.

But what was the settlers' legal position? Life in Outremer was made more attractive with the promise of certain freedoms, offered not only to Latins but to Armenians and Tranjordanian Christians. All non-noble Latin Christians (*bourgeois*) had their own court, the Cour des Bourgeois. First attested in 1131, these courts were under the authority of the local viscounts. The *coutumes* of the Cour des Bourgeois, mentioned on p. 96, give us information about their functions in the thirteenth century. Through these and other legal texts we can see that in Outremer the female settlers, too, enjoyed greater freedoms than in Europe. In a land so dominated by war, male mortality was particularly high. Therefore the women had a relatively high dowry, which they could dispose of freely after the death of their husbands. Similarly, noble women were allowed to choose a new husband with relative freedom. The feudal lord could present three candidates to the widow, but the lady was not forced to accept any of them if this implied a loss of honor.

These freedoms and the specific conditions under which the crusader lordships were founded played a role in giving the inhabitants a strong sense of identity. In a famous passage of his *Historia Hierosolymitana*, Fulcher of Chartres narrates how faded the memory of their old homes had become by twenty years after the conquest of 1099.

Settler self-identity

Passage from the *Historia Hierosolymitana*

From Fulcher of Chartres, ed. Hagenmayer, p. 748.

We who were formerly westerners are now easterners; he who was a Roman or a Frank has here become a Galilean or a Palestinian; he who regarded himself as an inhabitant of Rheims or Chartres now feels himself to be a Tyrian or Antiochene. We have already forgotten our places of birth. . . . Other [Latins] have married, not only women from their earlier homeland, but also Syrians and Armenians—even Muslim women, although of course only the baptized ones.

The new "settler identity" could only come into being because in Out-remer various identity-creating elements stood at the settlers' disposal. Three elements appear to have been particularly important: a common language, central places, and effective symbols. French soon joined Arabic as a trade language; not coincidentally, the assizes of the kingdom of Jerusalem were also composed in this language. Among outstanding, identity-giving places the holy city, and particularly the Church of the Holy Sepulcher with the tomb of Christ, was preeminent. Here the highest religious authority of the kingdom resided—the patriarch; here the monarchs were crowned and buried. Along with other famous edifices in Jerusalem like the Tower of David and the Dome of the Rock, the Church of the Holy Sepulcher was depicted on official "significance-bearers" of the kingdom; it could be found, for example, on seals and coins. Finally the symbols: for all four crusader lordships equally, the symbol *par excellence* was the cross, in the name of which they had been conquered and founded. In the kingdom of Jerusalem the most important relic of the land—the relic of the True Cross—had equal standing with the Sepulcher. It was carried in important processions and more than thirty times was carried into battle as a war standard.

Regressive development of identity

The most important of these points of reference were lost in the great catastrophe of 1187. The relic of the True Cross fell into Muslim hands and was never recovered; after the defeat of 1187 it was also difficult to maintain a sense of being a people that rightly and at God's will possessed the Lord's kingdom. The changed circumstances of the thirteenth century only deepened the identity crisis. The rulers were more and more rarely present in the kingdom, and nobles moved to the newly created Latin states of Cyprus or Constantinople. On the whole, the last century of the "crusader states" can be seen as a "regressive development of identity" (Hiestand 1995: 75).

Certainly the cities also played their part. Thanks to territorial losses, society in Outremer of necessity had a one-sidedly urban character in the thirteenth century, and in the large centers the Italian merchants formed an important group with markedly particular interests and loyalties. Those among them who lived in the quarters nonetheless remained citizens of their home cities and therefore only shared to a limited degree in the settler identity of Outremer. The Italian immigrants formed a special case. They repeatedly claimed the special rights of quarter inhabitants, sometimes or temporarily with success. They consequently regarded themselves as Pisans, Venetians, or Genoese, even if they had been born in the Holy Land. Perhaps this led to conflicts of loyalty; certainly it made the integration of Italian immigrants into crusader society more difficult.

Visitors: merchants and pilgrims

We have already spoken of the Italian citizens in Acre and Tyre. They remained in Outremer long term. The so-called seasonal merchants, by contrast, arrived in the Levant in the spring with the great trading fleets and left again in the fall. They did not transport just merchandise in their ships, but also a great many pilgrims. It is estimated that every year thousands of pilgrims arrived in the Levant. Like the seasonal merchants, they too usually stayed only a few weeks or months—just long enough to visit the most important shrines in the kingdom of Jerusalem.

The pilgrimage centers

In Christian eyes, Outremer—and especially the kingdom of Jerusalem— signified, more than any other region, a direct relationship to the biblical history of salvation. Here the events had occurred that were familiar to the faithful from the Bible. As a result, the number of pilgrim centers was especially great. The majority of pilgrims were Christians, but Jews, too, traveled to the Holy Land during the crusader era. The most important goal for Christians was the tomb of Christ in the Church of the Holy Sepulcher in Jerusalem. The scratched graffiti of medieval pilgrims can still be seen there. In and around the holy city pilgrims could also visit many Old Testament locales, such as the site of Solomon's Temple or the Tower of David. There were also innumerable spots connected to the New Testament. With every step, pilgrims were reminded that they found themselves where Christ himself had once stood. Some of the pilgrims composed travel journals or full-scale pilgrim guides, which sometimes give an impression of the holy places and life in Palestine during the crusader era. These texts played a role in making the Holy Land come alive for people in the Latin West.

The traders and pilgrims had more in common than the short time they spent in Jerusalem. Both groups were very important for the crusader lordships—economically, militarily, and socially. We have already seen that the traders' and pilgrims' business, the taxes they paid and the money they spent during their residence, played an important role in the survival of the "crusader states" (see "Trade and cities," p. 91). Many of them also seized the opportunity to fight for their fellow Christians while in the East. So the Latins of the Levant usually waited for the arrival of the great spring fleets before setting out on campaign. But the presence of foreign visitors was not always in the settlers' interest. The regular, months-long presence of outsiders also brought an additional element of unrest to the Levant. The foreigners often came to the East with preconceived notions, for example about Muslims and dealings with them. Now they encountered the realities. The guests had to process the culture shock, and for their part they had to be

Effects of trade and pilgrimage on the crusader lordships

assimilated until their departure. This seasonal and months-long presence of foreign Christians thus also made heavy demands on the crusader lordships.

The Churches of Palestine

The Latin Church

It has already been stressed that Outremer held an outstanding position in Christian religious thought. The special aura of the Holy Land and its direct connection to holy events had an influence on Palestine's Churches. In this section I will first deal with the Latin Church of the "crusader states," with particular attention to the patriarchate of Jerusalem. The following subsection on the religious orders in part considers the breadth of religious life in Outremer, but also examines those institutions that were founded in Palestine and spread from there throughout Christian Europe. The conclusion provides an overview of the Christian Churches of the Near East and their relations with one another.

The Greek Church

Latin foundations had already been established in the holy city before the crusaders took Jerusalem; in the mid-eleventh century merchants from the southern Italian port city of Amalfi had founded a hospice, dedicated to care for the poor and sick, in the city center not far from the Church of the Holy Sepulcher. This hospital of St John was, however, an exception. In the first place, it was Greek Orthodox and eastern Churches that dominated Christian life in Jerusalem before 1099, not the Latin Christians. The superior of the Church of the Holy Sepulcher, for example, was the Greek Orthodox patriarch of Jerusalem, who represented the Christian quarter of Jerusalem and who since the mid-eleventh century had been installed by the patriarch of Constantinople. In the summer of 1099, one of the first questions after the conquest was the position to take toward the incumbent Greek Orthodox patriarch. Probably contrary to the pope's original plans, after a short period of uncertainty the crusaders decided to create Latin structures independent of Constantinople (see "The creation of the crusader lordships," p. 45). The crusaders' political estrangement from Byzantium may have contributed to this decision. So, contrary to all canon law, parallel Church structures were formed, and often two bishops (a Greek and a Latin) resided in the same city. Jacques de Vitry, an important authority for the early ecclesiastical history of the "crusader states," was one of the authors to report on this situation.

> **Jacques de Vitry** (*c.* 1160/70–1240), bishop and historian, was commissioned to preach the Albigensian crusade by Innocent III (r. 1198–1216) in 1213. Three years later he was elected bishop of Acre. In 1225, though, he abdicated and left the Holy Land to enter papal service in Italy, becoming a cardinal in 1228. About 450 of Jacques' sermons are extant, as well as letters, a *vita* of Marie d'Oignies (d. 1213), and the *Historia Hierosolimitana abbreviata*. This last work is, next to William of Tyre's chronicle, a main source for the history of the kingdom of Jerusalem and its Church. Jacques planned the work in three sections, but only completed two. The first, the *Historia Orientalis*, is a description of Jerusalem, the Holy Land, and Islam; the second, the *Historia Occidentalis*, is an ecclesiastical history of the West.

When establishing the new Latin Church organization, the founders fell back on the structures of the pre-Islamic period, but with new emphases. Jerusalem, first raised to a patriarchate in the fifth/sixth century, was elevated over the older patriarchal see of Antioch and provided with a series of re-founded or newly created bishoprics. Jacques de Vitry reports that because of the costs and available personnel a reestablishment of all the old episcopal sees was out of the question; thus sometimes several dioceses were consolidated under a single bishop. At the same time, though, religiously significant places like Nazareth or Bethlehem were elevated to archbishoprics or bishoprics. In the late twelfth century the patriarchate of Antioch was comprised of six archdioceses and eleven to thirteen dioceses; the patriarchate of Jerusalem included four archbishoprics and nine or ten bishoprics. A web of parish churches was also created, which, however, was not particularly dense.

The structure of the Latin Church

The new organization of the Church was not accomplished without friction. After all, the West was for the most part ignorant of the ecclesiastical situation in Syria and Palestine, and Rome's grip was made weaker by its great distance from Outremer. As early as 1120 a council was called at Nablus; among other issues it dealt with specific canon law problems within the new crusader holdings. More tedious was the dispute between the patriarchates of Jerusalem and Antioch for control of the archdiocese of Tyre. Pope Urban II had decreed that ecclesiastical provinces should follow the political boundaries between lordships— which in the case of Tyre went against older ecclesiastical divisions. While Jerusalem had the upper hand in this dispute, control of Tyre remained a point of controversy, one of several in the ecclesiastical history of Palestine, that still had not found a lasting solution when crusader rule came to an end.

Jacques de Vitry is not only a good source for this conflict; he, based on William of Tyre, also reports on the beginnings of the Church and of the cathedral chapter of Jerusalem. In the unsettled days directly after the

The patriarchate of Jerusalem

conquest, the crusader leaders chose Arnulf of Chocques (or of Rohes, d. 1118), Robert of Normandy's chaplain, as leader of the cathedral church in Jerusalem. But he was soon supplanted by Daimbert, archbishop of Pisa and papal legate (d. 1106/07). Daimbert attempted to form Jerusalem into an independent ecclesiastical lordship. This was no trivial matter, because it affected the Church's future role in the kingdom of Jerusalem and the eastern patriarchate's position within the universal Church. Daimbert fell into conflict with King Baldwin I over this question and he too was soon deposed (1101). One can see from this and later episodes that in Outremer the bishop was by no means a free agent. As Rudolf Hiestand (1995) has put it, "With a few exceptions, the Church of the Holy Land was a 'royal Church.'"

Arnulf of Chocques had remained influential, and in 1112 was elected for a second time to the patriarchate. While he was patriarch, the Jerusalem cathedral chapter became a community of regular canons. This means that the clerics now followed a rule, ate communally, and owned no personal property. These regular canons of the Holy Sepulcher performed the liturgies at Christ's tomb and watched over the relics, especially the relic of the True Cross. These tasks brought them many donations from the faithful—an essential basis for the power of Jerusalem's Latin Church. The patriarch of Jerusalem became the most important ecclesiastical landholder of the kingdom and, among other resources, disposed of over a quarter of the holy city and many settlements. In times of crisis, he owed the service of a military contingent of 500 soldiers. From this fact, it has sometimes been falsely concluded that the patriarch was the grand master of a military order.

The exceptional ecclesiastical, economic, and military importance of the patriarchs also gave them wide-reaching opportunities to exert political influence, especially during the many times when the throne was vacant or the subject of contention. Patriarchs like Warmund of Picquigny (r. 1118–28) or William of Messines (r. 1130–45) were outstanding personalities who played a decisive role in the kingdom's fate. The poor state of our sources keeps us from examining the workings of the Latin Church in the crusader lordships in greater detail. The same is true of Outremer's intellectual life. Still, authors like William of Tyre, Rorgo Fretellus, or Gerard of Nazareth show that Outremer was capable of making independent cultural contributions.

The Latin Church in Palestine after 1187

It may seem astonishing, but the loss of Jerusalem in 1187 did not cause a long-term weakening in the political position of the patriarchs of Jerusalem. True, they had lost their mother church—the Church of the Holy Sepulcher—and a significant part of their earlier revenue. But the frequent absence of the kings of Jerusalem increased their authority and provided new opportunities to influence events. The patriarchs took up residence in Acre, played an active role in politics, and thus can properly be categorized along with the barons among the *de facto* rulers of the kingdom in the second half of the thirteenth century. However, the patriarchs were transformed more and more from heads of the Latin clergy into agents of papal interests in the Levant.

In general, the losses of 1187 constituted a decisive turning point for the Church in Outremer. Many dioceses, monasteries, and other religious foundations were lost, so their clergy were compelled to move to Acre, where the resultantly large clerical element must have made a particularly strong imprint on the city's image. Many bishops, lacking personnel and economic means, lived cheek by jowl in Acre. Besides the growing threat, this congestion may have been a reason why some ecclesiastical institutions moved out of the Levant. Before the fall of Acre, many Church organizations had already erected daughter houses on Cyprus or the European continent as possible places of refuge. These new foundations made it possible for many of Outremer's religious establishments to continue their life in exile after 1291.

The religious orders

Few sources are still extant that shed light on Outremer's religious institutions. There are just a few cartularies (manuscripts with copies of documents), and at most only fragments of the local archives have survived. One must bear this fact in mind when trying to describe or investigate these churches, monasteries, and other foundations. The loss is all the more deplorable since the Holy Land, as one would expect, was filled with a great many Christian foundations. They were an expression of the outstanding religious importance of Judea, Samaria, and the Galilee. Most of the Christian religious establishments went back to Late Antiquity and the Byzantine period; still, after the crusader conquests many were rebuilt or expanded. New regular communities (i.e., dedicated to a communal religious life) were also formed in the Holy Land.

The period of the first crusades was an epoch of revolutionary change in Latin monastic life (see "New orders and religious movements," p. 27). One must ask here whether—or how quickly—these developments made themselves noticeable in Outremer. Four tendencies can be discerned. First, some reform movements won little acceptance in the Levant, while, second, others enjoyed considerable success. Third, Outremer also produced a series of unique forms of regular (communal, rule-based) life, which in turn were transplanted to the West. Fourth, there was a series of religious foundations that did not belong to any order. In this category one should include especially the Holy Land's many communities of hermits.

Among the first group, the exponents of the reform movement that were only barely or not at all able to establish themselves in the "crusader

The varying presence of religious institutions in Outremer

states," were the Cistercians and the new eremitical orders. Benedictine-reformed congregations like the Cluniacs also failed to establish themselves in the East. The Benedictine monasticism of the crusader lordships was much more traditional in nature, as exemplified by the monasteries of St Paul in Antioch, St Mary's in the valley of Josaphat, or the Benedictine monastery of St Anne in Jerusalem. Matters were completely different in the case of the canonical reform movement—the regular canons were able to win a secure niche in Outremer. Thus already in the first half of the twelfth century the Premonstratensians had houses in Ramla and near Jerusalem, while the canons of St Ruf possessed houses in Tripoli. The canonical reform struck most intensively in the foundation or refoundation of cathedral chapters and individual collegiate churches as communities of canons. On the Temple Mount, on Mount Sion, in Hebron, and in other spiritually important locations communities of Augustinian canons (following the Augustinian Rule) were founded. The canons were put in charge of parish churches and chapels, through which they had a significant impact on the Palestinian Church. Some cathedral chapters, too, like those of Bethlehem or Nazareth, adopted the Augustinian Rule. Perhaps the regulation with the most important consequences was that of Jerusalem's cathedral chapter. Until 1114 the cathedral clergy were so-called secular canons, as they followed the rule established in Aachen in 816, but from 1114 on they were committed to personal poverty and a common life (*vita communis*). Other religious foundations in Palestine followed the example of the Church of the Holy Sepulcher. The strong impact of the regular canons was an "import" from the crusaders' homelands, of course, but it can still be regarded as a major characteristic of the Church and the religious life in the "crusader states."

Orders of canons in the Holy Land	Thanks to the generosity of the faithful, some of the newly founded Latin cathedral chapters succeeded in founding dependent daughter houses—called dependencies or filiations—in Europe. This was true, for example, of the chapter of the Church of the Nativity in Bethlehem, St Mary's in Nazareth, and especially the Jerusalem cathedral chapter. This last corporation not only created its own federation but also developed into an independent order of canons: the Order of the Holy Sepulcher. At its height, hundreds of foundations, churches, and chapels belonged to this order, ranging from Portugal to Poland, and England to Sicily. It was only one of the ecclesiastical institutions that originated in the crusader lordships and spread from there to the West, to enrich the history of Latin religious life.

Many other important monasteries, collegiate churches, and chapters found a new home in Apulia, Calabria, Cyprus, Sicily, or the smaller islands of the eastern Mediterranean after the loss of Jerusalem. For the most part, they already controlled dependencies there in the twelfth century. Two examples can illustrate this process. The Nazareth chapter followed its bishop to Barletta in southern Italy in 1187, where its members performed the liturgical service and supervised their remaining churches and possessions in Europe. For their part, the canons of the church of Bethlehem developed into a mendicant order, the little-known *fratres stellati* or Bethlehemites, after the loss of the crusader lordships. All of these religious institutions of Outremer continued to help keep Jerusalem-centered piety and longing alive far from the Holy Land. It was only the growing enmity between rival orders at the end of the fifteenth century, the Reformation, and other obstacles that finally brought the history of these long-exiled cathedral chapters to an end.

Before this, at the beginning of the thirteenth century, the first mendicant orders had been created (see "New orders and religious movements," p. 27). Franciscan convents were founded in Antioch, Jerusalem, and other cities of Outremer. But much better known is the journey that St Francis of Assisi (d. 1226), the order's founder, made to Palestine in 1219 in the course of the crusade against Damietta (1217–21). His intent was to convince Muslims with words rather than the sword. Jacques de Vitry tells in his *Historia Occidentalis* that the Ayyubid sultan al-Kamil (r. 1218–38) did indeed receive the pious, crusader-venerated Francis, but was not persuaded. Still, Francis's presence in the Levant had an important long-term impact. In part thanks to his journey, the Franciscans developed a many-sided role in the Near East as papal legates (representatives), bishops, and missionaries.

The mendicant orders in the Near East

The Dominican Order was also present in Palestine until 1291, in the form of convents in Jerusalem, Acre, Tyre, Antioch, etc., and also in the form of individual friars who became bishops. As in other border regions of Latin Christendom, there was indeed a certain predominance of mendicant, especially Dominican, bishops in Outremer. Until the mid-thirteenth century Dominican friars took an active part in dealings with the representatives of other Christian confessions in an attempt to reunify the eastern Christians with the Roman Church. They were ultimately unsuccessful. While the Augustinian Hermits made barely a ripple in Palestine, the Holy Land had (and still retains today) a constitutional significance for the fourth and last of the great Latin mendicant orders. For the Carmelite Order was born in the Holy Land, or more specifically, on Mount Carmel, from which the order took its name.

The newly formed lordships of Palestine, finally, contributed a further new creation of the Latin Church: the military orders. This is the religious institution of the crusader lordships that existed for the longest time after 1291. They will receive a detailed discussion in Chapter 5.

The Carmelites

Sometime in the twelfth century hermits settled on Mount Carmel, south of Haifa. They sought an ascetic life of poverty and withdrawal from the world, following the example of the Old Testament prophet Elijah. At the beginning of the thirteenth century they received their own rule from the patriarch of Jerusalem, but it was a new rule, composed in 1247, that provided the foundation for the community's later transformation into an international order by de-emphasizing its eremitical elements in favor of apostolic life and pastoral care. The loss of the kingdom of Jerusalem caused the order's eventual transference to Europe, where by the end of the thirteenth century it already comprised about 150 convents. By this time it had established itself as the fourth of the great mendicant orders, despite occasional animosity from rivals. More and more the Carmelites' main field of activity was the city, pastoral care, and study. Still, they never forgot their eremitical origins and never tired of recalling their beginnings in the Holy Land.

The eastern Churches

Multiplicity of the eastern Churches

Before their arrival in the Holy Land, the Christian confessions of the Near East had been unknown to most Latins of Outremer. Now the Latins needed to learn to distinguish between the Syrian Orthodox (also called Jacobites), Maronites, Copts, Armenians, Nestorians, and others. The differences between these confessions were usually based on their understanding of the person of Christ (Christology). The crusaders had to discover that Copts and Jacobites were so-called Miaphysites (more commonly: Monophysites). Both groups believe that Christ has only one nature—divine—and not, as presented in Latin and Greek Christendom, both divine and human natures. Only very few crusaders may have known who Jacob Baradaios was, the miaphysite monk and founder of the Syrian Church (d. 578) who gave the Jacobites their name. St Mero (d. *c.* 410), too, would have been for the most part unknown to them, because the Maronite Church that he had created had been condemned as heretical by the Greek Orthodox hierarchy. The Maronites did indeed accept Christ's double nature, but ascribed to him only a single, divine will (monothelitism). Both the Jacobites and the Maronites were based in Syria—the Jacobites in western Syria and Edessa, the Maronites in Lebanon and the Galilee.

The Latins also had to ascertain that an indigenous Christian Church had developed in Egypt in a tradition that went back to St Mark, a group that also believed in the single nature of Christ, and was known as the Coptic Church. And in Baghdad, the spiritual leader of the apostolic Church in the East, called the Nestorian Church after the fifth-century Syrian patriarch Nestorius, had his residence. The Nestorians believed that Christ had a twofold but unmixed nature, a stand rejected by the Miaphysites as well as by the other Christian confessions. And on their way to Jerusalem the crusaders crossed Armenia, which had also developed its own Church in the late second century. The Armenian Church had maintained its independence from Byzantium despite all attempts to dominate it, but had a relationship with the pope. Its members could also be found in the crusader lordships.

All of these confessions except the Maronites rejected the dogma of Christ's twofold nature, which had been promulgated in 451 at the fourth ecumenical council in Chalcedon. They can therefore be grouped together under the term "non-Chalcedonians." This set them apart, not just from the Latins but also from the Greek Orthodox Church. Greek Orthodoxy was by far the most numerically significant Christian confession in the Levant. Its relationship to Rome had rapidly deteriorated in the few decades before the First Crusade. Among other issues, the reason for this lay in the controversy over the *filioque* that broke out afresh in 1054. The heart of the dispute was the Latin doctrine according to which the Holy Spirit proceeded from the Father "and the Son" (*filioque*). Many adherents of the Byzantine imperial church were Arab-speakers, so-called Melkites or Surians. The number of confessions, in short, was bewildering. Jacques de Vitry gave a detailed description of their characteristics in his *Historia Orientalis* (Chapters 74–78), which helped spread this information to western audiences.

Besides ecclesio-political conflicts and the disputations of learned theologians over Christological differences, there were points of friction in daily co-existence between the Churches, rising from the different liturgies used by the various groups. These were differences recognizable to theologically uneducated Christians. Liturgical disagreement seems to have led to conflicts between members of the different eastern Churches more often in the northern crusader lordships than in the kingdom of Jerusalem. For example, an issue of contention was the date on which Easter should be celebrated. This dispute also affected the Church of the Holy Sepulcher, the central locus of all Christians' Easter celebrations, mostly taking the form of each side disparaging the other. Another difference that was immediately noticeable to all believers—in this case an issue between Greeks and Latins—was the "azymite" question: whether the eucharist should be celebrated with leavened or unleavened bread. The Greeks insisted on the former and the Latins on the latter. On this point confessional differences could literally be tasted, and in Outremer a number of treatises were composed arguing the issue. Still, on the whole there is evidence of only relatively few conflicts between the Latins and other Christian faith communities.

Relations between the Christian Churches

The Greek patriarchate, about which only a few twelfth-century sources are extant, continued to exist after the conquest of 1099. Until they were reestablished in Jerusalem at the beginning of the thirteenth century, the patriarchs lived in exile in Constantinople. From there, they still continued to claim lawful leadership over the Jerusalem Church. However, the crusaders did not drive out the lower-ranking Greek Orthodox clergy, who were allowed to celebrate their liturgy in the Church of the Holy Sepulcher. In the principality of Antioch, where a much larger proportion of Greek Orthodox lived than in the kingdom of Jerusalem, the Greek Church maintained a relatively strong position. This foundation of parallel ecclesiastical structures is remarkable and makes the "crusader states" the first place that effectively carried out the schism between the eastern and western Churches. Through the rest of the Middle Ages there were repeated attempts to heal this rift, just as there were many efforts to join the eastern Churches to Catholicism. In 1181 an agreement did indeed achieve union with the Maronites.

The relationship between the Latins, the Syrian Orthodox, and the Armenians was also on the whole good. The Latins accepted the ecclesiastical independence of the old eastern Churches and there was cooperation in spite of religious differences. The Syrian Orthodox Church had traditionally suffered the enmity of the Greek Orthodox Byzantines and had therefore welcomed the seventh-century Muslim conquest, an event that had brought them wide-reaching religious freedom. Under Latin rule, too, the animosity between Greeks and non-Chalcedonians endured. The two groups competed for influence and relations with the Latin rulers. Their rivalry took the form of mutual blame and defamation.

Eastern Christian monasticism

The old eastern and Greek Orthodox communities enjoyed a rich ecclesiastical and religious life. There is evidence of many non-Latin monasteries in Outremer; they were part of a long tradition and were often vibrant cultural centers. Greek Orthodox monks lived in places like the monasteries of SS. Sabas, Theodosius, and Euthymius in the Judean desert, at St Symeon's near Antioch, on Mount Tabor, and above all in the famous monastery of St Catherine's, Mount Sinai, one of the undisputed religious and spiritual centers of this region. Syrian Orthodox (Jacobite) monks lived in the monasteries of Gavithaca in Cilicia and Bar-Sauma in Edessa. In this period the Syrian Orthodox patriarch Michael the Great (1126–99) was active at Bar-Sauma, from whose important chronicle we know something about the religious life of the old eastern Churches. Michael's depiction is supplemented by the work of Gregorius, called Bar Hebraeus (1226–86).

Changes in the thirteenth century

The situation of the Churches in the crusader lordships altered a great deal in the course of the thirteenth century. In the Muslim-conquered regions the Greek Orthodox Church regained its earlier position, while the influence of other Christian religious groups waned. The Latins forfeited many bishoprics, so their Church had a predominantly urban character. The power of the Latin patriarch of Jerusalem increased, but the other bishops were poor in both economic provision and personnel. The ecclesiastical life of Outremer came to an abrupt end in 1291. The clerics—those who escaped Acre with their lives—were forced into exile. For centuries the papacy continued to claim authority in the Holy Land by appointing so-called "titular" bishops, even though the dioceses, in Muslim hands, were not administered. Only a few institutions succeeded in returning to Palestine.

4

The European crusades

711	July 23: defeat of the Visigoths at the river Guadalete
711–16	Muslim conquest of the Iberian Peninsula
1085	Conquest of Toledo by Alfonso VI of Castile-León
1086	Christians defeated by the Almoravids at the Battle of Sagrajas
1107/08	Crusade proclaimed against the Wends
1118	Conquest of Zaragoza by Alfonso I of Aragón
1147–49	Wendish crusade; military campaigns under King Afonso Henriques I of Portugal, King Alfonso VII of Castile-León, and Count Raymond Berengar IV of Barcelona
1168	Conquest of Rügen by the Danes
1195	July 9: Almohad victory over the Christians at Alarcos
1199	Crusades proclaimed against Livonia and Markward of Annweiler
1209–29	Albigensian crusades
1212	July 16: Christian victory over the Almohads at Las Navas de Tolosa
1228–48	Conquest of Mallorca (1228) and Valencia (1238) by King Jaime I of Aragón; conquest of Córdoba (1236) and Seville (1248) by Ferdinand III of Castile-León. Christian expansion to the Algarve coast
1230–85	Conquest of Prussia by the Teutonic Knights
1239	Crusade proclaimed against Emperor Frederick II (repeated in 1244)
1242	April 5: defeat of the Teutonic Knights by Alexander Nevskii at Lake Peipus
1260	July: defeat of a Danish-Swedish-German army by the Lithuanians at Durben
1265–68	War for the throne of Sicily between Charles I of Anjou and the Hohenstaufen
1282–1302	War over Sicily between Charles I of Anjou and Aragón (1285: crusade against Aragón)
1302 on	Several crusade proclamations against Italian cities
1307	Crusade against the *Apostolici* under Fra Dolcino

1386	Polish-Lithuanian union
1410	July 15: Poles and Lithuanians defeat the Teutonic Knights at Tannenberg/Grunwald
1420–34	Hussite crusades, several defeats of the Catholics
1454–66	Thirteen-year war between the Teutonic Knights and the Prussian League; ends 1466 with the Second Peace of Thorn
1465–67	Renewed crusade against the Hussites
1492	January 2: Granada surrenders to the Christians. Exile or forced baptism of the Spanish Jews and Muslims
1525	Secularization of the Teutonic Knights

The Iberian Peninsula

Why should the Iberian Peninsula, the Baltic, and wars against heretics appear in a book on the crusades? Wasn't Palestine the goal of all crusaders? The crusades *par excellence* were indeed those waged in the Near East—modern historians and medieval people agree on this point. But the Latin Church also offered indulgences for fighting against other opponents, and in these cases, too, troops were collected from different lands and pledged themselves to the campaign with an oath. Therefore, in this chapter three crusade zones will be briefly presented. Most similar to the crusader lordships of the Near East was the situation on the Iberian Peninsula. There, too, the fight was against Muslims; there, too, three religions lived together in a single region under Latin rule. Although conflict with the Muslims did not, as has been asserted, form the "red thread" of Spanish and Portuguese history, it did serve to make the Christian lordships west of the Pyrenees distinctive from the rest of Latin Europe. In the following section I will provide a short overview of the Hispanic lordships of the Middle Ages and present the so-called *reconquista*, dividing it into two phases (711–1095 and 1095–1492). The goal of the section is to show similarities, differences, and interactions between the crusades in the Near East and those in what is now Spain and Portugal.

Resistance and reconquista

The year 711 was a major turning point in Iberian history. In the early summer of that year a Muslim army under Tariq ibn Ziyad crossed the Strait of Gibraltar and on July 23, 711 annihilated the Visigothic army at the river Guadelete. The invaders—mostly Islamized Berbers and their Arabic co-religionists—succeeded in bringing almost the entire Iberian Peninsula under their sway. The Muslims named the region they ruled al-Andalus and elevated the old cathedral city of Córdoba into the capital of an emirate. Over time this emirate freed itself from the central control of the Baghdad caliphate, and in 929 Emir 'Abd ar-Rahman III

The Muslim conquest

115

(r. 912–61) founded an independent caliphate, that of Córdoba. Al-Andalus was very heterogeneous both ethnically and religiously. Berbers dominated in some regions, while Arabs predominated in others, and there were further divisions within these communities. Many Jews also lived on the peninsula, and even the majority population, the subject Christians, were divided between descendants of the Visigoths and of the Hispano-Romans.

The establishment of the Christian kingdoms

Only the mountainous, barely accessible border regions in the furthest north of the peninsula remained under Christian rule. In the course of the eighth through eleventh centuries, five Christian lordships were established here (see Map 2). In the Asturian-Cantabrian region, the kings of Asturias emerged from the ranks of the exiled Visigothic nobility. In the ninth century they expanded their territory southward and took, among other areas, the town of León. From the beginning of the tenth century, this city became the center of what from that point can be called the kingdom of León. To León's south, the county of Castile gradually freed itself from the king's authority in this period. By the beginning of the eleventh century Castile had finally established itself as an independent kingdom. Navarre, on its eastern border, developed into a principality whose leaders successfully claimed the royal title in the early tenth century. Just like the kings of León, they had to accept a formerly dependent county—Aragón—breaking free from their control and becoming a kingdom in 1035. Last of the five Iberian Christian states was the county of Barcelona. Unlike the other four, Barcelona had been part of the Carolingian Empire, one of several Catalan counties that formed its southern border. In the course of the eleventh century the counts of Barcelona grew into the dominant power of the eastern Pyrenees. These five states—León, Castile, Navarre, Aragón, and Barcelona—were transformed in the high Middle Ages. The Catalan-Aragonese crown (or simply the crown of Aragón) was formed by means of a dynastic alliance between the rulers of Barcelona and Aragón in 1137. The county of Portugal also won its independence from León and in 1143 officially rose to the rank of a kingdom. Finally, Castile and León were united from 1038 to 1157, and again, permanently, in 1230. The co-existence of these independent kingdoms (Portugal, Castile-León, Navarre, Aragón) makes it fundamentally impossible to generalize about "Spanish" history. One must keep this reservation in mind when considering the process known as the "*reconquista*."

The reconquista

"*Reconquista*" is the term generally applied to the conquest of formerly Christian-ruled territories from the Muslims. The *reconquista* was not an ongoing war, but rather a succession of long periods of peace interspersed with shorter crises. It has been suggested that this later label (the term comes from the nineteenth century) has added an ideological content retrospectively to what was really just a simple process of military expansion. But contemporary evidence shows that the Christians did indeed have the idea of winning back lost political and religious unity. In the kingdom of Asturias, for example, King Alfonso III's (r. 866–910) circle was especially dedicated to the memory of the lost Visigothic kingdom and propagated the idea that it must be reestablished. This "neo-Gothicism" was an important foundation for the expansion of the tenth and eleventh centuries. It caused people to view the geographic boundaries between the religions as provisional up until the end of the conquest. The Christian rulers repeatedly felt obligated to sign treaties with one another that defined their expansion areas in anticipation of future conquests.

The idea of a religious war was only indirectly linked to neo-Gothicism. The majority of early sources describe the conflict with the Muslims bare of any religious content. But there are a few other sources that give the *reconquista* a theological foundation. In tenth- and eleventh-century historical works like the *Chronica Gothorum* and the *Chronica de Sampiro*, the conflict is portrayed as God's will and thus a sanctified war. Just as in the Levant, here too some Christians looked to the re-establishment of a disturbed Christian order. For the conquered regions were formerly Christian territories, in which a fully established ecclesiastical system had existed before the Muslim conquest. To be sure, for a long time this view was apparently not so widespread that it had a great effect on the Christian advance; still less did it attract foreigners to fight in Spain. The fronts were not as clearly drawn as they often appear in hindsight. Local magnates—whether Muslim or Christian—allied themselves with one another in shifting coalitions, in which religion was often a secondary consideration. The best example of the co-existing cooperation and conflict in the eleventh century is the case of Rodrigo Díaz de Vivar, El Cid.

Holy war or border conflict?

El Cid (from the Arabic *al-Sid*, "the lord," 1043–99) was the name the Muslims gave the Castilian noble Rodrigo Díaz de Vivar. The life of this vassal of Sancho II and Alfonso VI of Castile has been passed down in the *Historia Roderici* (mid-twelfth century) and in the less-reliable *Poema del mío Cid* (late twelfth/early thirteenth century). These works describe the Cid's ever-shifting position: Rodrigo fought in his lord's name against Christians, took part in intra-Islamic battles between the lords of Seville and Granada, but also supported the Muslims of Zaragoza against the Christian king of Aragón. In 1094 he assumed lordship over Muslim Valencia. There he actually renounced the fealty he had hitherto always kept to Alfonso VI, established an independent state, and defended it successfully against Muslim attacks. There could hardly be a clearer expression of how particular the situation was on the interconfessional border. The history of the Cid Campeador (from *campi doctor*—victorious fighter), who died on July 10, 1099, is also an enlightening example of the opportunities open to militarily and politically adept warriors in the religious borderlands.

The Cid's battles against the Muslims were still for the most part an affair limited to Spain. In this period, though, the conflict also began to attract Christians from the far side of the Pyrenees. There are a number of reasons for this development. First, the dynastic and feudal alliances of the Hispanic ruling houses led to contacts with foreign lineages. Second, from the eleventh century onward, the major pilgrimage center Santiago de Compostela in Galicia attracted a growing stream of pilgrims along the so-called *Via sancti Jacobi* (Way of St James). And third, papal interest in the Iberian Peninsula was also growing in this period. For a long time the Roman Church's impact had been limited to the Carolingian-influenced eastern Pyrenees. But in the second half of the eleventh century its sphere of influence expanded. In 1068 the kingdom of Aragón placed itself under papal protection and adopted the Roman liturgical rite. Soon Castile, León, and Navarre followed suit, and clerics close to the papacy assumed important ecclesiastical functions. The affiliation to the Roman Church system can also be seen in relations with the Muslims. In 1064, for the first time a large contingent of French knights participated in the siege and conquest of the Aragonese town of Barbastro. Pope Alexander II supported this endeavor by granting indulgences and presenting the battle for Barbastro as particularly just, willed by God, and legitimate.

The Almoravids
In these eleventh-century battles, the Christians profited from the political and military weakness of al-Andalus. Granted, the field marshal al-Mansur billah (in Spanish Almanzor, d. 1002) was able to register major successes one more time, but a generation after his death the caliphate of Córdoba dissolved into a series of small states called the Taifa emirates (1031). These were often compelled to buy themselves free from Christian attacks by paying tribute (so-called *parias*) or to make pacts with the Christians. Nonetheless, the Christian-ruled regions continued to expand. The temporary high point of this development was reached on May 6, 1085, when a Castilian-Leonese army under King Alfonso VI succeeded in seizing control of the former Visigothic capital, Toledo. But the victory had unexpected consequences: the threatened Muslims turned for aid to co-religionists from Africa, the Almoravids (Arab. *al-murabitun*). These were fundamentalist Berbers, particularly dedicated to the idea of jihad (see "Crusade and jihad," p. 75). They inflicted a crippling defeat on Alfonso VI's troops at Sagrajas on October 23, 1086 and soon assumed the rule of al-Andalus for themselves. Between then and 1095 they conquered nearly all the Taifa emirates; the Valencian lordship of the Cid also fell victim to their expansion. An epoch of Spanish history had closed. It had been marked by the predominantly secular and political motivation for the *reconquista*. Now the conflict became more firmly based on religion on both sides, and the fronts hardened.

The reconquista's *European dimension*

With the Almoravid expansion on the Iberian Peninsula (1085–95), the second phase of the *reconquista* began. The Almoravids brought a religiously charged approach to warfare to al-Andalus, a perspective that also exerted an influence on Christendom. The papal engagement on behalf of the Iberian Peninsula took hold, and more foreigners traveled west to fight the Muslims. Among them were some later participants in the First Crusade, such as Count Raymond of Toulouse. But it should not be overlooked that various non-religious factors determined foreign participation in fighting, doubtless including hope for plunder or land, political circumstances, and other motives such as feudal ties to Hispanic rulers. Nonetheless, the battles were at the same time an expression of a sharpened opposition between religions on the Iberian Peninsula, an opposition that began to appear attractive to circles beyond the Pyrenees. Already at the end of the century at least some elements of the crusade movement can be discerned on the Iberian Peninsula, such as the emphasis on war for the faith, the vigorous participation of the papacy, the offer of indulgences, and the participation of foreigners in the battles. The Iberian situation seems above all to have had a strong impact on papal attitudes toward the use of force against Islam. It cannot, however, be demonstrated that the *reconquista* directly caused the proclamation of the First Crusade, nor can one simply call the Iberian campaigns of this period crusades. For some of the constitutive elements of the crusade (see "Holy war, knighthood, and pilgrimage," p. 14; "Papacy, piety, and indulgence," p. 23) were still missing in Spain. For example, there was no question of individual, complete forgiveness of sins, nor did the participating warriors swear an oath or mark themselves with the cross. But on the question of the indulgence, an important step had indeed already been taken before the conquest of Jerusalem: between 1096 and 1099, Urban II specifically promised the remission of all penalties of sin (*remissio peccatorum*) to the Christians who helped recover the Catalan city of Tarragona. The link between warfare against Muslims and the plenary indulgence was thus first fully established on the Iberian Peninsula.

Reconquista and crusade

Other crusading characteristics, however, reached Spain by way of the crusades in the Near East. In 1101 King Pedro of Aragón fought for the first time under the banner of the cross, when he confronted the Muslims at Zaragoza. He also had a market town there named after the war-cry of the first crusaders (Júslivol, from *Deus vult*—"God wills it"). In 1114 the Christians who set out to conquer the Balearic Islands were expressly granted indulgences, a papal legate accompanied the campaign, and the participants marked themselves with the sign of the cross. For the conquest of Zaragoza in 1118, too, foreigners were called to help and indulgences were promised. By this time at the latest, the campaigns on the Iberian Peninsula had taken on the character of a crusade, at least in the eyes of the papacy and the foreign fighting men. It

The influence of the First Crusade on the Iberian Peninsula

was only logically consistent that in 1121 the fighters in Spain were specifically granted the same indulgences as crusaders in the Holy Land; at the First Lateran Council in 1123, regulations were made for those who took the cross "in order to go to Jerusalem or Spain." Spain also saw the first crusade bull for recruiting crusaders. At almost the same time that the Palestinian military orders were founded, "militias" appeared in Spain that combined a religious life with warfare against the Muslims. It is thus possible to see a reciprocal give-and-take between the Levant and the Iberian Peninsula. Both were recognized as crusade regions.

Literary texts contributed to this assessment. The *Chanson de Roland*, the *Rolandslied*, and the so-called *Pseudo-Turpin* (*Historia Karoli Magni et Rotolandi*) describe Charlemagne's campaign on the Iberian Peninsula three centuries earlier as a crusade, and some *chansons de geste* also sang of Christian battles in *Hispania*. It is true, though, that only a few sources indicate an authentic crusader attitude among the local Hispanic Christians. This is not surprising. One can observe the same phenomenon among the inhabitants of Outremer after the establishment of the crusader lordships; for the Christians living in the area, the conflicts usually took on the character of border wars. But in major campaigns, crusade propaganda and crusading zeal can also be discerned in some local sources.

The campaigns of 1147–49

The years 1147/48 saw truly decisive participation by foreign crusaders. At the same time as the crusade against Damascus and a large crusade in the Baltic, the Hispanic kings undertook a series of offensives against the weakened Almoravid state. In Portugal, the Christians took Lisbon (October 1147); in the same month the Castilian king conquered the important port city of Almería. Soon thereafter, the Taifa emirates of Tortosa and Lleida submitted to the Catalan-Aragonese crown (December 1148 and October 1149). The monarchs had foreign assistance in these endeavors. Afonso Henriques I of Portugal (r. 1128–85) took advantage of the presence of crusaders from the lower Rhine and England, who were on their way to the Holy Land, for the conquest of Lisbon (October 24, 1147). Several months later, some of the English crusaders took part in Count Raymond Berengar IV of Barcelona's (r. 1131–62) seizure of Tortosa. A Genoese fleet supported them and was decisive in the undertaking's success. Unquestionably, the campaigns of 1147/48 were a high point of foreign participation in the *reconquista*.

After these successes, the Iberian monarchs apparently took steps to ensure that the presence of foreign crusaders remained limited. This forms an essential difference between the Levantine crusades and those of the Iberian Peninsula: while the Latins of the Near East actively sought the assistance of their European co-religionists and also needed it desperately, the Hispanic Christians apparently were not dependent on outside support to the same degree. Certainly there were initiatives like that of King Louis VII of France, who in 1159 wanted to join Henry II of England to aid the Hispanic Christians. Foreign crusaders also took part in various campaigns (such as in 1212 at Las Navas de Tolosa, 1217 in Portugal, and 1309 at Gibraltar). But it is significant that the initiative of 1159 came to nothing, because the native monarchs did not agree to it. On the whole, the international appeal of the *reconquista* cannot compare with that of the crusades in the Near East. This qualification does not change the character of the Iberian Peninsula as a crusade region, it only expresses its relative weight as part of the crusading movement.

Al-Andalus underwent yet another change in rule in the mid-twelfth century—the Almoravids were forced from power by the Almohads. The Almohads (Arab. *al-muwahhidun*) were, like the Almoravids, Sunni reformers, but belonged to another Berber tribe. They conducted jihad first of all against the Almoravids, whom they accused of laxity and heresy. They conquered Morocco with extreme brutality in the period up to 1148, and by 1172 had also subjugated al-Andalus. The Almohads reaped their greatest success against the Christians on July 9, 1195 at Alarcos against the troops of Alfonso VIII of Castile (r. 1158–1214). The defeat led the Christians to surmount their internal disagreements and plan a common attack against the Muslims. Pope Innocent III gave them strong support, making the campaign known far beyond the borders of Spain through crusade bulls, processions, and intercessory prayers. Thus a sizeable contingent of foreign, mostly French, crusaders joined the united armies of Castile, Aragón, and Navarre. Although most of the foreigners left when they were forbidden to sack conquered towns, still the native Christians were victorious over the Almohad army at Las Navas de Tolosa on July 16, 1212.

The Almohads

After the Battle of Las Navas de Tolosa, the Muslims in Spain had no more major military successes. Consequently, this battle is accepted as the final turning point in the history of the *reconquista*, even if this does not seem to have been clear to contemporaries. At this time, the papacy began separating the *reconquista* from the eastern crusades—Innocent III wanted to direct all available forces toward a campaign to free Jerusalem. Therefore, in the crusade bull *Quia maior* of 1213, he revoked the indulgences that had previously been granted to Christians for fighting on the Iberian Peninsula. With this move he annulled the equation of the two campaigning zones that had existed implicitly since the beginning of the twelfth century. This policy change of 1213 certainly played a part in slowing the expansionist drive. But the death of several rulers and internal disputes also kept the victors of Las Navas de Tolosa from continuing their expansion immediately. The conquests continued only after a twenty-year "breather." The new offensive was highly successful: under King Ferdinand III, the Castilians conquered the most important

The thirteenth-century expansion

cities of Andalusia in a series of campaigns, including Córdoba and Seville (1236 and 1248). Jaime I "the conqueror" (r. 1213–76) achieved similar gains for the Catalan-Aragonese crown—Mallorca was occupied in 1228 and in 1238 the powerful kingdom of Valencia fell. Lastly, in Portugal the expansion movement reached the Algarve coast by 1248. In barely twenty years, the kingdoms of Portugal, Castile, and Catalonia-Aragón had conquered nearly all of al-Andalus, thus cementing their own hegemony over the Iberian peninsula. Only in the mountainous Sierra Nevada region of southern Spain could Muslim rule hold out—the emirate of Granada, ruled by the Arabic Nasrid dynasty. For more than two centuries this state adroitly played its position between the Muslim Marinid state to the south (in modern Morocco and Algeria) and the Christians in the north.

The end of the reconquista

In the first half of the fourteenth century the *reconquista* was again fanned into flame. An Aragonese-Castilian army seized Gibraltar from the Marinids in 1309, and on October 30, 1340 a Portuguese-Castilian force won a major victory at the river Salado. Crusaders, promised indulgences, took part in both campaigns. In later periods, too, Christians crossed the Pyrenees to Spain to fight the Muslims; the expeditions were by this time strongly superimposed with chivalric ideals. Many knightly participants were apparently more concerned with honor and adventure than with their spiritual well-being. After the union of Castile and Aragón under the "Catholic kings" Ferdinand II and Isabella (1469), Granada, too, the last Muslim state on Iberian soil, fell to Christian hands after a ten-year war. With its surrender on January 2, 1492 the *reconquista* had reached an end. Still, the idea lived on and served as a foundation and justification for the Spanish expansion to the Americas.

New political, ecclesiastical, and social structures

During the expansion, the Christians on the Iberian Peninsula faced challenges similar to those of their co-religionists in Palestine and Syria. They had to restructure conquered regions both ecclesiastically and politically. A related task was the settlement of Christians in depopulated or already-inhabited regions. Lastly, it was also necessary to clarify the legal position of the subjugated populace.

The first issue, the reestablishment of an ecclesiastical framework, appeared at first glance to be a simple task, because a fully developed Church organization had already existed at the time of the Muslim conquest. But, as in Palestine, things had changed on the Iberian Peninsula during the centuries of Muslim rule. Political interests were often different than in Visigothic times. Thus, among other changes, some episcopal sees were transferred to different cities. For example, Santiago de Compostela, which had risen to prominence as a pilgrimage center thanks to its possession of the tomb of St James, won the episcopal dignity from nearby Iria. More controversial was the erection of new archdioceses. The new political entities wanted their own ecclesiastical centers, and so archbishoprics were created for León, Portugal, and the Catalonian-Aragonese crown. The pilgrimage center Compostela won this honor for León in 1120 (finalized in 1124) despite the bitter opposition of the long-established Castilian archdiocese of Toledo; Braga in Portugal (1100) and Tarragona in Catalonia (1118) enjoyed similar success.

The creation of new political structures went hand in hand with this developing Church organization. In the first decades of the *reconquista* the so-called *presura* (Lat. *aprisio*) were still operated; that is, regions were conquered by private initiative without governmental control. Soon, however, the rulers succeeded in bringing the conquest process under their authority. From the ninth century on, it was they who summoned warriors to campaigns of conquest and they who divided up and distributed the conquered territories. Starting in the second half of the twelfth century, the military orders won ever-greater possessions, because their participation made military success more likely. The monarchs, however, took care that the dominance of the military orders did not become too great by issuing large land grants to other ecclesiastical institutions, nobles, and relatives.

This process of parcelling out the land brings us to the third task of the conquerors—settlement. Already at an early stage the *reconquista* was accompanied by efforts at resettlement, known as *repoblación*. The majority of these settlers were from the Iberian Peninsula, emigrating Christians from Muslim al-Andalus or co-religionists from the northern regions. But foreigners, especially French, also settled along the *via sancti Jacobi* to Santiago de Compostela. In the course of the eleventh to thirteenth centuries Christians settled the newly conquered areas in several waves. In the border regions of Castile-León, for example, a line of fortified cities was created, the populace of which for the most part engaged in stock raising. Since the danger of sudden raids was particularly great in this region, the communities had to be able to act independently. They created their own military units, called *milicias*, which also had important military functions for the *reconquista*. Settlement in these advance posts was made attractive for the Christians, the territorial lords issuing charters that secured relatively generous liberties. In the border regions these privileges were also collected in normative texts, the *fueros*.

The *repoblación* (resettlement)

123

Fuero

On the Iberian Peninsula *fuero* is the name given to collections of customary law. Cities' legal codes are also called *fueros*. These texts could contain the actual privileges granted by the lord of the city, but also more precise regulations about tax obligations or the constitutional life of a particular locality. The *fueros* described the principles of civic autonomy in the border districts. Some of them won a position as exemplars for other communities, so that they built up their own town law "families." The *fuero* of Cuenca, composed immediately after the town's conquest in 1177, is an influential and particularly detailed example. It includes precise rules for the organization of razzias and for distribution of the plunder taken, but also deals with the election of city officials and other matters.

The position of the subjected peoples In the newly conquered areas, the settlers encountered Muslims and Jews who were already resident. Relationships with them were regulated on the Iberian Peninsula very much as they were in the Near East. In both places, there was not tolerance but rather a pragmatic interaction with people of other faiths. The much-employed term *convivencia* (living together) suggests a higher degree of cooperation and exchange than existed in reality. The interests responsible for the co-existence that occurred in both the East and on the Iberian Peninsula is better described with the term *conveniencia*—expediency. The Muslims under Christian rule, called *mudéjares*, were second-class citizens, even more so than the Jews. They had to pay a head tax, were forbidden to bear arms, and were gathered together in their own residential quarters. For example, in Andalusia the subjected Muslims were ordered out of the cities and their houses were divided among the victors in the so-called *repartimiento*. Still, the Iberian Muslims could, for the most part, practice their religion without major interference and had the protection of the law. The *fueros*, like that of Cuenca, are also important sources for investigating the co-existence of the three monotheistic religions on the peninsula. In these texts, Muslims and Jews were explicitly invited to settle and were recognized, not indeed as legal equals, but as subjects with vested rights.

There was as little missionary activity on the Iberian Peninsula as there was in Outremer. Still, some Christianization gradually occurred. Probably the most important reason for adopting Christianity was the legal discrimination practiced against Muslims and Jews, as well as the continuation of Christian rule. Despite these tendencies toward conversion, at the end of the *reconquista* in 1492 there were still large Jewish and Muslim populations on the Iberian Peninsula. They fell victim to the Catholic kings' (Isabella I of Castile, r. 1474–1504; Ferdinand II of Aragón, r. 1461–1516) efforts to achieve confessional unity. In 1492 the Jews were ordered into exile unless they gave up their religion, and a little later the *mudéjares* were baptized by force. In 1609 the descendants of these former Muslims were also finally banished from the land.

The Baltic lands

The internationalization of war against the heathen of the Baltic lands

The Christian conquest of the Baltic lands was also part of the general expansion movement of the high Middle Ages. The process began before the First Crusade with the Christianization of much of Scandinavia and campaigns against the western Slavs, but was influenced in the twelfth century by developments in the Near East. At first, elements of the crusades were adopted in the Baltic lands, and finally the expansion there developed into a crusade movement. The earliest evidence of this transformation appears in a crusade proclamation from 1107/08. In this document, the secular and ecclesiastical authorities of eastern Saxony called on the Christians of Westphalia, Flanders, and the lower Rhine for support in battle against the pagan Slavs east of the Elbe. The warriors were explicitly compared to the crusaders in Palestine and the region to be conquered directly equated to the holy places: "Our Jerusalem [the territory to be conquered], which was free from the beginning, is reduced to slavery by the heathens' savagery. Its walls fell down because of our sins" (Constable 1999: 207). The relation to the crusades leaps to the eye, but it still took until the year 1147 before the papacy elevated the Christian expansion in the Baltic to the level of a crusade. After 1147, Baltic crusades were repeatedly equated to those of the Levant (1171, 1199, 1240, 1249, etc.), and were also granted identical indulgences (the *remissio peccatorum*). Participation in a crusade in the eastern Mediterranean could be substituted with one against the pagans in the Baltic. To be sure, the last papal crusade indulgence for this region was issued in 1265, but in the following period the Teutonic Order held out the prospect of indulgences and right up to the fourteenth and fifteenth centuries the warriors themselves often called themselves *peregrini*, swore crusader vows when they set out, and thus showed that they regarded themselves as crusaders. How important a role the crusader movement played in this region can be seen for instance in the origin legend of the Danish flag, the Danebrog, with its white cross on red ground: the flag is supposed to have fallen from heaven as a sign of divine support during a battle near Reval (Tallinn) against the pagan Estonians on June 15, 1219, and to have won the Christians a victory. Admittedly, by the end of the late Middle Ages the Baltic crusades had lost much of their crusading character, but from the twelfth century to the fourteenth one can certainly regard the Baltic lands as a crusade region.

The Baltic as a crusade region

125

Bearers of the expansion

The Baltic crusades were not waged by a single power, such as the Teutonic Order, and no more than the Christians involved did the pagans form a single homogeneous group. A large number of different tribes and peoples confronted the Christians. At the beginning there were west Slavic peoples or the tribal confederations of the Liutizi, Pomeranians, and so on. The eastward expansion brought conflict with a series of Baltic tribes: Prussians, Lithuanians, Kurs, Semgallians, Livonians, and Estonians. For their part, at least five Christian groups can be distinguished: secular magnates, the Church, the Teutonic Knights, the cities, and finally individual crusaders without connections to the other groups. The secular powers in the Baltic included the Roman-German Empire—not just its monarchs but also northeastern magnates such as the dukes of Saxony. The kings of Denmark and Sweden were also involved. These two royal houses, only recently Christianized themselves, now pushed ahead with the subjection of the pagans. Lastly, the Polish magnates on the Baltic, especially the dukes of Masovia, should be named. The Church's expansion was for the most part conducted by the large archbishoprics of Hamburg-Bremen and Lund. Soon ecclesiastical structures also developed in the newly conquered regions (see "Settlement, colonization, and mission," p. 131), and they too took a hand in events. And lastly the papacy played an important role as a distant but influential factor, decisive in both ecclesiastical and political penetration of the region. The Teutonic Order will be discussed in Chapter 5. The Teutonic Knights became the leading power in the Baltic in the mid-thirteenth century, carving out their own territory, the so-called *Deutschordensland* (State of the Teutonic Order) in a series of conflicts against Christian as well as pagan opponents. A series of urban centers played a role, especially in the early phase of the Baltic crusade movement. Their economic significance is obvious, but they were also important for the crusades, providing both men and transport. Among them, Lübeck stands out, the main point of entry for many foreign crusaders making their way eastward. These crusaders formed their own subgroup within the Baltic crusade movement—individuals who decided to make the journey, some in hope of loot or adventure, others seeking salvation or the forgiveness of sins. At the very end of the Middle Ages many western European nobles also traveled eastwards every year to participate in the campaigns against the Lithuanians. These tours, commonly called "journeys to Prussia" (*Preussenreisen*), were a unique mixture of chivalric adventure quest and campaign in the service of religion.

Phases of the expansion

The Christian expansion into the Baltic lands can be divided into three phases (see Map 3). The first phase includes the period from 1107/08 until the establishment of the Teutonic Knights in the Baltic in about the year 1230. The second phase lasted from 1230 until the conquest of Pomerelia and the establishment of the order's headquarters at Marienburg in 1308/09. The final phase lasted until the Polish-Lithuanian union of 1386. The historians of the Teutonic Order provide important evidence about the first two phases.

The chronicles of the Teutonic Knights

The literature associated with the Teutonic Knights was to a large extent composed in the vernacular, but some chronicles were written in Latin. Of outstanding importance among them is a chronicle completed in 1326 by Peter of Dusburg, one of the order's priests, which was translated into German about ten years later. This work gives an account of the subjection of Prussia as well as the first stages of the crusades against the Lithuanians and was intended not only to legitimate the campaigns of conquest but to recruit new crusaders. Older than Peter of Dusburg's work is the anonymous "Livonian" verse chronicle, completed in 1290. This chronicle consists of 12,017 rhyming couplets, making it the most extensive poem produced in the Teutonic Knights' milieu. It describes the battles against the northern Baltic tribes from 1180 to 1290.

The first phase of the Baltic crusade is marked by the activities of the northeastern magnates of the Roman-German Empire, the Danish and Swedish kings, the missionary bishops of Riga, and the religious Order of the Sword-Brothers. The most important stages of this phase are the so-called Wendish crusade (1147), the conquest of Rügen (1168), and the occupation of Livonia (beginning in 1197/98). The Wendish crusade of 1147 was a campaign by Saxons, Danes, and Poles, who attacked both the Wends (a Slavic tribe that lived east of the Elbe) and the Baltic Prussians. The papacy and some participants regarded this campaign as the opening of a third confessional front to set alongside the Iberian Peninsula and the Near East. The success of this Wendish crusade was limited, but in 1168 the Danes were able to complete the conquest of Rügen. At the mouth of the river Düna, 700 km northeast of Rügen, a Livonian bishopric was created in 1186 under the authority of the archdiocese of Hamburg-Bremen. Under the energetic leadership of Bishop Albrecht of Bekeshovede (r. 1199–1229) the city of Riga was founded in 1201, followed a year later by the Order of the Sword-Brothers. The knights of this order played a vital role in the subjugation of much of Livonia in the following three decades, receiving in return one-third of the conquered land in freehold. In the same period crusaders under the leadership of King Valdemar II of Denmark (d. 1241) attacked northern Estonia. Soon tensions developed between the bishop of Riga, the Sword-Brothers, and the Danes. After the bishop's death (1229) and the annihilating defeat of the Sword-Brothers at the Battle of Saule on September 22, 1236, the latter were incorporated into the Teutonic Order, which rose to become the leading power in Livonia.

First expansion

The second phase of the conquest was shaped by the Teutonic Order. The Knights were given lordship over Kulmland on the Vistula in the

Consolidation of lordship

period 1225–30. From this base they launched the conquest of the parts of Baltic Prussia that bordered them to the north and east. Despite two rebellions (1242–49 and 1260–74) the expansion was completed by 1285. In the north, in Livonia, the Sword-Brothers were incorporated, thus enabling the creation of a second state. Estonia, on the northern border, was divided between the Teutonic Knights (in the south) and Denmark (in the north), although the order's defeat by Prince Alexander Nevskii of Novgorod (1220–63) at Lake Peipus on April 5, 1242 prevented further eastward expansion. Ever since, Lake Peipus has formed the border between Latin and Russian Orthodox Christianity. The Teutonic Knights worked hard, but ultimately failed to unite Prussia and Livonia. Between the two lay the pagan Samogitia, the western edge of Lithuania. In the attempt to conquer this region, in July 1260 a Danish–Swedish–German army suffered a severe reverse at the Battle of Durben. Instead of further eastward campaigns, the Knights now turned their attention to the west. In 1308/9 they took advantage of the dynastic and political weakness of Christian Pomerelia to occupy the land, with its center Gdansk. The order established a new headquarters in the nearby Marienburg in 1309.

Lastly, in the third phase of expansion the fighting front moved northward. Northern Estonia and Reval (Tallinn) were purchased from the Danes, but the Teutonic Knights did not expand further against the Christian Russians. The sole remaining non-Christian enemy was the Lithuanians. Their existence made it possible for the Teutonic Knights and the crusaders who joined them to fulfill their original *raison d'être*; that is, to wage war for the faith. Year after year nobles from central and western Europe traveled eastward every spring to take part in the "journey to Prussia" (*Preussenreise*), the annual campaign against the Lithuanians. These expeditions, first attested in 1304, were conducted throughout the fourteenth century and even continued for a few decades after Lithuania accepted Catholic Christianity in 1386. Finally, people even in distant lands realized that the war was no longer being waged against pagans, so the crusaders and *Preussenreisen* gradually faded away.

The Teutonic Knights and their state

State formation by the Sword-Brothers

What made the Baltic different from all the other expansion zones of Latin Christendom was the strong political control by religious organizations. Nowhere else did military religious orders rule over such consolidated and independent territories. The Teutonic Order developed into the greatest power in northeastern Europe after the Hanseatic League. It had already tried several times to build states—for example in the Holy Land and in Transylvania (see "Foundations and beginnings of the military religious orders," p. 145). But in fact the Teutonic Knights were not the first military order to accomplish this goal in the Baltic. As early as 1210 the Sword-Brothers made an agreement with the bishop of Riga that they would hold one-third of Livonia and Latvia—formally as a fief, but free of all obligations and duties except defense. The Order of the Sword-Brothers was allowed to present candidates for parishes, and its priests as well as the other members of the order were freed from paying tithes. In fact, the Sword-Brothers were the first military order anywhere to establish their rule over a territory successfully. The Teutonic Order assumed these rights in 1236 and later expanded them. The following pages will tell of the establishment of the order's lordship in Prussia and Livonia. One must also, however, assess the role of other powers in the region, which often gave support but later also appeared as opponents of the order. The object of the following pages is to sketch out the ecclesiastical, political, and economic powers in the State of the Teutonic Order (*Ordensstaat*) and the transformation of their relations to each other in the late Middle Ages.

Unlike the Levant or the Iberian Peninsula, east of the Oder there were no older ecclesiastical structures that could serve as a foundation for a new Church organization. In the early period, the archdioceses of Bremen-Hamburg and Lund were the dominant powers in the creation of a new organization. Soon, however, the papacy seized the initiative. Due to this intervention, in 1243 the diocese of Prussia was divided into the four bishoprics of Kulm, Pomesania, Ermland, and Samland. In Livonia, too, new episcopal sees were established in Dorpat, Ösel-Wiek, and Kurland in the first half of the thirteenth century. Lastly, in 1255 a new archdiocese was founded at Riga for the whole region. Some of these bishoprics, but especially the archdiocese of Riga, controlled vast territories. However, the bishops' sphere of power was strictly limited: the Teutonic Order often possessed direct control over the bishoprics, since their cathedral chapters were incorporated with the order (as in Kulm, Pomesania, Samland, and Kurland). That meant that the cathedral canons and the bishops—unless the pope named someone else— were priest-brothers of the Teutonic Order. In other bishoprics, the order could only acquire this privilege in part (e.g., Riga, Reval).

Ecclesiastical organization

But how was the Teutonic order able to establish itself successfully in the Baltic in the first place? Their attempt to build a state in Hungary failed in 1225 (see "The spread of the military orders," p. 151). In 1225/26 Duke Conrad I of Masovia (*c.* 1187–1247) invited the order to take control of Kulmland in modern Poland, as a base from which to fight the pagan Prussians. Grand Master Hermann von Salza (*c.* 1179–1239) had learned his lesson from the order's failure in Hungary, so in 1226 he won a privilege from Emperor Frederick II, the famous Golden Bull of Rimini, that granted the order lordship over Kulmland and all territory that they could conquer in the land of the Prussians.

The Teutonic order's state-building

At first the duke of Masovia, Bishop Christian of Prussia, and the military order of Dobrin (created by the two in 1228) were rivals for the rule

---

The Golden Bull of Rimini

Probably between 1230 and 1235, Emperor Frederick II granted to Hermann von Salza, grand master of the Teutonic order, a ceremonial charter, sealed with a gold seal (*bulla*). In it, the emperor permitted the order to take possession of Kulmland, given to them by Duke Conrad of Masovia, as well as future conquests in Prussia, complete with judicial rights and sovereignty. The authenticity and purpose of this undated document were long a subject of debate. It can now be accepted without reservation as genuine, but the document should not be regarded as a conscious effort to found a state. It is only together with other documents that the Golden Bull of Rimini created the constitutional parameters for the development of Teutonic order lordship in Prussia.

---

of Prussia. The Teutonic Knights were only able to set about the military endeavors they planned when the most important competitors had been swept out of the way. First they received a guarantee from the duke of Masovia similar to the Golden Bull of Rimini, then they procured a papal confirmation, after which Bishop Christian's claims were cleared away, and finally by 1237 the older Prussian-Baltic military orders (of Dobrin and the Sword-Brothers) were incorporated into the Teutonic order.

Administration
In the course of the ongoing conquest up to 1285, the order's gains had to be secured. So the territory was studded with castles. It is estimated that by 1400 the Knights had constructed over 260 "Teutonic order castles" in their state. These fortified centers were usually built to a common type: four-winged with an inner court and equipped with outbuildings. These served as trade locales, storage rooms, and living quarters, bearing witness to the castles' role for economy and settlement. To fulfill these goals, an efficient administration was a necessity, and the order proved itself to be a true master at the task. A good courier system and regular visitations assured that communication between the individual houses and headquarters was preserved despite the distance involved, and many different officials were charged with administrative tasks. The state was under the authority of two landmasters (of Livonia and Prussia), with the grand master taking over the function of the Prussian landmaster after 1309. The individual houses, with their surrounding territory, were controlled by so-called commanders; the steward was responsible for economic interests, the forestmaster was in charge of the woods, and so on. Record-keeping was developed intensively, and careful registers were often kept of activities. The Knights themselves carried out these administrative functions. They were nobles, for the most part recruited from other parts of the Roman-German Empire—in other words, foreigners to the territory. However, their numbers suffered a steep decline in the fifteenth century, so that increasingly the order's convents were

converted into houses under the leadership of a single knight. At the same time, the influence and self-identity of other Baltic powers rose. This tension ultimately led to the end of the "State of the Teutonic order."

Two powers in particular confronted the order: the cities and the local nobles. In the course of the settlement movement of the thirteenth century (described in "Settlement, Colonization, and mission," p. 131), many cities were founded, with privileges granted by the Teutonic order. Over time, the cities' interests diverged more and more from those of the order. The townsmen and women identified themselves rather with the interests of the Hanseatic League, the most important economic force of the region, and many cities joined the League (including Gdansk, Königsberg, Riga, and Reval). The Hanse dominated Baltic trade (dealing in furs, leather, wood, and grain, among other products). Since the Teutonic order itself traded in grain, amber, and other goods, and in some spheres had a very different perspective from the cities' interests, conflicts were inevitable. The cities demanded a larger say in government, because of their economic clout, but remained unheard. So they found allies among the secular nobles. A local aristocracy had risen in the course of the fourteenth and fifteenth centuries, growing from the more important free Prussian farmers and Christian soldiers who had settled. They were critical of the foreign Teutonic Knights and in the fifteenth century won the right to a say in political affairs. The military situation gave their voice more weight: ever since the Lithuanian ruler had accepted Christianity in 1386 and had taken the throne of Poland, the order had been under increasing pressure. After its defeat at the Battle of Tannenberg/Grunwald on July 15, 1410 the pressure grew even more intense. Nobles and cities had to finance the wars and used this fact as leverage to make their demands. The two groups united in the so-called Prussian League in 1440, and from 1454 to 1466 they made an alliance with the Polish king to fight the order. The war ended with the order's defeat, the second Peace of Thorn (1466), and the partition of the Teutonic state. Pomerelia and Kulm (with Gdansk and Marienburg) were lost to the order. Forced to fall back on their eastern possessions and robbed of purpose, the *Ordensstaat* maintained its *de facto* independence, but its end as an ecclesiastical lordship was sealed. In 1525 Prussia, under Albrecht of Hohenzollern-Ansbach (1490–1568), was converted into a secular duchy; Livonia followed its example in 1561.

Fifteenth-century conflicts

Settlement, colonization, and mission

Like the Levant and the Iberian Peninsula, the Baltic region was marked by the interrelationship of crusade and settlement. Many people came from the west to the newly conquered territories. The majority of the settlers were from the middle Elbe, Westphalia, and Flanders. This

The "eastern settlement"

settlement movement in the Baltic was a part of what is called the "eastern settlement" (*Ostsiedlung*), a term used to described the occupation and acculturation of large parts of central-eastern Europe by German monks, farmers, artisans, and merchants. Evaluation of the process is a very controversial issue in both German and international scholarship. In part it has been regarded favorably as part of the Europe-wide phenomenon of agrarian development and thus as a particular element of a larger movement. Other parts of Europe, such as the marshy region of the Netherlands, were also opened up for settlement from the twelfth century. Many of these regions display structural similarities, ranging from the initiative taken by feudal lords in the use of tenant systems and liberties for the settlers to the societal consequences of the colonization process. What made the Baltic different from other regions was the stark ethnic and religious chasm between the natives and the newcomers.

Large-scale colonization movements require careful planning, and one can trace such initiatives in the regions conquered by crusaders. Potential settlers had to be informed that migration would bring them improvements in their living conditions, greater liberties, and fewer dues. In the territories east of the Elbe an official known as the "locator" was responsible for advertising and carrying out the new settlement.

The locator

The locator was not the actual landlord, but rather an independent entrepreneur. He made a (location) contract with the lord, which usually assured him and his descendants a particularly large land grant, fewer taxes, and often portions of the village revenues, too. Sometimes the agreements went even further, including the right to operate a mill, or sell alcohol, or the office of village mayor. Thus the former locator and his descendants assumed judicial functions and the accompanying revenues as well as often taking on a role as village headmen.

The settlers

The settlers were also won over with special rights and above-average grants. The land, given freely for settlement, was divided into "hides" that were usually at least twice as big as the holdings of the Prussian farmers. The free "hide tax farmers" also paid fewer taxes than the native "hook tax farmers." Their farms were hereditary and could be sold; the farmers were not legally bound to the land. The settlers were also assured a certain degree of communal organization and therefore the foundations for self-rule. Thanks to these privileges, an agrarian middle class, the so-called "little freemen," developed, composed of settlers as well as the Prussians who had voluntarily submitted to the conquerors. The nobles of the Teutonic order state constituted a second group among the free. This group, called "great freemen," consisted of locators, crusaders who settled, and upwardly mobile farmers. The little freemen mostly lived according to Kulmian law, a typical colonial law code that assured the farmers far-reaching liberties. Thus it is also possible to regard the German eastward settlement as, to a large extent, a colonization by German law.

The same was true of the cities. Locators were also active in some of them, and the centers were attractive places for migration thanks to their far-reaching rights. The cities that followed German law usually possessed self-government and their own jurisdiction, trade privileges, and artisanal privileges as well as far-reaching rights for the citizens. One can group these cities into "urban law landscapes" or "urban law families": most cities that were founded in the Teutonic order state adopted the Magdeburg law code, while a few took that of Lübeck. In Prussia several subgroups of the Magdeburg code developed. The so-called Kulm Laws of December 28, 1233 were especially influential. They codified the rights and freedoms, as well as the obligations, of the citizens of Kulm and Thorn. The Kulm Laws were an exemplar for other cities and supported Prussia's organizational development. However, these privileges were not intended for all inhabitants of the cities, but only for the citizens. These were usually German-speaking settlers, not natives.

The cities

But what peoples did the conquerors come into contact with? Much is still unknown or unauthenticated about the religion and lifestyle of the pagan Prussians, Lithuanians, Kurs, Semgallians, Livonians, and Estonians, because for the most part the written sources were produced by the Christian victors. Archaeological excavations have certainly demonstrated that these peoples created more differentiated and better-organized governmental structures than is widely assumed. It is also a telltale sign that they successfully opposed conquest and evangelization for such a long time. One must make a clear distinction between the various expansion zones: Prussia and Livonia were penetrated by Christianity and stamped with middle European culture to very different degrees. After its bloody conquest, Prussia was systematically settled with foreigners from the Roman-German Empire, Poland, and Pomerania. The land was opened to agriculture and a dense settlement web developed. Still, it would be completely false to regard the Teutonic order state as a "missionary state"—the order was primarily concerned with creating an independent territorial lordship, and its missionary efforts were confined within very narrow limits. But even though the difference between native Prussians and foreigners remained large, a stronger acculturation took place there in religious, political, and economic terms than in Livonia. In the latter, settlement for the most part remained limited to the cities, the immigrants were mostly merchants and other city-dwellers, or combatants. In this border region between the Russian, Swedish, Lithuanian, and German spheres of influence, the fronts often fluctuated, as the local magnates' frequent political realignments attest. This region was not of central importance to the Teutonic Knights, either politically or economically, and the order's

Contact with the conquered peoples

missionary efforts were even more circumscribed than in Prussia. Lastly, between Prussia and Livonia lay Lithuania—the border region of minor wars and sudden raids, the land of the late medieval *Preussenreisen* and crusades.

Baltic/Near East: similarities and differences

In closing, let us attempt to lay out similarities and differences between the Baltic lands and other crusade regions. It is notable that a few crusades in the Near East had a counterpart in the Baltic—the Wendish crusade of 1147 is the most conspicuous example. One can also point to the year 1171, when an English–French–German crusade to the Holy Land was preached while at the same time the Scandinavians were enjoined to crusade against the Estonians. In 1219, crusaders fought simultaneously before the walls of Damietta and in Estonia. Crusades were preached and crusader indulgences promised for the Baltic, the Near East, and the Iberian Peninsula alike, and in all three regions military religious orders played an outstanding military and political role. As in the Levant, nautical conditions led to a certain regularity of campaigning in the Baltic: in one case it was prevailing winds, in the other melting ice that made the spring fleets to the crusade regions possible. On the Iberian Peninsula, in the Levant, and in the Baltic the crusaders were followed by settlers who occupied and also opened up the land. Once there, they developed forms of co-existence with the subjugated natives. These enjoyed fewer rights than the conquerors, but could claim the protection of the law. However, certain features were unique to the Baltic lands. In contrast to other crusade regions, non-Christian religions were officially not tolerated. The position of the Teutonic order as territorial ruler was particularly remarkable: nowhere else did a military religious order succeed in gaining so much power. And lastly, the grand masters of the Teutonic Knights, just like the Hispanic monarchs, succeeded in dominating and directing the crusade movement in their region.

Enemies within

The Albigensian crusades in France

Crusade and fighting heretics

To most modern eyes, crusades against Christians seem to be a contradiction in terms—isn't war under the sign of the cross always against non-believers? Did not the crusaders who bore weapons against their co-religionists pervert the whole idea of crusade? Some contemporaries also viewed the issue in this light. Critics of the crusades against heretics in the thirteenth and fourteenth centuries reproached the crusaders with neglecting their true task—war against the Muslims. Others rejected the notion that these wars had any higher purpose and regarded them as aggression plain and simple. But from another perspective, it was perfectly consistent that Christians should proceed against heretics, schismatics, and Christian enemies of the Church. Indeed, from a historical perspective fighting against heretics was not a corruption of the original holy war idea at all, because the Augustinian doctrine of just war had in fact developed from an issue of conflict with internal foes (the Donatists) (see "Just war—holy war," p. 13). Only later was this theory applied to external threats. The situation was the same in Islam—the Persian author of the *Bahr al-Fava'id* (mid-twelfth century) even asserted that it "is worth seventy wars to shed the blood of one heretic." The supporters of these wars argued that if struggle against enemies of the faith in distant lands was already accepted as a meritorious deed, then the same struggle in one's homeland must be all the more pleasing to God. Did not the enemy within threaten the very unity of the Church? Innocent III, one of the most important popes of the Middle Ages, took precisely this stand.

Innocent III (r. 1198–1216) carried papal authority and actual papal power to new heights. He convened the momentous Fourth Lateran Council in November 1215, at which one of the most important items on the agenda was the eastern crusade. Innocent saw crusading entirely as a war in God's service and as a struggle of all Christendom to restore the lost unity of the Church. This view found ample expression during the eighteen years of his pontificate, during which he had crusades preached not only for military endeavors in the Levant, the Iberian Peninsula, and the Baltic, but also against the Cathars in southern France and opponents of the papacy in Sicily. In all cases, the crusaders were expressly promised the same indulgence as a fighter going to Jerusalem. Without a doubt, Innocent III made crusading his personal concern like few other popes.

This point of view was important in the famous Albigensian crusades of 1209 to 1229. They were waged in southern France, where the city of Albi gave its name to a heretical movement that is also called Catharism. The Albigensians/Cathars were not monotheists like Christians or Muslims. They did indeed believe in Jesus, but did not regard him as the savior. Central to their belief was the idea of *two* divine principles—one good and spiritual, while the other was evil and material (dualism). This doctrine was similar to that of the dualistic Bogomils in the Balkans, and indeed there is evidence linking the two—we know that about the year 1167 a Bogomil named Niketas helped to organize the Albigensian Church at a Cathar "synod" held at Saint Félix-de-Caraman. The Cathars rejected the Roman Church as well as the doctrine of the Trinity. They believed themselves to be a schismatic movement that remained Christian, one that separated itself from the institutional Church and created an anti-church with its own bishops, deacons, and so on. Their opponents regarded them as heretics, since they followed deviant positions on doctrinal questions. Modern scholars, too, debate whether Catharism was a form of Christianity, a heresy, or an independent religion.

The Cathars

135

Among the authors who report the course of the Albigensian crusades, three stand out. First is the Cistercian monk and crusader Petrus of Vaux-de-Cernay (*c.* 1182–after 1218), who in his *Historia Albigensis* tells of Cathar doctrine and the conflict with the Cathars with unconcealed partisanship for the crusaders. Similarly critical of the heretics, but more balanced, is the *Chronica* by the southern French Guillaume de Puylaurens (*c.* 1201/2–before 1287). The third work, the *Cansò de la Crozada*, was produced by two authors while the Albigensian wars were still going on. The first writer, William of Tudela (d. *c.* 1214), displays great sympathy for the harried southern French, but is still on the side of the crusaders, whom he likens to the participants in the First Crusade. The work's anonymous continuator wrote in about the year 1228; he presents the campaign as an unjustified war of conquest in the guise of a crusade.

With the help of these and other sources it is possible to reconstruct the course of the Albigensian crusades in detail. The Catholic Church had long been aware of the growing popularity of Cathar beliefs: efforts to combat the *cathari* had been urged ever since the Third Lateran Council of 1179. In 1204 Pope Innocent III unsuccessfully encouraged the French king Philip II to take steps to correct the situation in southern France. When, in January 1208, one of the count of Toulouse's followers murdered a papal legate (Pierre de Castelanau), Innocent called not just for steps against heresy but for a full-scale crusade against the heretics. He allowed the warriors to mark themselves with the sign of the cross and granted them the full remission of sins, the *remissio peccatorum* (see "Just war—holy war," p. 13). Innocent addressed his appeal to all the faithful, but ultimately it was mostly northern French nobles who made the journey to the culturally and politically very different south of France.

Philip II could not take part in the crusade because he was involved in a war with the king of England, so at an early stage military leadership fell to the northern French noble Simon de Montfort (1165–1218). In the course of the year 1209/10 he and a core force of northern French knights, along with crusaders who joined him for short periods, conquered the vice-county of Béziers-Carcassonne. The attackers were exceptionally bloodthirsty. When they conquered and looted Béziers on July 22, 1209, there were reports that several thousand citizens were killed, and the sources also tell of atrocities on other occasions. From 1211 on, the center of crusade operations was the county of Toulouse. This focus led to the involvement of King Pedro II of Aragón (r. 1196–1213), the most powerful ruler of the eastern Pyrenean region. Pedro had nothing to do with the Albigensians and their doctrines. In fact, after his victory over the Muslims at Las Navas de Tolosa he was regarded as a crusading hero. But because of dynastic obligations and concern about northern French expansion he came to the aid of his Toulousain kinsmen. In the Battle of Muret on September 12, 1213,

Simon de Montfort's troops defeated the Aragonese-southern French army, leaving the king dead on the field. This left the county of Toulouse open to the victor, whom Pope Innocent in 1215 declared to be the lawful overlord of the regions the crusaders had conquered. Despite defeat and the pope's decrees, new southern French resistance formed under the leadership of the young count of Toulouse, Raymond VII (r. 1222–49), Simon de Montfort was killed during the siege of Toulouse in 1218, and crusade efforts soon dwindled. The crusade was only rekindled when Simon's son resigned his claims in favor of the French king Louis VIII (r. 1223–26) and Count Raymond VII was excommunicated. After several military successes the northern French brought the Albigensian crusades to an end with the treaty of Meaux-Paris of April 12, 1229. Count Raymond was restored to Christian communion, swore to go on a crusade to the Holy Land, and accepted a marriage alliance between his heiress and King Louis' brother. In 1271 the county reverted directly to the French crown.

The events of 1209–29 show that the Cathar wars were indivisibly linked to the struggle for power in southern France. From the perspective of canon law, the conflict was beyond question a war against heretics, proclaimed as a crusade since 1208. However, from the perspective of the southern French Christians involved—the majority of southern French remained true to Christianity despite Catharism's popularity—it was a war of conquest. They did not accept the role of enemies into which they were forced, but saw themselves as part of the Church and therefore used feudal law as the basis for their opposition. It is clear in fact that crusading motives indeed rapidly took second place to expansionism. A clear sign of this is the fact that the conquest and later annexation by no means succeeded in extirpating the Cathar heresy. Again and again reports appeared of Cathar centers and Cathar resistance. The heresy was only wiped out in southern France in the course of the thirteenth and fourteenth centuries. The instruments used for the task were not warriors, but two ecclesiastical institutions—the mendicant orders and the Inquisition. The first presented a counterweight to the exemplary life of the Cathar clerics through their life of poverty and pastoral care. The second, in conjunction with the secular powers, proceeded against the remaining heretics. The clergy, using their own means, brought the crusaders' work to completion.

Political motivations

Late medieval crusades against religious movements

The Cathars continued to pose a challenge for the Church in various areas in the fourteenth century, since large communities of dualist heretics survived in northern Italy and especially in the Balkans. Pope Gregory IX even planned to call the Hungarians to a crusade against the Bosnian Cathars, but the Mongol invasion of the Balkans in 1241 forced all other plans into the background. In Italy, too, plans for a military

The heresy of Fra Dolcino

action against the Cathars were abandoned. But in that region a different anti-heretical crusade took place. Its target was the sect of the *Apostolici*, founded in 1290. Members of this group advocated a life of poverty and separation from the institutional Church. Under Fra Dolcino (d. 1307) of Novara, who at the beginning of the fourteenth century called for open opposition to the Church, the movement spread—especially in Lombardy and the Piedmont. Pope Clement V (r. 1305–14) called the faithful to a crusade against the heresy in 1307. In a swift campaign the crusaders destroyed the sect; its leaders were burned at Vercelli on June 1, 1307.

The crusade against the Hussites

The only really major anti-heretic crusade of the late Middle Ages was the campaigns waged against the Hussites. In this crusade, just as with the Albigensian crusades of the high Middle Ages, religious, material, and political motives came together to an exceptionally high degree. The Hussite wars contributed in a fundamental fashion to Czech nationalism and had important consequences for the Roman-German Empire, which undertook the first attempts at a reform of the imperial governing structure because of the severe military threat the Hussites posed. These wars could be regarded as crusades, since the papacy proclaimed them to be so and provided indulgences, crusade propaganda, and money, and the troops were equipped with crusade symbols (banners, etc.). Besides, at least in the early stages of the wars the crusading armies were quite international in composition. The first army of 1420 already had a disproportionate German element, though, and over time the conflict took on the character of an imperial enterprise.

The Hussite movement took its name from the Bohemian-Czech theologian Jan Hus, who was summoned before the Council of Constance in 1414 to defend his teachings. When he refused to recant the points of his teaching that the council condemned, he was burned on July 6, 1415 in Constance.

Jan Hus (c. 1369–1415) was a preacher in Prague who followed the teachings of the English theologian John Wyclif (c. 1330–84). Like Wyclif, Hus regarded the Bible, the canons of the ancient Church councils, and the Church fathers as the only sources of Christian doctrine. Therefore he encouraged the translation of the Bible into the vernacular (Czech). Hus denied ecclesiastical authority and claimed an authority for divine law that transcended secular power and its laws. In all of these matters, Hus remained entirely within the context of Church reform; he was not concerned with social change. Thus Hus was not a Hussite.

Hussite doctrine

Hus's death provoked an uprising in Bohemia. Three sectors of the populace in particular comprised the Hussite movement—the minor nobility, the urban lower class, and the lesser clergy—which rapidly took on strong socio-political and nationalist characteristics. Early criticism of the Church's wealth developed into fundamental enmity against the rich. Encouragement of Bible-reading in the vernacular led to a strong Czech national feeling that aimed at removal of the Germans from the kingdom of Bohemia. After the German king Sigismund (r. 1410–37) became ruler of Bohemia in 1419, opposition grew. The Hussites demanded that the laity be allowed to receive the eucharist in both forms (bread and wine), a position known as utraquism, which the Council of Constance rejected and King Wenceslas of Bohemia (r. 1363–1419) forbade. The communion chalice for laypeople became one of the main demands of the movement, which coalesced from a number of diverse groups. Some of them, like the Picards or the Taborites, expected the imminent end of the world and the beginning of a new kingdom of peace; they aspired to a community of mutual love and the sharing of goods in common. Others, like the Prague Hussites or the so-called Orebites, were more moderate. Most groups, however, agreed to a common creed, the "Four Prague Articles," on May 27, 1420: they demanded the chalice for the laity, free preaching, that the Church reject secular power, and also the punishment of all mortal sins.

The Hussites issued the Four Prague Articles in direct reaction to the Hussite crusade. On March 1, 1420, Pope Martin V (r. 1417–31) had proclaimed the crusade and specifically called on King Sigismund and the German imperial princes to suppress the heresy. A united army moved against Prague that same summer. In the early stages, the most important Hussite military leader was Jan Žižka of Trocnov (*c.* 1360–1424), an impoverished southern Bohemian member of the lower nobility. His most important military support was the so-called field army. This was a standing army that consisted particularly of soldiers from the lower classes with minor nobles in command. The Taborites and Orebites also maintained field armies, 6,000 and 4,000 men strong. Not only were they able to hold their own against the crusaders but also, after 1428, launched expeditions against Saxony, Silesia, Poland, Austria, and Hungary, laying large areas waste under the leadership of their second significant general, Procopius the Great (d. 1434). By that period at the latest, the Hussites had grown into a first-rate political problem for the empire. Their military successes can to a large extent be attributed to a strategic innovation—the wagon forts.

The Hussite wars

The wagon forts

The wagon forts were mobile defensive constructions. They consisted of war wagons that were bound together and equipped with cannon. Placed under a captain, they could be defended by about 12–20 soldiers. Since the wagon fort often consisted of several hundred vehicles, there was room for both foot soldiers and cavalry to take shelter within them. The wagon forts' great mobility made it possible to erect round or square defenses almost at will in a very short time, which could also act as firing stations during the battle. Other armies too adopted the wagon forts, which remained in use until well into the early modern period.

Hussite
successes

Thanks especially to the wagon fortresses, the Hussites garnered a series of spectacular victories over the crusade armies between 1420 and 1431. These years saw five crusading hosts launched against Bohemia. Between May and November 1420 a large crusade army campaigned under King Sigismund, supported during a second campaign from August 1421 to January 1422 by the troops supplied by a number of imperial princes. Both campaigns were military disasters for the crusaders. In October 1422 contingents from Brandenburg, Meissen, Franconia, and the Rhineland, under the leadership of Margrave Frederick I of Branden-burg (r. 1417–40), had little success, but at least were spared a defeat. During the fourth campaign in July/August 1427 the Hussites inflicted another severe defeat on Margrave Frederick at Tachov. Finally, between June and August 1431 three crusade armies from the Roman-German Empire yet again brought war to Bohemia. Although their leadership was imposing—the margrave of Brandenburg, the duke of Austria, and Cardinal Giuliano Cesarini (1398–1444)—they suffered reverses just as their predecessors had. In the end, all the crusades failed. The crusaders regularly lost to the Hussite armies, whose fighters for their part regarded themselves as "God's champions" (*Boži bojovníci*).

The so-called Basel Compacts of 1433 should be regarded as a reaction to these military failures. They were an agreement reached by a Hussite delegation led by Procopius the Great (d. 1434) and an ecclesiastical deputation that met during the Council of Basel; the Compacts were announced in 1436. They proposed a compromise between Hussites and Old Believers: in Bohemia the laity was permitted communion in both kinds. The agreement split the Hussite movement in two, with the moderate nobles and Prague Hussites on one side and the radical social revolutionaries on the other. In the civil war that now broke out, the radical army under Procopius the Great was defeated on May 30, 1434 in the Battle of Lipany. Subsequently, the Czechs recognized Emperor Sigismund's claim to the Bohemian throne. Still, a series of Hussite uprisings occurred, and the papacy never approved the Basel Compacts. As late as 1465–67, the papacy proclaimed yet another new crusade against the Hussites, although the ensuing expedition brought no military success. The movement only came to an end with the Reformation, when the new churches absorbed the Hussites.

The Church's secular enemies

At first glance, there seems to be a fundamental difference between crusades against heretical movements and those against Christian powers. In the first case, the issue was defense of the faith; in the second it was a matter of political power. But in the discussion of the Albigensian and Hussite wars it already became clear how strongly political considerations permeated the crusades in France and Bohemia. Wars against secular enemies of the Church were understood, for their part, as a struggle to see God's will fulfilled—not just by the popes but also by other contemporaries. For was not a person who set himself against the Church automatically an enemy of the faith? But there were also plenty of critics of these undertakings, and already in some medieval canon law commentaries a distinction was made between heretical and non-heretical enemies of the faith. In the late Middle Ages, the crusades against enemies of the papacy took on unique forms that only distantly resembled the original crusades to the Near East. To be sure, certain important elements remained at a formal level, such as the crusade proclamation or the promise of an indulgence, but other elements were completely atypical. For example, there was a strong dependence on mercenaries—for whom the idea of indulgence would have been unimportant—or the papacy's interests in the secular rule over central Italy. In many senses, the crusades against secular enemies of the Church are only situated on the fringes of crusade history.

Crusades or papal wars?

This limited character is nowhere so evident as in Italy, the main region in which these crusades were waged. The Appenine Peninsula was divided roughly into three political regions in the high and late Middle Ages. The German emperors nominally ruled the north, which is thus often called "imperial Italy." In practical terms, the cities and territories of this area asserted their freedom in face of claims by the German kings and achieved far-reaching autonomy. The *patrimonium Petri*, the papal state, occupied the majority of central Italy. Finally, in the south lay the kingdom of Sicily, which also included southern Italy. The Normans ruled this state in the twelfth century, but in 1194 it passed to the Hohenstaufen and in 1268 to the Angevins. From 1282 the Angevin dynasty and a cadet branch of the Aragonese royal family, which was able to take possession of the island, fought for control. It was especially northern and southern Italy that became crusade showplaces in the late Middle Ages: focal points of conflict were Sicily in the thirteenth century and various states in the north in the fourteenth.

The potential for conflict in this situation lay in the unique legal position of Sicily and the papacy's secular interests, for since the middle of the twelfth century the popes had repeatedly claimed suzerainty over the

The struggle for Sicily

141

island. Consequently, those Sicilians who rebelled against this legal claim were automatically the Church's enemies. The island's position as a southern outpost of Christendom in the Mediterranean and as supply base for the crusader lordships increased its importance. Twelfth-century popes already presented this argument when they called for crusades against Sicilian rulers, such as in 1135 against the Norman king Roger II (r. 1130–54) and in 1199 against the loyal Hohenstaufen regent Markward of Annweiler (d. 1202). But none of these initiatives had much practical result; it is more accurate to speak of crusade proclamations than of actual crusades. The same is true of the war that Pope Gregory IX inaugurated against Frederick II in 1229. In this case there were in fact military actions, but the troops fought under the banner of St Peter rather than the sign of the cross, and there was no mention of an indulgence. However, only shortly after this unsuccessful war a crusade army was indeed mobilized with the promise of indulgences. Its opponents were rebels against ecclesiastical authority in the northwest of the Roman-German Empire, the peasants of Stedingen.

The peasants of Stedingen

The peasants of Stedingen inhabited the lower course of the Weser, to the northwest of Bremen. In this region, only brought under cultivation at a late date, the peasants refused to pay taxes and tithes to the archbishop of Bremen-Hamburg at the beginning of the thirteenth century. After they defeated an episcopal army, the peasants were excommunicated in 1227 or 1229 and declared to be heretics in 1229/30. A first crusade undertaking in 1233 was for the most part a failure. But in 1234 a second expedition was given a broader footing: the peasants were accused of witchcraft and the crusaders were promised the *remissio peccatorum*. By these means a large army was assembled, which on May 27, 1234 annihilated the peasant forces at Altenesch.

Perhaps it was the crusading experiences in the empire that induced Pope Gregory IX in 1239 to present his war against Emperor Frederick II much more strongly in terms of a crusade. The emperor was not only excommunicated but demonized as a heretic and Muslim collaborator. Other thirteenth-century popes carried this precedent further. In 1244 Innocent IV (r. 1243–54) also proclaimed a crusade against Frederick, as did his successor Alexander IV (r. 1254–61) in 1255 against Frederick's son Manfred (1232–66). When the papacy designated the French king's brother, Charles of Anjou (1226–85), as the Church's champion against the Hohenstaufen in southern Italy, it supported his campaign repeatedly with the tools of crusade, until in 1268 Hohenstaufen rule had finally been shattered. And when the Aragonese put Charles I of Anjou's rule as king of Sicily (r. 1268–85) into question in 1282, the popes once again turned to these tried and true weapons: on January 13, 1283 Pope

Martin IV (r. 1281–85) proclaimed a crusade against Aragón. A large, mostly French crusading army crossed the Pyrenees into Spain in 1285— a venture that ended in failure. Although the Sicilian problem was resolved diplomatically in 1302, the end of the Angevin–Aragonese war by no means marked the end of the "Italian crusades."

In 1309 the papal curia moved to Avignon in southern France. During the seventy-seven years of this "Avignon exile," the popes lived far from their own papal state. Despite their absence, they were deeply immersed in the struggles between the Ghibellines (enemies of the papacy) and the Guelfs (papal supporters) in Italy. Popes also proclaimed several crusades in this context, such as in 1309 against Venice, 1321 against Ferrara, and 1324 against Mantua. There were particularly numerous proclamations against powerful Milan (most notably in 1322, 1360, 1363, and 1368). But in the meantime the transformation mentioned above had taken place. These Italian crusades were first and foremost mercenary wars that made little attempt to mobilize foreigners. What is more, they diverted energies from other crusade fronts. In 1363 Pope Urban V (r. 1362–70) assured his representatives in Italy that he would not push ahead with any crusade in the East as long as the Visconti of Milan remained undefeated. In this case, it is obvious that crusades against secular lords hindered crusading to the East. In the period of the Great Schism (1378–1417), various military conflicts were declared to be crusades—such as in 1383, when English troops fought in Flanders in the name of the Roman pope, or in Galicia and Portugal in 1386/87. However, these conflicts belong to the context of the Hundred Years War, not of wars for the faith. The great era of crusades against secular enemies of the Church had definitely come to an end.

The "political crusades" of the fourteenth century

5

The military religious orders

before 1080	Amalfitan merchants found St John's Hospital in Jerusalem
before 1120	Hugh de Payens founds the Templar community
1113	Papal approval of the community of St John (Hospitallers)
1129	Council of Troyes: Confirmation of the Templars' customs
c. 1130	Creation of the Hospitaller Rule
c. 1135	The Hospitallers militarize
1139	Bull *Omne datum optimum*: papal approval of the Order of Knights Templars
1142	First mention of the Order of Lazarus
1154	Bull *Christiane fidei religio*: approval of the Order of St John
1158	Establishment of a confraternity at the fortress of Calatrava
1175/76	Papal approval of the Order of Santiago and its rule. Papal confirmation of the confraternity of San Julián de Pereiro (later the Order of Alcántara) First mention of the confraternity of Évora (later the Order of Avís)
1187	Rule of the Order of Calatrava
1190	Foundation of a German hospitaller confraternity at the siege of Acre
1198	Militarization of the Teutonic order
1202	Foundation of the Order of the Sword-Brothers
1211	Confraternity of San Julián de Pereira subjected to the Order of Calatrava
1218	Conquest of the castle of Alcántara
1225	Teutonic order driven from Burzenland
before 1228	Foundation of the Order of Dobrin
1235/37	Order of the Sword-Brothers and Order of Dobrin incorporated into the Teutonic order
1307	October 13: arrest of the French Templars

1309	Headquarters of the Teutonic order transferred to the Baltic
1306–10	Order of St John conquers Rhodes
1312	March 22: dissolution of the Order of the Temple
1410	July 15: Battle of Tannenberg/Grunwald
1466	Second Peace of Thorn
1523	Knights of St John evacuate Rhodes
1525	Secularization of Prussia
1530	Knights of St John take up residence on Malta

Foundations and beginnings of the military religious orders

Preconditions for the rise of the military orders

Of all the institutions that grew from the crusades and the crusader lordships, the military religious orders had the longest life and greatest success. Thanks to their military might, wealth, and political weight they influenced events in Outremer more than any other corporate body. Over a dozen military orders came into being in the period up to the mid-thirteenth century, some of which spread over all of Christian Europe. In the following discussion I will attempt to present in a systematic manner the foundation of the various orders and their expansion. But first it is necessary to consider the various conditions from which they rose.

At first glance, it is hard to pin down the difference between a crusader and the member of a military order. Both took up arms to defend Christendom, both understood themselves to be *milites Christi* (warriors for Christ), and both hoped for a special heavenly reward for their endeavors. Both forms of life combined elements of the *vita religiosa* and pilgrimage. Many of the reasons that led people to participate in a crusade (see "Holy war, knighthood, and pilgrimage," p. 14; "Papacy, piety, and indulgence," p. 23) could equally well lead a man to join a military religious order. But for members of the military orders some of these reasons had a particularly great resonance. The following five factors were especially compelling: the idea of service to one's neighbor, the Christianization of knighthood, the ecclesiastical reform movements, the lay piety of the twelfth century, and the particular conditions in the lands that bordered on Islam. Certainly other motivations, such as political or economic interests, supplemented the military orders' *raison d'être*, but they cannot provide an adequate explanation for their creation.

The impulse to serve one's neighbor was fulfilled in a twofold manner— a military order's members provided armed protection to fellow Christians (in contemporary eyes this, too, was an act of Christian love of one's neighbor), and charitable work in hospitals. Both activities had

Crusader and knight of a military religious order

145

their origins in the context of pilgrimage. The original task of the oldest military order, the Knights of the Temple, was to protect Christian pilgrims on their way to Jerusalem. The idea of providing assistance or defense to fellow Christians also influenced the foundation of several Spanish military orders, which sought to defend newly conquered territory from the Muslims. On the other side of the spectrum, the Knights of St John, the Lazarites, and the Teutonic order, all of which developed from hospitaller confraternities, exemplify the charitable works of the orders.

The Christianization of the knightly class, which has already been mentioned (see "Knighthood," p. 16), was also a fundamental precondition for the rise of the military orders. Without the Church's growing acceptance of these warriors it would have been impossible to integrate them formally into the ecclesiastical organization as members of religious orders. This appears with particular clarity in a work that catches the essence of the military orders' novelty, the "Treatise in Praise of the New Knighthood" (*Ad milites Templi de laude novae militie*) by the Cistercian abbot Bernard of Clairvaux (see "The crusades to the Battle of Hattin, 1187," p. 47). This text repeatedly emphasizes that the Templar community gives knights the opportunity to employ their military skills for the sake of God and their neighbors.

Ecclesiastical reform movements and lay piety

Building on the model of pre-existing forms of religious life eased the military religious orders' integration into the structures of the Church. Two ecclesiastical reform movements in particular served as inspiration, the Cistercians and the canons regular (see "New orders and religious movements," p. 27). Most of the Iberian military orders were institutionally affiliated to the Cistercian order and thus lived in accordance with the Benedictine Rule. Many others, such as the Knights of St John and the Order of Santiago, chose St Augustine's rule for canons as the basis of their own order's rule.

The lay piety of the eleventh and twelfth centuries was probably a still weightier influence on the genesis of the military orders than the three reasons already named. For in their beginnings these orders were usually lay fraternities plain and simple. This is true of the first Templar community as well as of the Spanish *milicias*, from which orders of knights later developed. This is especially valid for the Hospitaller communities, which were only militarized at a later stage of development. These confraternities were fundamentally imbued with the idea of poverty in imitation of Christ. It is no coincidence that the first Templars called themselves *pauperes commilitones Christi*—poor fellow-fighters of Christ. Bernard of Clairvaux also particularly accentuated this characteristic. Thus in the military orders, four elements joined together in a symbiotic relationship: older views of church-led war against pagans, more recent monastic reform movements, the new lay piety of the twelfth century, and the aspiring knightly class.

> ### Military orders and *ribat*
>
> It has been argued that the first Templars modeled themselves on a Muslim prototype, the *ribat*. This term is used to describe Muslim conventual buildings that were defended by warriors. Some of these volunteer fighters only served for a limited period and combined military service with spiritual exercises. Their similarities to the Christian military orders are apparent, and the idea of direct imitation is reasonable. But no evidence has yet been found to support this assertion. The distinctive features of the military orders were not propagated solely in Islam. The communal, regulated life of laypeople fits in with the Christian confraternity movement, the idea of "meritorious violence" developed from older Christian roots, and even the armed service for a limited time that the first Templars were permitted can be detected in the Spanish militias. Yet, the question of Christian military order members adopting Islamic elements has still not been settled conclusively.

Apart from all the general spiritual, religious, and social bases of this new form of professional religious life, one last factor should not be overlooked, one that had decisive significance for the creation of the military orders: the immediate circumstances in Christianity's border regions. The foundation of the first confraternities to protect pilgrims or fortresses, but also the transformation of charitable foundations into military orders, was made in large part in response to a direct challenge. It was an attempt to provide an adequate solution to an actual situation that arose from the unique character of the crusader lordships or other border regions.

The union of religious life and armed conflict also provoked skepticism. Early sources reveal that doubt about this novelty existed not only outside but within the Templar community. In the Order of St John, too, until the mid-twelfth century there was opposition to setting aside service of the poor and sick in favor of military action. For the rest of the Middle Ages, criticism was never completely silenced. Over time, further arguments embroidered on this initial criticism and finally contributed to the amalgamation or dissolution of particular orders.

Charitable or military confraternities: the conditions of foundation

When looking at the history of the military religious orders—often centuries long and sometimes reaching even to the present—it is easy to overlook that these orders usually had their start as lay confraternities. These groups, which appear in the sources as *confraternitates, societates*, and other terms designating associations of like-minded people, admittedly lived according to religious principles, but without having

Confraternities and military orders

147

taken religious vows. Church authorities generally approved the confraternities, but the groups did not satisfy all the conditions necessary to be "orders": they all lacked papal approval and did not follow an approved rule. Nonetheless, approved orders could very well develop from confraternities, as was indeed the case with many military orders.

If one attempts to categorize the medieval military orders by content instead of just by locality, an important consideration is the type of religious confraternity from which each order sprang. According to this categorization, one can distinguish between two types of association— those dedicated to armed conflict from their origin (often called *militia(e)* in the sources) and those that originally cared for the sick and poor and only later assumed a military role. This distinction remained significant even when both types became militarily active to an equal degree. One can see this in the fact that some members of the orders as well as other contemporaries repeatedly referred to the respective order's original purpose. For all institutions that had their start as charitable foundations, service of the sick and poor in the order's own hospitals continued to play a much greater role than in the corporations of the first, genuinely military type (which also provided such care). The founding circumstances of the military religious orders will thus be discussed and counterpoised in the following pages, making use of this distinction. Still, it is impossible to deal with all the bewildering multiplicity of large and small, Palestinian, Baltic, and Hispanic military orders in equal detail. Instead, I will focus on the three most powerful corporations: the Templars, the Hospitallers, and the Teutonic Knights. One should bear in mind, though, that smaller or less durable institutions, like the Lazarites, the Order of St Thomas, the Order of Montesa, and others, also made their mark on the history of medieval religious orders.

The Knights Templars

The Order of Knights Templars is the archetypical example of a military order that sprang from a purely military confraternity. It had its origins as a confraternity of knights that came together in Jerusalem shortly before the year 1120 under the leadership of a Champagne noble named Hugh de Payens (*c.* 1080–1136/37). This group appears to have formed an alliance with the patriarch of Jerusalem and dedicated itself to protecting Christian pilgrims, who repeatedly suffered Muslim attacks on the road between the coast and Jerusalem. King Baldwin I (r. 1100–18) gave the knights some space in one of his palaces on the Temple Mount (Arab. *al-Haram as-Sarif*), the site of the original Temple of Solomon, from which the confraternity took its name. Probably the group was confirmed at a council of important secular and ecclesiastical officials at Nablus in 1120.

The new order's decisive break came nine years later, though, at a synod in the French city of Troyes. There, Hugh de Payens submitted the customs (*consuetudines*) that he and his brethren followed for the

The Spanish military orders

Of all the border regions of Christian Europe, it was the Iberian Peninsula that produced the most military orders. The conditions under which the four most important Spanish orders were founded—the orders of Calatrava, Alcántara, Santiago, and Avís—can be summarized briefly. In 1158 the fortress of Calatrava (which had been captured in 1147 by King Alfonso VII of León and Castile [r. 1126–57]) was under threat of being lost once again to the Muslims. So some Cistercian monks and laymen banded together to defend the castle. In 1187 the association of Calatrava received its own rule. The new order was placed under the Cistercian order, but retained considerable independence. Three other Hispanic military orders also developed from *militiae* (Sp. *milicias*); in other words, military lay confraternities. The Order of Alcántara goes back to such a *milicia*, which was founded in about 1167; Pope Alexander III (r. 1159–81) confirmed the order in 1176. Although the order was able to expand its power, it was still subordinated to the Order of Calatrava in 1213, following the Rule of Calatrava from that time on. It was only in this period (in the year 1218) that the order received the castle and town of Alcántara, from which it took its name. The Order of Santiago, too, was not originally called by that name; it stemmed from the lay confraternity of *fratres de Cáceres*, which King Ferdinand II of León (r. 1157–88) founded in 1170 after he took the town of Cáceres (in the Extremadura). Only a year later did this group, as the community of St James, subordinate itself to and enter into a sort of brotherhood with the cathedral chapter of Santiago de Compostela. In 1175 Pope Alexander III confirmed the order's rule, based on that of St Augustine, the last step to make the group a fully functional military order. The first mention of the oldest Portuguese military order also falls in this period (1176). It was founded in the city of Évora, conquered from the Muslims in 1165, and later received the town of Avís from which it took its name. Thus, within a few years four military orders came into being on the Iberian Peninsula. The number is still higher if one counts ephemeral foundations like the Order of Trujillo or that of Montjoie. These associations were, however, incorporated into the already-named institutions after a few decades.

assembled clerics' approval. At this point his foundation won acceptance at the highest level—even a papal legate was present. This support and the Templars' bid for support on their journeys to various European countries primed the pump—many men joined the Templars or made them donations. The means that were obtained in this way served as a basis for expanding the originally localized foundation beyond the boundaries of Jerusalem and Palestine. All that was still lacking was approval from the Holy See, which came in 1139 in the seminal bull *Omne datum optimum*. The path was open for development into an international order, the *Ordo Militiae Templi Hierosolimitani*.

Military orders were not confined to Outremer or the furthest western rim of Europe. On the other end of the continent, in the Baltic region,

Military orders
in the Baltic

religious corporations also formed in the early thirteenth century, the Order of the Sword-Brothers and the Order of Dobrin (see "The Teutonic Knights and their state," p. 128). A Cistercian monk and some north-German knights founded the Order of the Sword-Brothers in 1202 for the protection of newly converted Christians from the non-Christian Livonians, placing the organization under the bishop of Riga's authority. At first the order was able to expand its power and territory significantly and even to establish its own lordship. After an annihilating defeat at the hands of the pagans, though, the Sword-Brothers were incorporated into the Teutonic order in 1237 at the pope's behest. The Order of Dobrin was created in the locale of that name on the river Weichsel at the instigation of Bishop Christian of Prussia and Duke Conrad of Masovia. It was intended for campaigning against the Prussians, a non-Christian Baltic tribe. Yet it too was incorporated into the Teutonic order in 1235.

Which brings us to the military order that had the strongest ties with the Baltic—the Teutonic Knights. Despite that connection, they neither originated in the Baltic region nor were they even dedicated to warfare originally. The order had its inception as a Hospitaller confraternity, founded by northern German crusaders in 1189/90 during the siege of Acre and placed under the protection of the Virgin Mary. This charitable confraternity militarized swiftly. As early as 1198 the members adopted the Templar Rule alongside the Hospitaller Rule they had followed hitherto, and shortly thereafter Pope Innocent III granted them formal approval as a military order. In their early years, the Hospitallers still asserted their claims on the new foundation, but the Teutonic Knights successfully warded off these demands under the adroit leadership of their high master Hermann von Salza. Consequently, the community, not least thanks to Hohenstaufen support, was able to establish itself among the military orders of the crusader states as the *ordo fratrum hospitalis sanctae Mariae Theutonicorum Hierosolimitanorum*. Until the fall of the kingdom of Jerusalem, this order's administrative and spiritual center was in Palestine, not the Baltic.

The Order of St John (the Hospitallers)

Smaller military orders, too, like the Lazarites (who cared for lepers) or the Order of St Thomas developed from charitable confraternities. But this overview will focus on the foundation that was the first to make this transformation and thus served as a model for all later groups: the Order of St John. This order developed from a hospital that merchants from the southern Italian port city of Amalfi founded sometime before 1080 at the monastery of Santa Maria Latina in Jerusalem. After the conquest of 1099 these Hospitallers, like the Templars, appear to have entered into a still-unclear legal relationship with the patriarch of the nearby Church of the Holy Sepulcher. Nonetheless, in 1113 Paschal II (r. 1099–1118) recognized them as an independent foundation with the bull *Piae postulatio*, and in about 1135 (scholars disagree on the date) the Hospitallers were entrusted with military duties. It apparently took decades before the members of the community themselves were willing to recognize military service as an equally important task as their charitable duties; even the bull Pope Anastasius IV (1153/54) issued approving the order, *Christiane fidei religio* of October 21, 1154, does not speak of it. After 1160 the order's increasing military commitment at first caused financial and internal crises, but in the 1180s the way to militarization won general agreement in light of the crusader lordships' needs. From the beginning of the thirteenth century on, hospital work took a back seat to military activities. Nonetheless, the Knights of St John continued their original ideals appropriately in their hospital in Jerusalem. Until the fall of Jerusalem this structure could house 2,000 patients, both male and female, and thus made an essential contribution to the care of needy inhabitants and pilgrims. The Hospitallers would never have been able to fulfill these charitable duties if they had not—like the other Palestinian military orders—been able to count on an extensive network of houses in the Latin West, which served as recruiting and supply bases and through which they contributed decisively to the survival of the crusader states. This network will be described in the following section.

The spread of the military orders

Until 1291, the center of all Palestinian military orders was the Holy Land. During the first kingdom of Jerusalem, until the loss of the holy city in 1187, the Templars' mother house was on the Temple Mount and that of the Order of St John was in the nearby Hospital of St John Locating the orders' headquarters in Jerusalem is understandable because of the city's outstanding significance, both as political center and because of its particularly venerable status. It is not a coincidence that the treatise "In Praise of the New Knighthood" includes a detailed description of the holy places of Jerusalem. Indeed, even the non-Palestinian military orders maintained a presence in the Holy Land. Some Spanish military orders or *milicias* were oriented at least ideally toward Palestine or acquired possessions there. The loss of Jerusalem in 1187 forced a displacement of the mother houses; the Templars and Hospitallers moved their headquarters to Acre, and the Teutonic Knights, starting in the late 1220s, built up the nearby castle of Montfort as their center of operations. Nonetheless, the loss of most Palestinian possessions was a heavy blow and also had an effect beyond the crusader lordships in the East.

Under these circumstances, the European daughter houses of the orders took on a special significance. All of the military orders of the Holy Land held a larger or smaller number of such filiations or dependencies, which supported the mother houses above all through the *responsio* (see box). This network of branch houses reached from Portugal to Poland, from Scotland to Sicily. The network might be narrower or broader

The military orders' sphere of activity

depending on the order and also varied in degree of communication within a given institution. The Knights of St John controlled the widest, most inclusive network, with hundreds of houses in Palestine and all lands of the Latin West. The Knights Templars were admittedly distributed widely in Europe, but their possessions were particularly concentrated in what is now eastern France, Catalonia, Aragón, and Portugal, as well as eastern England, Tuscany, and Latium. In the first decades of its existence, the Teutonic order, by contrast, was especially well endowed outside of Palestine, in southern Italy and the German Empire, before new possibilities opened up for it to expand into Kulm and Pruzzenland, what later became the order-state (*Ordensstaat*) of Prussia. Among the great military orders, the Spanish ones were most limited geographically. There is, admittedly, evidence of dependencies of the orders of Santiago and Calatrava in southern Italy and France, but essentially their sphere of influence was focused on the Iberian Peninsula, and here too concentrations of possessions can be observed.

The *responsio*

The dependencies carried out a variety of functions for the orders' central command. Their most important task was to collect and transport materials to support their respective headquarters in Palestine. The houses had to turn over a portion of the goods they produced or received as donations to the mother house. This portion, called the *responsio*, was usually a third of their income. Only on the Iberian Peninsula was the share smaller, since here a large part of the orders' possessions lay in the border regions of Christendom, where means were also needed to fight against Muslim adversaries. Military material, especially horses and weapons, also passed to Outremer along these channels. Lastly, the dependencies also functioned as recruiting stations, from which brothers of the order could be dispatched to other houses or to military service in the East.

The organization of the military orders

Carrying out these tasks was made easier by the hierarchical organization of the orders. At the local level the individual house (*commanderie, encomienda, Kommende*) was the most important element. In agricultural regions such a house was little more than a large farm with attached chapel, but it could also take the form of a fort with numerous buildings. At the regional level the commanderies were joined together in "provinces" (called bailiwicks in the Teutonic order), which, depending on order and region, could be aligned with counties but also with kingdoms, and thus usually followed existing political borders. All of these provinces were answerable to the master and high officials of the order. The organization of the military orders was thus in fact international and for the time of their creation, the twelfth century, ground-breaking. The ability of this international organization to function was facilitated by the fact that most military orders were freed from the jurisdiction of local bishops; in other words, "exempt." Thus in canonical terms they were subordinate only to the pope. They did not have to pay tithes and the local clergy could not control them. A series of extra privileges expanded these liberties, including the grant of free burial and freedom from interdict (a ban on taking part in the sacraments and suspension of religious services). It is hardly surprising that these privileges, repeatedly granted by popes, gave rise to difficulties with the secular clergy. The conflicts continued throughout the entire Middle Ages. There were repeated attempts to control the orders' activities at the local level through individual lawsuits, though in most cases the orders were able to defend their most important rights. With secular powers, by contrast, the military orders got along well, by and large, although the closeness of their dealings varied from order to order. The degree of proximity to royal power an order enjoyed might serve as the central question for the following sketch of the most important military orders.

For example, the Templars and Hospitallers were extremely important supports for the kingdom of Jerusalem, and not just militarily. The masters of the military orders were members of the Haute Cour, the court assembly, and usually served as advisors to the current ruler. The kings' dealings with the orders were correspondingly intense until the loss of Jerusalem in 1187: the rulers did not hesitate to interfere directly in the orders' affairs and may also have had a direct role in the election of order officials. This began to change early in the thirteenth century, as the kings were more rarely—and from 1229 on almost never—present in the kingdom. At this point the military orders, along with the patriarchs of Jerusalem, assumed the role of *de facto* rulers. They were the only ones who were able to provide for a standing military power, and possessed not only military knowledge but also the necessary political awareness to secure the ongoing existence of the crusader lordship in hard times. The military orders in general worked together to fulfill this function, although they sometimes came into conflict with each other. Precisely because their political power in Palestine was so great, the final loss of Acre in 1291 was a particularly heavy blow. Admittedly, from their emergency stations on Cyprus the orders' members still hoped for a reconstitution of their old lordships, but soon they had to acknowledge that they had now been thrown back onto their European possessions.

Relationship to the kings of Jerusalem

In their early stages the Teutonic Knights were even more strongly obligated to secular potentates, especially the Hohenstaufen emperors, than the Templars and Hospitallers. Of all the military religious orders, this group underwent the most astonishing transformation. We have already seen their development from charitable confraternity to order; still more unusual was their spread and development beyond the Holy Land. In 1211 the opportunity arose for them to take over new holdings and rights of lordship in Burzenland (Siebenbürgen) in modern Romania, when King Andrew II of Hungary (r. 1205–35) of the Arpad dynasty invited the order to support him in fighting the Cumans, a nomadic

The Teutonic order in Hungary

153

Turkish tribe that inhabited the areas beyond the eastern borders of his kingdom. He consequently granted the Knights extensive revenues and important fortifications in the frontier region. The Knights were indeed able to establish themselves in Burzenland, but in 1225 King Andrew drove them from his kingdom. It is hard to establish the particulars behind this decision, but it appears that on the one hand the king feared that the Knights wanted to carve out their own lordship on the borders of his kingdom and on the other hand his step was a response to his barons' resentment of the growing German influence at court. Shortly thereafter, a new opportunity presented itself for the order to win its own territory, this time in Kulmland. How they did so has already been described (see "The Teutonic Knights and their state," p. 128). In this new territory the Teutonic Knights gained a greater degree of legal and political independence than any other military order.

Military orders and kingship on the Iberian Peninsula
Of all rulers, the Hispanic kings consistently exercised the highest degree of political influence on the region's military orders. Just as they tried to regulate the progress of the Christian conquests, the kings watched over the institutions that evolved in the course of the *reconquista*. During the first century of their existence, the orders of Calatrava, Alcántara, and Santiago served the kingdom of Castile and León as reliable supporters, while the Order of Avís played the same role for Portuguese monarchs. The military orders were essential in the great expansion thrusts of the early thirteenth century, including the conquest of Córdoba (1238) and Seville (1248). They received a rich reward for their aid when the land was partitioned. Only after mid-century—not coincidentally with the close of the great expansion—did the first cracks appear in what until then had been a close relationship. More and more, the officials of the major orders sought a political rather than just a military function in the consolidating lordships of the south. Tensions became ever more apparent, finally leading to an open struggle for power in the early fourteenth century—which the kings won.

The military orders in Palestine, on the Iberian Peninsula, and in the Baltic

The organization of the military orders

The universal base of all Christian orders was a commitment to keep the three "evangelical counsels": poverty, chastity, and obedience. But for the actual arrangement of the religious life normative texts were necessary. These are divided between the overarching definitions (the actual rule [*regula*] of the order) and the more specific prescriptions for daily life, the statutes or customs (*statuta* or *consuetudines*). The evidence of these normative texts will help us grasp the essential features of the medieval military orders in the following section, as we discuss (1) their organization, (2) the social and geographical origins of their members,

(3) their offices and dignitaries, and (4) the unique qualities of the orders' religious and liturgical practices.

The Templar and Hospitaller rules

The Templars' and Hospitallers' life was organized according to the rules of their orders, which in turn served as the basis for the rules of other military orders such as the Teutonic Knights. The Council of Troyes confirmed the customs of the first Templars in 1129, which developed further into a true rule, consisting of seventy-two chapters. It contained elements of both the Augustinian and Benedictine rules and was strongly imbued with the poverty ideal of the twelfth century. The brothers were to renounce all sorts of display, only to speak when absolutely necessary, and to eat in moderation. Truly innovative were the directives for military service—the rule set the number of horses allowed and also prescribed simplicity in armor. While in the field, exemption from fasting was permitted. The early seal of the Templars portrays these rules and ideals with particular clarity. Devoted to the ideal of *pauperes commilitones Christi*, two Templars are depicted mounted on a single horse. The first Hospitaller Rule was composed in the 1130s, during the reign of Master Raymond of Puy (1120–60). It is based on the Augustinian Rule and reveals the strong ongoing influence of the community of St John's charitable origins, placing special emphasis on following Christ's example in service to the poor.

The rules also dictated the habit—that is, the clothing—that members were to wear. It had a symbolic value. Thus only the full knight-brothers were entitled to a white habit, because, thanks to their vow of chastity, they had achieved a special degree of purity. Brethren of all the military orders wore some form of cross on their habit, differing in shape and color depending on the order. Besides this, the habit showed the wearer's rank, because, like all religious orders, the military orders were organized according to a functional hierarchical system. At least five groups can be distinguished: knight-brothers, priest-brothers, *servientes* (*seargents, sariant-brothers*), *milites ad terminum*, and finally the *confratres* or *consorores*. **The habit**

The full knight-brothers formed the military core of the order. With their profession (taking of the order's vows) they swore to lead a religious life according to the order's rule in the service of God and in war against God's enemies. They were obligated to obey and accept discipline from the order's leadership and were equipped with a set number of horses. The second group of members was the priest-brothers. These men were ordained clerics. Their duty was spiritual care of the order's other members and laypeople. In general they were in charge of the churches or chapels of each order. The third group of members was very similar to the knight-brothers, and was indeed subordinated to them—the *servientes* (or sergeants among the Templars **The members** and Hospitallers, sariant-brothers for the Teutonic Knights). Depending on the order and the particular conditions of the time they could have one or two horses, while the knight-brothers received at least twice as many. The *milites ad terminum* had a special position among the membership. These knights belonged to the order for only a short time (usually one year) and served it as a penitential act or to win spiritual grace. Similar motivations prompted the members of the fifth group, the *confratres* and *consorores*, to link themselves to a military order. These laypeople, also called *donati*, *oblati*, or *conversi* in the sources, made donations to the order, in return for which they were included in a given community's prayers. In exceptional cases they could also lead a semi-religious life in one of the order's houses or earn a livelihood there. Finally, a series of other people were connected to the military orders, without being true members in a technical sense. Among them were the menials and other servants (including soldiers), but also the physicians who were responsible for care of the sick in the charitably based orders.

Female religious

The orders' sisters had a special position. Among the Templars there were apparently female *donatae*, who in the long term, however, were unable to form themselves into independent institutions. The orders of St John, Calatrava, and Santiago, though, did indeed found female branches. Their convents were very different from the brethren's houses, since the women of the order lived cloistered from the outside world; the charitable element became much less important and the military element vanished completely. In the case of the Lazarites, but especially for the Order of Santiago, a way was finally found to integrate women religious in the order—married couples were accepted as full members. During certain periods of the year they lived separately from each other and in principle had to obey the three monastic vows of poverty, chastity, and obedience.

There was a clear connection between the hierarchy of members and their social origins. Bernard of Clairvaux in his treatise "In Praise of the New Knighthood" had lauded the egalitarian character of the first Templar community. But soon the order's members were recruited to a great extent from a clearly circumscribed social group—the nobility. By the thirteenth century at the latest, only those who could provide evidence of their noble birth were accepted as full knight-brothers, while less stringent standards were applied to the sergeants and other lower-ranking members. This tendency toward aristocratization can be seen in all the military orders. In terms of the knights' regional origins, however, there were significant differences between the orders. The Teutonic order's recruits came for the most part from the regions of the empire north of the Alps, especially Westphalia, the Rhineland, and Franconia. A similar concentration can be observed in the Spanish military orders, whose recruits came almost exclusively from the Iberian Peninsula. Even the truly international military orders, the Templars and Hospitallers, recruited particularly large numbers of members from a single region, France.

The orders' rules prescribed not only the hierarchy and the religious life within each order, but also laid out the functions and division of offices and dignities. All military orders had a highest representative, the master (Templars, Calatrava), grand master (Hospitallers), or high master (Teutonic Knights). He was usually elected by a group of senior officeholders (often limited to thirteen members) and served for life. Varying by order, though, was the number and title of the subordinate functionaries. In the three Palestinian military orders, two officials in particular served as the master's lieutenants in the order's central governance. The marshal (who was responsible for military matters) and the seneschal (Templars) or commandant or grand commander (Hospitallers, Teutonic Knights) served as the master's substitute if the need arose. Other specific functions were filled by the treasurer, the *drapier* (responsible for providing clothing), as well as the hospital master in the Hospitaller and Teutonic orders. A large number of further offices were necessary to assure the smooth operation of finances, governance, and supply.

The dignitaries and the convent met at regular intervals for general chapters at the mother houses, at which they took council about the order's affairs, elected new officials, and dealt with administrative issues. Besides the hierarchical organization there also existed a corporate element, which functioned as a check on the leadership's authority. The general chapter superseded the officials in importance and its membership was expanded to include the officials of the daughter houses. Besides these levels, the overseas possessions, organized into provinces, each had a leader, too, who exercised supervision over the heads of the individual houses, the commanderies. Regular chapters were also held at the provincial and local levels.

As in every major corporation, in the military orders everyday problems came up that had to be regulated in a binding and comprehensible fashion. This regulation took place at the general chapters, at which attendees also passed additions to the rule and formulated statutes. These "statutes" or "customs" (*retraints* for the Templars) codified generally accepted practices and form an important source for understanding the daily life and possible tensions within the military orders. These documents fixed, among other matters, how the knights ought to behave when visiting a city, how their horses should be tended, and how assistance should be provided for sick members. But they also established the penalties for the widest possible variety of offenses, such as throwing one's habit on the floor in a rage, spending a night outside of the convent, etc.—all conceivable misdeeds appear in their pages. The variously expanded statutes mirror not only the customary life in the orders' houses but also changes in the military orders over time. For example, from them one can even discern that all the military orders had practically abandoned one of the three basic vows of the religious life—the obligation to personal poverty—by the beginning of the thirteenth century at the latest.

Spirituality Not least in importance, both rules and statutes illuminate the brethren's spiritual and liturgical life, which displayed some unique features. The early Hospitaller and Templar institutional connection to the Church of the Holy Sepulcher found expression in their liturgy, which remained strongly influenced by that of the patriarchal church. A pronounced devotion toward Jerusalem found expression in various ways, such as on seals, and in specific cases even in architectural imitation of buildings in Jerusalem. It was supplemented by a marked veneration of the Virgin Mary, particularly visible among the Teutonic Knights and Templars in the dedications of many churches and chapels. Some military orders also promoted their own saints or successfully laid claim to others for their own institution. The Hospitallers serve as a good example of the former, who with St Ubaldesca (d. 1206) could point to a sister of the order who combined a holy life with service to the poor. The best example of the second variant is the Teutonic order, which succeeded by astute tactics with the Hohenstaufen and the pope to create a posthumous connection between their order and the saintly marchioness Elisabeth of Thuringia (or of Hungary) (1207–31, canonized 1234). The Knights created a shrine at Elisabeth's tomb in Marburg that attracted pilgrims from far beyond regional boundaries. Of all the military corporations, it was likewise the Teutonic order that took the most care for its own historiography and actively presented an image of its own history through the composition of chronicles of the order.

Military and economic significance

Despite their charitable activities in the hospitals, the most pressing duty of the military orders remained to wage war against enemies of the faith. The brethren were of decisive importance for the survival of the Christian lordships on the borders of Christendom because of two functions in particular: they provided armed contingents in the open field and served as commanders and garrisons of fortified places.

The knights as part of the field army Until the end of the twelfth century, the knightly levy of the kingdom of Jerusalem included around 600 Templars and Hospitallers, comprising about half of the whole army. The proportion of knight-brothers in Hispanic forces was much smaller; there is evidence of contingents ranging from twenty to a hundred knights. These too, however, often played a decisive role in battle. What particularly distinguished the knights of the military orders was their experience in waging war against the Muslims, their perpetual readiness, and their dependability. These factors were especially true in Outremer from the beginning of the orders: in contrast to crusader contingents, the members of the military orders were accustomed to their enemies' military tactics, geographical factors, and the climate. This knowledge might also have been the reason why commanders of the orders' contingents tended to be more cautious in the field than crusaders, for example avoiding pitched battles. They knew that they brought the crusader lordships into peril if they committed too many warriors in the field. This tendency, however, also brought misunderstanding and criticism down on their heads.

Despite this caution the knight-brothers in the Levant put their lives on the line often enough. More than half of the masters of the Knights Templars died in battle. At the annihilating defeat of Hattin in 1187 about 300 Templar and Hospitaller knights died. And it is estimated that at the Battle of La Forbie in 1244 no less than 1,000 knights of the three Palestinian military orders lost their lives. On the Iberian Peninsula, too, the knights of Santiago and Calatrava were in the foremost ranks at the great battles of the *reconquista*—Alarcos (1195), Las Navas de Tolosa (1212), and Alcácer do Sal (1217).

Members of the orders were therefore well trained for battle, since they were not subject to the time limitations that applied to vassals in a feudal levy. While the latter could only be pulled together for military service for a limited time, the orders created something not far from a "standing army" that played an essential role in the continuance of a Christian presence in Outremer. Another characteristic of the orders' knights, their discipline, was again a direct consequence of their structure. Here, too, the rules and statutes were very important. They dictated absolute obedience in military matters and meted out draconian penalties to violators. Offenses like turning one's horse from the enemy, letting the standard sink or fall, pressing forward ahead of the line during a charge, and so on, were harshly punished. The Templar rule and statutes regulate how the knights should behave in battle so precisely that they can be read as a handbook of medieval warfare.

Rules for military conduct

Because of these characteristics—their high level of experience, their military skills, their preparedness, and their discipline—their Muslim opponents understandably feared and hated the knights of the orders. This loathing is particularly evident after the Muslim victory at Hattin: Saladin had the captured Hospitallers and Templars beheaded "because they were the most proficient warriors among the Franks," as the chronicler al-Atir put it. The orders did not fight solely against those of other faiths, though. Various sources report that they also took the field against Christians. On occasion the military orders even came to blows against each other, for example during the War of St Sabas (1256–59). On the Iberian Peninsula, in 1385 at the Battle of Aljubarrota, contingents of one and the same order, the Hospitallers, even served on both sides.

Among the members of the orders, the full knights with their heavy armor and several horses were especially important militarily, because the frontal, massed charge of a well-armored contingent of knights was the crusaders' favored tactic in pitched battle. Below the full knights, not

Military ranks

just in the orders' hierarchy but in military rank, were the sergeants, whose armor was not as heavily plated. These troops were supplemented by the *turcopoles*, lightly armed horsemen recruited from the native populace, who served for pay. They and the Muslim archers of the Spanish military orders were particularly important because their opponents were also equipped with lighter arms and armor. The heavily armored, rather immobile knights of the orders were supported by squires, who could also take part in battles. Finally, one must name the orders' vassals as part of their fighting force. Especially on the Iberian Peninsula the vassals provided a significant body of troops which, however, had to perform military service for only short periods. Besides the land forces, the military orders also had seamen in their service. In this regard the Hospitallers are particularly noteworthy, since they developed into a significant maritime power in the eastern Mediterranean.

The castles of the military orders

When they were not in the field, the most pressing military duty that members of the military orders had to face was to secure the borders by building and garrisoning castles. It is no coincidence that many of the Spanish military orders were named after these fortified centers (Calatrava, Alcántara, Montesa). Some crusader castles can still be seen on the Iberian Peninsula (especially between the Tajo and Guadalquivir rivers), on the Baltic, or in the Near East (above all in the former crusader lordships of Tripoli and Antioch). Especially famous are Crac des Chevaliers in Syria and the Marienburg near Gdansk.

Crac des Chevaliers and the Marienburg

In 1142 the Hospitallers purchased Crac des Chevaliers (Qal'at al Hisn al-Akrad) in Syria from one of the count of Tripoli's vassals. The enormous installation was built in successive stages and at the end of the century was provided with projecting corner towers, a 130-meter-long entry ramp built on arches, and an outer curtain wall. By the middle of the thirteenth century its garrison of about sixty horsemen was only a small fraction of the 2,000 inhabitants, who included foot soldiers, artisans, slaves, and so on. Crac des Chevaliers provides a vivid example of the mingling of European traditions with eastern elements that is characteristic of some of the castles of Outremer. It fell to the Mamluks in 1271. The Marienburg, not far from Gdansk, is another good example of the military orders' fortifications. The Teutonic Knights began building the castle in 1274 and two years later received rights over the neighboring market town of the same name. This fortification, built primarily from brick, became the chief house and administrative center of the Teutonic order in 1309. In following years, it was expanded into one of the largest defense systems in Europe. It fell to the kingdom of Poland in 1457.

The Marienburg convincingly illustrates that the orders' castles were economic centers in addition to their military purposes. In the castles, the orders' income was collected, guarded, and further distributed as occasion rose. The wealth that gathered in such places was considerable, because in the course of the twelfth and thirteenth centuries the military orders developed into extraordinarily prosperous institutions. The Order of Santiago, for example, controlled more than 200 towns and villages and 23,000 square kilometers of land by the end of the fifteenth century. Before the Battle of Hattin, the Templars possessed over a third of the principality of Antioch and half of the county of Tripoli, besides extensive possessions in the kingdom of Jerusalem. One should point out, though, that maintenance of the castles alone devoured enormous amounts of money and ongoing warfare sapped the orders' wealth.

The revenue of the military orders came for the most part from five sources: their real estate, their rights, raising livestock, trade and banking activities, and finally the proceeds of military activities, such as loot and payment of tribute. This wealth was based first of all on donations made by pious Christians, then on privileges granted by rulers and popes, and finally on conquests in the border regions. Especially on the Iberian Peninsula, the military orders were granted a percentage of all captured territory, normally 10–20 per cent. The grant of particular rights—such as to administer justice, collect tolls, or operate mints— also brought the orders considerable revenues. Supplementing this income were the proceeds of leases, taxes, and other payments drawn from their extensive properties, because the orders not only held existing settlements but also founded new towns and villages and brought in settlers. This is especially true of the Iberian Peninsula and Prussia. Besides these traditional revenue sources, the orders engaged very successfully in animal husbandry, especially in sheep-raising and horse-breeding. While the latter also supported their military mission, the sale of wool fetched good profits.

The income of the orders

In the case of the Palestinian military orders one can make a clear division between their possessions in their outposts at the boundaries of Christendom and those in the European "hinterland." Part of the revenue flowed in the form of *responsiones* for support of the outposts. The Templars and Hospitallers transported these payments to Outremer in their own ships. The logistical and financial network established for this process, along with other already-mentioned characteristics of the military orders—the union of supranational structure, closeness to rulers, financial know-how, and military potential—recommended the orders for their role as international trade and credit institutions. Funds could be deposited securely at one house of the order and paid out at another; loans taken out in foreign lands could be paid back to officials at the local house after the borrower's return. The Templars had such a good reputation for safeguarding items deposited with them that at times even the French crown jewels were safeguarded at the order's Paris headquarters. In time, these economic ties to the kingdom of France proved to be disastrous.

Criticism, control, and dissolution: the military orders in the late Middle Ages

In hindsight, the fall of the crusader lordship of Outremer's last bastion, Acre, on May 18, 1291, was a turning point in the history of the Palestinian military orders. The knights lost their true field of operations and their original reason for existence. They had not given up the locales remaining to them without a fight—the Templars, for example, lost almost the entire contingent of knights posted at Acre. Admittedly, the orders failed to evacuate the populace in their own ships in time, but they cannot be blamed for the fall of Outremer. The true cause was much more the superior might of the Mamluk enemy and lack of support from the Latin West.

Criticism of the
military orders

Some contemporaries saw the matter otherwise, though. After the loss of Acre the number of people who reproached the military orders with lack of mission grew. They vehemently reiterated old criticisms. In the twelfth century William of Tyre and Jacques de Vitry had already reproached the Templars and Hospitallers for their wealth and had criticized, from their own position as bishops, the fact that the exempt military orders cut into the Church's revenues. Other authors, like Walter Map (*c.* 1140–1210) or Matthew Paris (*c.* 1200–59) went much further in their criticism, asserting that in Outremer the personnel of the orders had not merely adopted the outward customs of the East but were only half-hearted in their attacks on the Muslims. According to these and other contemporaries, the knights were proud, greedy, and militarily simply no longer in a position to carry out an effective reconquest of Outremer. And finally churchmen like Roger Bacon (*c.* 1219–*c.* 1292) complained that the military orders had not paid adequate attention to conversion of the infidel. This was true enough: evangelization was never a priority for the orders, since their primary task was military activity against enemies of the faith. The situation was not essentially different even in the Baltic. Admittedly, during their brutal advances against the native non-Christian populace the argument was made occasionally that the subjected Slavs should indeed be given the option of converting, but still the orders do not seem to have taken evangelization very seriously.

Reform
proposals

Contemporaries did not limit themselves to criticism by any means; some also proposed plans to improve the situation. In the many reflections on how to win back the Holy Land—that is, how to achieve the *recuperatio Terrae Sanctae* (see "Attempts to win back the Holy Land," p. 58)—authors also made recommendations for the reform of the military orders. Many bishops welcomed the idea of amalgamating the Templars and Hospitallers into a new, more effective military order, a plan formulated in response to an inquiry by Pope Nicholas IV (r. 1288–92). The Mallorcan theologian Ramon Llull (1232–*c.* 1316), for example, suggested in his *Liber de fine* (*c.* 1300) that the new order be given the name "Order of the Holy Spirit" and be placed under a warrior king, a *rex bellator*; other authors such as Pierre Dubois (*c.* 1250–*c.* 1321) and later Philippe de Mézières (*c.* 1327–1405) formulated similar proposals. But the orders, despite all criticisms and their losses in Outremer, retained the structures they had already developed. However, they now had the tasks of establishing new headquarters outside of the Holy Land and of finding new spheres of activity. Each of the orders went about this task in its own fashion.

While the Lazarite Order, after a few false starts, established a new center in Boigny (France) and continues to the present as a charitable institution, the other orders that had begun as hospital organizations did not initially revert to their original duties. The Hospitallers made their way first to Cyprus and from there successfully conquered the Greek-ruled island of Rhodes between 1306 and 1310. They fortified their new possession very strongly, built it up as a home base for an important fleet, and transformed it into the order's new center of operations. From this lordship the Hospitallers were able to play an active role in eastern Mediterranean politics, to rule Smyrna for nearly thirty years (1374–1402), and to engage in naval warfare against the Muslims. In January 1523 the order evacuated Rhodes under pressure from the Ottoman Turks, but in 1530 they received the island of Malta from Emperor Charles V (r. 1519–55), where they operated their own independent state until 1798.

The creation of independent states

The Teutonic Knights were even more successful in establishing their own territory. Even before the fall of Acre there had been voices in favor of transferring the order's activities to the Baltic, although at first the high master resided in Venice. The order's leadership only decided to move headquarters to the Marienburg in 1309. A year before that, the Teutonic Knights had conquered Christian Pomerelia, furthering plans to create a state in Prussia. Because plans to unite all military orders were floating around at the time, the Knights were under strong pressure to act, and conflicts with the non-Christian Lithuanians offered a suitable field of activity. The rise and decline of the Teutonic *Ordensstaat* has already been described ("The Teutonic Knights and their state," p. 128); it ended in 1525 with its secularization under the first "duke in Prussia," Master Albrecht von Hohenzollern-Ansbach (r. 1510–25).

By that time, the Order of Knights Templars was only a distant memory. As the first of the three Palestinian military orders, it fell victim of the changed circumstances after 1291. Two factors in particular weakened the Templars' position. In contrast to the Lazarites, Hospitallers, and Teutonic Knights, the Templars' original purpose was war against enemies of the faith; thus criticism of their inability to hold Acre was

Criticism of the Templars

especially loud. But above all, the Templars failed to establish a territorial base of their own on the borders of Christendom. The true focal point of the order lay in France, home of the first brethren and also of the order's founder. Most of the Templar dependencies lay in France; there the order's wealth was particularly great. The Templars were also particularly close to the French royal court. The end of the Templar Order at the hands of King Philip IV shows how dangerous this proximity could become.

The end of the Knights Templars

On October 13, 1307 the French Templars were arrested in a secret action, at the command of King Philip IV (r. 1285–1314). The charges against them were heresy, worship of idols, and homosexual practices. Through confessions won by interrogation and torture, several Templars confirmed the accusations. The pope (Clement V, r. 1305–14) was ill and in too weak a political position to counter the king's initiative effectively; thus at the Council of Vienne on March 22, 1312, the order was formally dissolved. The recantation of many high-ranking members, including Grand Master Jacques de Molay, changed nothing. The order's possessions were for the most part transferred to the Hospitallers—a macabre twist of the plans to consolidate the orders. In France the king secured a lion's share of their wealth for himself, while in Portugal and Aragón the possessions— and apparently also the members—of the Templar Order found a new institutional form in the royally founded Order of Christ and in the Order of Montesa. Grand Master Jacques de Molay, however, was executed in 1314 as a relapsed heretic. The oldest military order had ceased to exist. What motivated Philip IV to eradicate the Templars with such vigor is still the subject of debate. It appears that he may have personally believed the accusations; possibly he also wanted to place himself or one of his sons at the head of a new military order. Perhaps the Templars merely stood in the way of the king's efforts to centralize his power. Then again, the king, indebted to the order, might have seen in its dissolution a chance to renege on his own obligations and at the same time increase his income. This question of motivation and the dramatic end of the Knights Templars still fascinates some authors today, their fantasies bearing exotic fruit in contemporary literature.

The end of the Spanish military orders

The Spanish military orders had always been under the close control of the Castilian and Aragonese kings. With the end of the great campaigns of the *reconquista* they gradually lost their reason for existence. By the end of the fifteenth century the kings had succeeded in claiming for themselves the office of grand master; now the orders were also formally incorporated into the crown and secularized under the Catholic monarchs Ferdinand and Isabella (r. 1474–1516). Admittedly they continued to exist as institutions, but they had become honorary corporations into which nobles were received in return for their service at court—as such they played a not unimportant role in the social structure of the Spanish crown. Today, successor institutions to the medieval military religious orders still exist. Some of them, like the Order of St John or the Lazarites, are still dedicated to care of the sick; others are concerned with missionary work and education.

6

The aftermath

The heritage of the crusades

Intercultural contacts

Opinions vary on the question of how much the crusades contributed to exchange between the Latin, Greek Orthodox, and Islamic cultural worlds. Beyond a doubt, the crusades, with their battles and military expeditions, played their part in the alienation between Christianity and other religions. This is true of both the Islamic and Byzantine worlds. The conquest of Constantinople in 1204 marked the nadir of Latin–Byzantine relations. Even though many Latins gave their lives to defend Constantinople from the thirteenth through the fifteenth centuries, the events of 1204 left such a deep impression that even in the mid-fifteenth century memory of the Latin conquest prevented Christians from making common cause against the Ottoman Turks. The crusades brought great suffering to both fighters and noncombatants, both Christian and Muslim. Like all wars, they were brutal and contemptuous of human life. But the crusades did not make the Christian–Islamic world more violent: it was a violent world that brought the crusades into being.

Cultural exchange and transfer

It is equally beyond question that the crusades and the creation of the crusader states increased the number of contacts between the two religions. New interreligious border regions came into being, in which the mercantile cities in particular functioned as places of encounter. In such locales, a certain amount of exchange was inevitable. After the Muslim defeat at Ascalon (1153) at the latest, Muslims were no longer a serious threat to Christian sea travel in the Levant. In the following period, the Italian merchant cities enjoyed a hegemony over trade in the eastern Mediterranean. They opened the markets of the Levant to the West. Did these exchange processes also encompass the transmission and adoption of foreign learning? Indeed, one can name a fair number of cultural acquisitions that found an entry into the Latin West via the Muslim world. Arabic loanwords from the world of trade, such as "bazaar," "check," "tariff," or "arsenal," or words from the sciences like "algebra" or "algorithm" can be cited in this context. Artistic achievements, especially in the decorative arts, as well as skills in working metal, textiles, ceramics, and leather can be shown to have been adopted from the Islamic world. It is possible to identify exchange processes from the Muslim perspective, too, although the Latin Christians had relatively little to offer the Muslims by way of culture. In military technology, for example, encounter with the foreign warriors led to important innovations ranging from the introduction of armored horsemen to changes in siege technology and castle construction. The religious border was thus more permeable than one might assume.

But how much of all this cross-cultural influence found its way to the West via the crusader lordships of the Near East? Scholars have for the most part agreed that comparatively few such exchange processes took place in the crusader lordships of Palestine and Syria. Other contact zones served as points of entry for foreign learning to a far greater degree. For several centuries Sicily and southern Italy remained strongly imbued with the culture of the subject Muslims who lived there, and in many Islamic ports of the Mediterranean Christian traders came into contact with Muslims and their culture. Admittedly, the Christians in Alexandria, Tunis, and other centers lived separated from the native populace in their *funduqs* (see "Visitors: merchants and pilgrims," p. 103), but they engaged actively in trade with Muslim businessmen. The longest and most intensive intercultural exchange occurred on the Iberian Peninsula. Here one can see a variety of reception processes that went well beyond the adoption of Islamic learning. The Christians also gained access to long-unknown ancient texts, Arabic translations of Greek authors that were translated into Latin at Toledo and other Iberian towns. Of all the crusading regions, the Iberian Peninsula was beyond doubt the most important for intercultural exchange. This should not come as a surprise, because here Christendom was never driven away again after its conquests, so the exchange process could take place over a longer period and with less disruption than in Palestine and Syria. In the East, the Muslim reconquest not only removed direct Christian presence but included large-scale destruction, which possibly obliterated evidence of Christian-Islamic contacts that had indeed existed.

Sicily and Spain as contact zones

Despite such losses, some evidence remains of the crusader lordships' own cultural life and accomplishments, some of which also spread to Europe. In Jerusalem, Antioch, and Acre authors of the caliber of William of Tyre, Rorgo Fretellus, and Gerard of Nazareth were active, while in the artistic realm the transplanted westerners developed their own centers of book illumination and sculpture. Some knowledge of this work reached the West. For example, in Sicily and Umbria the art of the crusader states probably influenced local artistic production. Frederick I Barbarossa is said to have successfully besieged a Lombard city thanks to the expertise of a fortifications expert from Jerusalem. And an eye doctor from the holy city, apparently trained in Arabic,

Cultural influences of the crusader lordships

introduced the revolutionary idea of inserting embryonic tissue into wounds to help heal them. The transport of relics and reliquaries from the Holy Land to the West constituted a unique form of cultural transfer. Silversmiths and goldsmiths in Jerusalem enclosed particles of the True Cross in reliquaries, which were sent to select people; they made westerners who could not travel to Palestine mindful of the holy city through their shape and ornamentation. One can also speak of cultural transfer in the art of castle-building, because there is evidence that especially since the 1160s Christians integrated Muslim elements in fortification technology. Especially notable are the stepped curtain walls of the great Syrian crusader castles, a style soon adopted in the Latin West.

The true significance of the crusader lordships of the Near East in terms of intercultural exchange, though, might have lain less in the export of objects and technological innovations than in the realm of perceptions and attitudes. On the Muslim side, an important consequence of the crusades was the strengthening of the concept of jihad during the course of conflicts with the crusaders. On the Christian side, the expansion of the late eleventh century and the early twelfth played an essential role in bringing the East into the consciousness of Latin Christendom. It now won a position in imagination, in art, and in the literature of the Latin West—and not just negatively or as a counterfoil. The holy places achieved a new, concrete significance beyond their biblical sense. Now, besides the heavenly Jerusalem of Revelation and the biblical Jerusalem of the Old and New Testaments, there was a sense of the actual Jerusalem, the capital of a kingdom of the same name. Its conquest in 1099, the *liberatio* of the holy city, was liturgically celebrated in several regions of Europe in the Middle Ages and thus acquired a place in the calendar of holy days; similarly, its loss in 1187 was a milestone in the West's collective consciousness. Jerusalem and the crusades thus became elements in the medieval reckoning of time.

Self and the other
The most important consequence of the crusades for all the cultures engaged in them may not lie in the realities of reception, transfers, or attitudes toward foreigners, though. The encounter with Islam showed the Latin West its own characteristics, for perceptions of the other and of oneself go hand in hand. The First Crusade would not have succeeded militarily at all were it not for an unprecedented alliance of powers that transcended accepted political boundaries. Similarly, the settlement and defense of the conquered territory for nearly two centuries was only achieved through repeatedly renewed collective efforts. So it may well be that the encounter with other cultures led not so much to a greater understanding of the other as to a truer self-knowledge—with all of its consequences, both positive and negative. The crusades at the most fundamental level led both Christendom and Islam to self-discovery.

The crusades as myth

The crusades are among the historical phenomena that still survive today in the collective consciousness and in general linguistic usage. "Crusade" appears in altered form as a catchword in advertising, the media, and politics, and to some degree as a synonym for any concerted action in favor of a set goal. On the other hand, though, the term is also used to refer to the historical crusades—with extremely varied associations and levels of significance. This differentiated response can already be seen in the Middle Ages.

In the twelfth and thirteenth centuries the appeal to the crusades as a historical phenomenon can be seen in a number of sources—in chronicles and documents, sermons and poetry. These texts assured that the First Crusade soon attained the level of myth. For these witnesses already made the leap from remembering events to writing history, and thus interwove the ideas and values of their own time. What images of the crusades do these sources sketch? The first thing that stands out is that Christian contemporaries generally regarded the undertaking in a positive light. One can further observe that in the historical discourse, the many crusades to win or defend the holy places, the many expeditions summoned by popes against the enemies of Christianity, were reduced for the most part to the First Crusade. A third point is that the texts usually stress the exemplary character of the First Crusade's great heroes. Thus, reference to the crusades was often bound up with an invitation to imitation.

Today, by contrast, things are completely different: today crusades and crusaders are by no means something upon which one looks back with nostalgia—on the contrary. In the meantime the crusades have in general come to be regarded as brutal, pillaging, and unjust wars against peoples who were superior both culturally and morally. This valuation, too, has its prehistory: criticism, or at least distance, already characterized the position of some earlier writers, from Voltaire (1694–1778) to David Hume (1711–76). But it is in recent times that rejection of the crusades has become a commonplace. In particular, three historical developments or occurrences of the twentieth century appear to be responsible for this shift in perspective: the general secularization of western Europe, increasingly critical judgment of the colonialism of the nineteenth and twentieth centuries, and the genocide of the European Jews under the Nazis.

The negative myth of the crusades

The general secularization and criticism of the Church often led to a high regard for Islam. This can already be seen in *c.* 1800 with authors like Gotthold Ephraim Lessing (1729–81) or Sir Walter Scott (1771–1832); it was surely not a coincidence that this reassessment occurred at the same time as the Ottoman Empire declined in power. The collapse of the colonial system, for its part, let the crusader states appear as prefigurements of what now came to be regarded as an unjust political model. In this case the crusades provided a myth of integration, in that they served and serve critics of the colonial age as an added argument. One could, observing them functionally, even label them foundational myths of a better, purified Europe. The supposed direct line between the Holocaust and the crusades, in turn, was propagated soon after the Second World War by some historians and later continued with such success that in certain recent accounts an almost causal relationship has been drawn between the anti-Jewish atrocities of the Middle Ages and the anti-Semitic (in other words, racially motivated) mass murders of the twentieth century.

The idea of crusade in the nineteenth century

The negative myth sketched out here first became a broadly accepted reality after the Second World War. Attitudes were still completely different in the 1930s and 1940s, when most people still regarded the idea of crusade as a positive force, employed as a catchword by an amazing variety of political parties and positions. The term was used as shorthand not only for medieval military engagements but also for modern ones. In the broadest sense, "crusade" had positive connotations, as a selfless struggle for higher ideals against an evil, apparently more powerful opponent. US president Eisenhower spoke of the Allies leading a "crusade in Europe," the Spanish dictator Francisco Franco Bahamonde (1892–1975) labeled his revolt against the republican government as *cruzada*, and Hitler, too, made indirect recourse to the image when he gave his assault on the Soviet Union the code name "Operation Barbarossa."

The instrumentalizing of the crusade idea in the twentieth century was a reflection of the upsurge of research on the crusades in the second half of the nineteenth century. The conditions of the age also had a direct impact on scholarly attitudes about the medieval crusades. The political circumstances of an era characterized by European nationalism and growing colonial rivalry led some historians to regard the crusader lordships as forerunners of the modern colonies or spheres of interest. All European powers developed their own images of the crusades at one time or another, as skewed in perspective as they were effective. It was these positivist colonial crusade myths of the nineteenth century, not the medieval texts, that created the preconditions for the anti-colonial negative- and counter-myths of the twentieth century.

The multilayered term "crusade"

Thus, the myth of the crusades was and is a phenomenon that has embraced all Europe. Its effectiveness, though, has by no means been limited to Christian Europe, but reaches far beyond the continent and religious boundaries. In the Jewish world, the Jerusalem massacre of July 1099 is still embedded in modern memory as part of the history of a religion, but also in the long history of a people's suffering. The crusaders' pogroms, to which the Jewish communities of the Rhineland fell victim, have remained a symbol of Ashkenazi suffering up to the present through tales and tradition. Even more evident is the mythic content of the crusades in the Islamic world. The 200-year-long Christian presence—or, from the Muslim perspective, occupation—left deep traces in the collective consciousness, which, as modern Islamicists and scholars of the Near East attest, still endure to the present. Already at the end of the nineteenth century the Ottoman sultan Abdülhamit II (r. 1876–1909) described the policies of the European great powers explicitly as "neo-crusades" against which it was necessary to offer resistance. In scholarship and literature Saladin was raised to the level of a champion against the western occupiers. A subsequent application of this concept to the current political situation in the Near East has occurred by regarding the state of Israel, despite all historical logic, as a successor of the Christian crusader states—one of the most important, fictitious, current, and at the same time effective of the crusade myths. Recent events in the Near East, Central Asia, and the United States have demonstrated painfully that the idea of crusade in East and West, in the most varied political situations, has lost none of its potency.

These few words may suffice to underscore two points: the unbroken importance of the crusade myth and its multilayered quality. Today, this myth still serves the most widely varied goals. It is an emblem of cruelty and violence, but also a symbol of sacrifice and idealism, and, last but not least, was a prefiguration of European arrogance and expansion.

Select bibliography

Encyclopedias, periodicals, and bibliographies

Andrea, A.J. (2003) *Encyclopedia of the Crusades*, Westport, Conn.: Greenwood Press.
Crusades, 1 (2002–   ) *The journal of the Society for the Study of the Crusades and the Latin East. Each annual volume includes a detailed bibliography of current crusade research.*
McEaney, J.F. (2002) *Crusades: A Bibliography with Indexes*, Hauppauge, N.Y.: Nova Science Publishers. *A handy bibliography of crusade research.*
Mayer, H.E. (1965) *Bibliographie zur Geschichte der Kreuzzüge*, 2nd edn, Hannover: Hansche Buchhandlung. *Fundamental bibliography of earlier crusade research.*
Mayer, H.E. and McLellan, J. (1989) "Select Bibliography of the Crusades," pp. 511–665 in H.W. Hazard (ed.) *History of the Crusades*, vol. 6, Madison: University of Wisconsin Press. *A useful compilation of the state of research up to 1989.*
Sacra Militia, 1 (2000–   ) *A periodical dedicated to the history of the military orders.*
Strayer, J.R. (ed.) (1982–89) *Dictionary of the Middle Ages*, 13 vols, New York: Scribner. *The standard English-language reference work on the European Middle Ages.*
Vauchez, A., *et al.* (eds) (2000) *Encyclopedia of the Middle Ages*, Chicago, Ill.: Fitzroy Dearborn. *A useful recent encyclopedia of medieval life and thought.*

Primary sources

Albon, G. (1913) *Cartulaire général de l'Ordre du Temple, 1119?–1150*, Paris: H. Champion. *The early charters of the Order of Knights Templars.*
Andrea, A.J. (ed.) (2000) *Contemporary Sources for the Fourth Crusade*, Leiden: Brill. *Latin sources on the conquest of Constantinople in translation, along with critical editions of two texts.*
Anna Comnena (2001) *Alexias*, D.R. Reinsch and A. Kambylis (eds), 2 vols, Berlin: W. de Gruyter. English translation: *The Alexiad*, trans. E.R.A. Sewter, Harmondsworth: Penguin, 1969. *The First Crusade from the Byzantine perspective.*
Benjamin of Tudela (1995) *The World of Benjamin of Tudela: A Medieval Mediterranean Travelogue*, trans. Sandra Benjamin, Madison, Wisc.: Fairleigh Dickinson University Press. *The twelfth-century crusader lordships from the perspective of a Spanish Jew.*

Crusade Texts in Translation (1998–), Aldershot: Ashgate. *A new series of translations of relevant sources, including eastern ones.*

Delaville le Roulx, J. (ed.) (1894–1906) *Cartulaire général de l'Ordre des Hospitaliers de St-Jean de Jérusalem (1100–1310)*, 4 vols, Paris: E. Leroux. *An important charter collection, covering more than just the history of the Hospitallers.*

Documents relatifs a l'histoire des Croisades (1946–95) 17 vols, Paris: Académie des Inscriptions. *A continuation of the* Recueil des historiens des croisades *with relevant texts and documents.*

Edbury, P.W. (trans.) (1995) *The Conquest of Jerusalem and the Third Crusade: Sources in Translation*, Aldershot: Ashgate. *Texts on the events of 1180–92 in English translation.*

Fulcher of Chartres (1913) *Historia Hierosolymitana (1095–1127)*, ed. H. Hagenmeyer, Heidelberg: C. Winter. *The standard edition of one of the most important crusade chronicles.* English translation: *A History of the Expedition to Jerusalem, 1095–1127*, trans. F. Ryan, New York: W.W. Norton, 1969.

Gabrieli, F. (ed.) (1969) *Arab Historians of the Crusades*, Berkeley: University of California Press. *Relevant Arabic sources in English translation.*

Geoffrey de Villehardouin (1963) *The Conquest of Constantinople*, in *Chronicles of the Crusades*, trans. M.R.B. Shaw, Harmondsworth: Penguin. *An important work on the conquest of Constantinople in 1204.*

Guibert of Nogent (1996) *Dei gesta per Francos, et cinq autres textes*, ed. R.B.C. Huygens. Corpus Christianorum Continuatio Medievalis 127A, Turnhout: Brepols. *Standard edition of one of the important crusade chronicles.*

Hagenmeyer, H. (ed.) (1901; reprint 1973) *Epistulae et chartae ad historiam primi belli sacri spectantes. Die Kreuzzugsbriefe aus den Jahren 1088–1100*, Innsbrück: Wagner'sche Universitäts-Buchhandlung/Hildesheim: G. Olms. *Letters from participants in the First Crusade.*

Hiestand, R. (ed.) (1972–85) *Vorarbeiten zum Oriens pontificius*, 3 vols, Göttingen: Abhandlungen der Akademie der Wissenschaften. *Papal charters for the Templars, the Hospitallers, and the Church of the crusader states, with suggestions for further reading and commentaries.*

Hill, R. (ed.) (1962) *The Deeds of the Franks and the Other Pilgrims to Jerusalem*, London and New York: T. Nelson. *Text and translation of one of the most important crusade chronicles.*

Housley, N. (ed. and trans.) (1996) *Documents on the Later Crusades, 1274–1580*, New York: St Martin's Press. *Translated sources on the late medieval crusades.*

Jean de Joinville (1963) *The Life of Saint Louis*, in *Chronicles of the Crusades*, trans. M.R.B. Shaw, Baltimore, Md.: Penguin. *On the crusades of Louis IX.*

Matthew of Edessa (1993) *Armenia and the Crusades: Tenth to Twelfth Centuries: The Chronicle of Matthew of Edessa*, trans. A.E. Dostourian, Lanham, Md.: University Press of America. *The Armenian view of the crusades.*

Raymond d'Aguilers (1969) *Le "Liber" de Raymond d'Aguilers*, trans. J.H. Hill and L.L. Hill, Paris: P. Geuthner. *Standard edition of one of the important crusade chronicles.*

Recueil des historiens des croisades (1841–1906) 16 vols, Paris: Impr. Nationale. *The most important source collection on the history of the crusades in the Near East.*

Robert of Clari (1936) *The Conquest of Constantinople*, trans. E.H. McNeal, New York: W.W. Norton. *A major source for the conquest of Constantinople in 1204.*

Röhricht, R. (1904; reprint 1960) *Regesta regni Hierosolymitani, MXCVII–MCCXCI*. Innsbruck. Reprint edn, New York: B. Franklin. *Collection of the charters of the Kingdom of Jerusalem; in Latin.*

Sandoli, S. de (ed.) (1978–84) *Itinera Hierosolymitana Crucesignatorum (saec. XII–XIII)*, 4 vols, Jerusalem: Franciscan Print. Press. *Christian descriptions of Jerusalem; Latin with Italian translation.*

Strehlke, E. (ed.) (1869; reprint 1975) *Tabulae ordinis Theutonici*, Berlin: Weidmann;

reprint Toronto: University of Toronto Press. *Fundamental source collection for the history of the Teutonic order.*

William of Tyre (1986) *Chronique*, ed. R.B.C. Huygens. Corpus Christianorum Continuatio Medievalis 63–63A, Turnhout: Brepols. English translation: *A History of Deeds Done Beyond the Sea*, trans. E.A. Babcock and A.C. Krey, New York: Octagon Books, 1976. *The most important historiographical work of the crusader lordships.*

Surveys of the crusades

Balard, M. (2001) *Croisades et Orient latin, XIᵉ–XIVᵉ siècle*, Paris: A. Colin. *A good overview with interesting use of sources.*

Bartlett, R. (1993) *The Making of Europe: Conquest, Colonization and Cultural Change 950–1350*, Princeton, N.J.: Princeton University Press. *A comparative study, fundamental for the "European expansion" of the high Middle Ages.*

Garcìa-Guijarro Ramos, L. (1995) *Papado, cruzadas, órdenes militares, siglos XI–XIII*, Madrid: Cátedra. *With emphasis on the reform papacy and the origins of the military orders.*

Hillenbrand, C. (1999) *The Crusades: Islamic Perspectives*, Edinburgh: Edinburgh University Press. *A current synthesis, well-grounded and richly illustrated.*

Lilie, R.-J. (2004) *Byzanz und die Kreuzzüge*, Stuttgart: W. Kohlhammer. *A broad overview from the Byzantine perspective.*

Mayer, H.E. (1988) *The Crusades*, 2nd edn, Oxford: Oxford University Press. (The original German text is now in its tenth edition: Stuttgart: Urban Taschenbücher, 2005.) *The standard work on the political history of the crusader lordships and the crusades in the Near East.*

Nicholson, H.J. (ed.) (2005) *Palgrave Advances in the Crusades*, New York: Palgrave Macmillan. *A new edited volume that reflects current research issues.*

Richard, J. (1999) *The Crusades, c. 1071–c. 1291*, Cambridge: Cambridge University Press. *An overview of the crusades in the Near East and the crusader lordships.*

Riley-Smith, J. (1990) *The Atlas of the Crusades*, New York: Facts on File. *Broad geographical and chronological coverage, with useful commentaries.*

—— (2005) *The Crusades: A History*, 2nd edn, New Haven, Conn.: Yale University Press. *Expanded and updated edition of a geographically and chronologically broad survey by the leading English historian of the crusades.*

—— (ed.) (1995) *Oxford Illustrated History of the Crusades*, Oxford: Oxford University Press. *A recent overview by a number of crusade historians.*

Setton, K.M. (ed.) (1955–89) *A General History of the Crusades*, 6 vols, Madison: University of Wisconsin Press. *A reliable and broadly conceived portrayal of the crusades and their effects.*

Winkelmann, F. (1998) *Die Kirchen im Zeitalter der Kreuzzüge (11.–13. Jahrhundert)*, 2nd edn, Leipzig: Evangelische Verlagsanstalt. *A short overview of Greek and Latin Church history.*

Christendom, Islam, and pagan lands to the end of the eleventh century

Brett, M. (1997) "The Near East on the Eve of the Crusades," pp. 119–36 in L. García-Guijarro Ramos (ed.), *La Primera Cruzada novecientos años después: el Concilio de Clermont y los orígenes del movimiento cruzado*, Madrid: L. García-Guijarro. *A good overview of the Islamic world at the time of the First Crusade.*

Holt, P.M. (1986) *The Age of the Crusades: The Near East from the Eleventh Century to 1517*, London: Longman. *A concise but reliable study of the Near East from the eastern perspective.*

Kedar, B.Z. (1984) *Crusade and Mission: European Approaches toward the Muslims*, Princeton, N.J.: Princeton University Press. *On Christian relations with the Muslims.*

Laiou, A.E. and Mottahedeh, R.P. (eds) (2001) *The Crusades from the Perspective of Byzantium and the Muslim World*, Washington, D.C.: Dumbarton Oaks. *Recent essays on the crusade movement and the eastern Mediterranean world, especially giving due credit to the Byzantine perspective.*

Holy war, knighthood, and pilgrimage

Erdmann, C. (1977) *The Origin of the Idea of Crusade*, trans. M.W. Baldwin and W. Goffart, Princeton, N.J.: Princeton University Press. *Pathbreaking study, still valuable today despite some revisions.*

Flori, J. (1998) *Croisade et chevalerie, XIe–XIIe s.*, Brussels: De Boeck Université. *A collection of articles on knighthood, holy war, and crusade.*

—— (2002) *Guerre sainte, jihad, croisade: violence et religion dans le christianisme et l'islam*, Paris: Seuil. *A new comparative study.*

Hehl, E.-D. (1980) *Kirche und Krieg im 12. Jahrhundert*, Stuttgart: Hiersemann. *A fundamental study of the ecclesiastical-theological position on war, especially the crusades.*

"Militia Christi" e Crociata nei secoli XI–XIII, Atti della undecima Settimana Internazionale di studio Mendola, 18 agosto–1 settembre 1989 (1992) Milan: Vita e pensiero. *A successful collection of articles on the idea of "militia Christi" in various institutions.*

Papacy, piety, and indulgence

Alphandéry, P. and Dupront, A. (1954–59) *Le chrétienté et l'idée de croisade*, Paris: Alban Michel. *A major intellectual history of the idea of crusade.*

Bull, M. (1993) *Knightly Piety and the Lay Response to the First Crusade: The Limousin and Gascony 970–1130*, Oxford: Oxford University Press. *Outstanding regional study of the idea of crusade in southwestern France.*

Constable, G. (1996) *The Reformation of the Twelfth Century*, Cambridge: Cambridge University Press. *Also relevant for the eleventh century.*

Cowdrey, H.E.J. (1984) *Popes, Monks and Crusaders*, London: Hambledon Press. *Important articles on the relation of the reform popes to the crusades.*

Hehl, E.-D. (1994) "Was ist eigentlich ein Kreuzzug?" *Historische Zeitschrift* 259: 297–335. *Overview of the state of research with insightful considerations of the idea of crusade.*

The First Crusade

Becker, A. (1964–88) *Papst Urban II. (1088–1099)*, 2 vols, Stuttgart: A. Hiersemann. *A fundamental study of the orginator of the First Crusade.*

France, J. (1994) *Victory in the East: A Military History of the First Crusade*, Cambridge: Cambridge University Press. *Outstanding presentation of the First Crusade, not limited to military history.*

Lilie, R.-J. (1987) "Der Erste Kreuzzug in der Darstellung Anna Komnenes," pp. 49–148 in *Varia II (Poikila Byzantina 6)*, Bonn: R. Habelt. *Compares the perspective of the Byzantine princess Anna Comnena with the Latin crusade reports.*

Lobrichon, G. (1998) *1099, Jérusalem conquise*, Paris: Seuil. *Comparison of the chronicles of the First Crusade.*

Phillips, Jonathan (ed.) (1997) *The First Crusade: Origins and Impact*, Manchester: Manchester University Press. *Collection of recent articles with a good bibliography.*

The crusades in the twelfth to fifteenth centuries

Eickhoff, E. (1977) *Friedrich Barbarossa im Orient. Kreuzzug und Tod Friedrichs I*, Tübingen: E. Wasmuth. *A study of the emperor's brilliant campaign.*

Housley, N. (1992) *The Later Crusades: From Lyons to Alcazar, 1274–1580*, Oxford: Oxford University Press. *Comprehensive study of the later medieval crusades.*

—— (2002) *Religious Warfare in Europe, 1400–1536*, Oxford: Oxford University Press. *A geographically wide-reaching, up-to-date study.*

Möhring, H. (1980) *Saladin und der dritte Kreuzzug: Aiyubidische Strategie und Diplomatie im Vergleich vornehmlich der arabischen mit den lateinischen Quellen*, Wiesbaden: Steiner. *A work with groundbreaking use of the Arabic and Latin sources.*

Phillips, J. and Madden, T.F. (eds) (2001) *The Second Crusade: Scope and Consequences*, Manchester: Manchester University Press. *Collection of recent articles with a good bibliography.*

Powell, J.M. (1986) *Anatomy of a Crusade, 1213–1221*, Philadelphia: University of Pennsylvania Press. *A concise but reliable examination.*

Queller, D.E. and Madden, T.F. (1997) *The Fourth Crusade: The Conquest of Constantinople*, with an essay on the primary sources by A.J. Andrea, 2nd edn, Philadelphia: University of Pennsylvania Press. *The standard work on the crusade against Constantinople.*

Setton, K.M. (1976–84) *The Papacy and the Levant, 1204–1571*, 4 vols, Philadelphia: American Philosophical Society. *A fundamental work on the relations between Byzantium and the West in the late Middle Ages.*

Theory, practice, and criticism of the idea of crusade

Brundage, J. (1969) *Medieval Canon Law and the Crusader*, Madison: University of Wisconsin Press. *An important study of the position of the crusades in canon law.*

Constable, G. (1998) "The Place of the Crusader in Medieval Society," *Viator* 29: 377–403. *An examination in light of other forms of expressing medieval piety.*

Hiestand, R. (1998) *"Gott will es!"—Will Gott es wirklich? Die Kreuzzugsidee in der Kritik ihrer Zeit*, Stuttgart: W. Kohlhammer. *A short and reliable overview.*

Maier, C.T. (1994) *Preaching the Crusades: Mendicant Friars and the Cross in the Thirteenth Century*, Cambridge: Cambridge University Press. *Draws on long-neglected sources on the idea of crusade in the late Middle Ages.*

Siberry, E. (1985) *Criticism of Crusading, 1095–1274*, Oxford: Clarendon Press. *A synthesis of criticism of the crusades.*

Tyerman, C. (1998) *The Invention of the Crusades*, Toronto: University of Toronto Press. *With detailed arguments about the crusades in the twelfth century.*

The crusades from the Islamic perspective

Atrache, L. (1996) *Die Politik der Ayyubiden. Die fränkisch-islamischen Beziehungen in der ersten Hälfte des 7./13/ Jahrhunderts, under besonderer Berücksichtigung des Feindbildes*, Münster: Rhema. *The crusades from the Muslim perspective.*

Hitti, P.K. (1985) "The Impact of the Crusades on Moslem Lands," pp. 33–58 in N.P. Zacour and H.W. Hazard (eds) *The Impact of the Crusades on the Near East (A General History of the Crusades,* vol. 5), Madison: University of Wisconsin Press. *On the short- and long-term consequences of the crusades.*

Irwin, R. (1989) "The Image of the Byzantine and Frank in Arabic Popular Literature of the Late Middle Ages," pp. 226–42 in B. Arbel *et al.* (eds) *Latins and Greeks in the Eastern Mediterranean after 1204,* London: Society for the Study of the Crusades and the Latin East. *On Islamic perceptions of foreigners.*

—— (1997) "The Impact of the Early Crusades in the Muslim World," pp. 137–54 in L. García-Guijarro Ramos (ed.) *La Primera Cruzada novecientos años después: el Concilio de Clermont y los orígenes del movimiento cruzado,* Madrid: L. García-Guijarro. *On the limited significance of the First Crusade for the Muslims.*

Sivan, E. (1968) *L'Islam et le croisade,* Paris: Librairie d'Amérique et d'Orient. *A fundamental study on the relationship between Islam and Christianity.*

Secular lordship

Edbury, P. (1991) *The Kingdom of Cyprus and the Crusades, 1191–1374,* Cambridge: Cambridge University Press. *The standard work on the history of Cyprus and the crusader lordships in the late Middle Ages.*

Lilie, R.-J. (1993) *Byzantium and the Crusader States, 1096–1204,* Oxford: Clarendon Press. *A fundamental study of Byzantine–Latin relations up to the conquest of Constantinople.*

Mayer, H.E. (1995) "Herrschaft and Verwaltung im Kreuzfahrerkönigreich Jerusalem," *Historische Zeitschrift* 261: 695–738. *A compact view of the lordship structures and de facto powers in the kingdom of Jerusalem.*

—— (1996) *Die Kanzlei der lateinischen Könige von Jerusalem* (Monumenta Germaniae Historica Schriften 40: 1–2), Hannover: Hahn. *A masterful and detailed study of governing structures.*

Murray, A.V. (2000) *The Crusader Kingdom of Jerusalem: A Dynastic History, 1099–1125,* Oxford: Prosopographia et genealogica. *An essential prosopographical study.*

Phillips, J. (1996) *Defenders of the Holy Land: Relations between the Latin East and the West, 1119–87,* Oxford: Oxford University Press. *On efforts to get assistance and diplomatic contacts between the crusader lordships and Latin Christendom.*

Prawer, J. (1980) *Crusader Institutions,* Oxford: Clarendon Press. *The standard work on rule and lordship in the kingdom of Jerusalem.*

Rozenberg, S. (ed.) (1999) *Knights of the Holy Land: The Crusader Kingdom of Jerusalem,* Jerusalem: Israel Museum. *Exhibition catalogue with short overview articles on the history of the crusader lordships in the Near East.*

Christians, Muslims, and Jews

Ellenblum, R. (1998) *Frankish Rural Settlement in the Latin Kingdom of Jerusalem,* Cambridge: Cambridge University Press. *A pathbreaking study of settlement patterns in the crusader lordships.*

Favreau-Lilie, M.-L. (1989) *Die Italiener im Heiligen Land vom ersten Kreuzzug bis zum Tode Heinrichs von Champagne (1098–1197)*, Amsterdam: Hakkert. *An authoritative work on the Italian mercantile cities in the Near East.*

—— (2001) " 'Multikulturelle Gesellschaft' oder 'Persecuting Society?' 'Franken' und 'Einheimische' im Königreich Jerusalem," pp. 55–93 in D. Bauer, K. Herbers, and N. Jaspert (eds) *Jerusalem im Hoch- und Spätmittelalter*, Frankfurt am Main: Campus. *A successful overview of recent research.*

Hiestand, R. (1995) " 'Nam qui fuimus Occidentales, nunc facti sumus Orientales,' Siedlung und Siedleridentität in den Kreuzfahrerstaaten," pp. 61–80 in C. Dipper and R. Hiestand (eds) *Siedler-Identität: neun Fallstudien von der Antike bis zur Gegenwart*, Frankfurt am Main: P. Lang. *Understandable and reliable study of the essence and transformation of self-identity.*

Kedar, B.Z. (1990) "The Subjected Muslims of the Frankish Levant," pp. 135–74 in J.M. Powell (ed.) *Muslims under Latin Rule*, Princeton, N.J.: Princeton University Press. *A good survey of the subject.*

Mayer, H.E. (ed.) (1997) *Die Kreuzfahrerstaaten als multikulturelle Gesellschaft*, Munich: R. Oldenbourg. *An up-to-date collection of articles with many new insights.*

Pahlitzsch, J. (2001) *Graeci und Suriani im Palästina der Kreuzfahrerzeit. Beiträge und Quellen zur Geschichte des griechisch-orthodoxen Patriarchats von Jerusalem*, Berlin: Duncker und Humblot. *On the interconfessional relations between Latins and Greeks.*

Shatzmiller, M. (ed.) (1993) *Crusaders and Muslims in Twelfth-Century Syria*, Leiden: Brill. *Case studies on the relations between Muslims and Latins.*

The Palestinian Churches

Elm, K. (1998) *Umbilicus Mundi. Beiträge zur Geschichte Jerusalems, der Kreuzzüge, des Kapitels vom Hlg. Grab und der Ritterorden*, Bruges: Sint-Trudo-Abdij. *A collection of authoritative articles on the Church and the religious orders in the crusader states.*

Hamilton, B. (1980) *The Latin Church in the Crusader States: The Secular Church*, London: Variorum. *A good, readable survey.*

Kirstein, K.-P. (2002) *Die lateinischen Patriarchen von Jerusalem: von der Eroberung der Heiligen Stadt durch die Kreuzfahrer 1099 bis zum Ende der Kreuzfahrerstaaten 1291*, Berlin: Duncker und Humblot. *The most recent study of the Latin patriarchate.*

Pahlitzsch, J. and Weltecke, D. (2001) "Konflikte zwischen den nicht-lateinischen Kirchen im Königreich Jerusalem," pp. 119–45 in D. Bauer *et al.* (eds) *Jerusalem im Hoch- und Spätmittelalter, Konflikte und Konfliktbewältigung—Vorstellungen und Vergegenwärtigungen*, Frankfurt am Main: Campus. *A comparative study of relations between the Christians of the Near East.*

The Iberian Peninsula

Engels, O. (1989) "Die Reconquista," pp. 279–300 in O. Engels (ed.) *Reconquista und Landesherrschaft. Studien zur Rechts- und Verfassungsgeschichte Spaniens im Mittelalter*, Paderborn: F. Schöningh. *The* reconquista *from the perspective of lordship.*

Jaspert, N. (2001) "Frühformen der geistlichen Ritterorden und die Kreuz-zugsbewegung auf der Iberischen Halbinsel," pp. 90–116 in K. Herbers (ed.)

Europa an der Wende vom 11. zum 12. Jahrhundert. Beiträge zu Ehren von Werner Goez, Stuttgart: Steiner. *On structural similarities between East and West.*

Lomax, D. (1978) *The Reconquest of Spain*, London: Longman. *A good, readable synthesis.*

Schwenk, B. (1992) *Calatrava. Entstehung und Frühgeschichte eines spanischen Ritterordens zisterziensischer Observanz im 12. Jahrhundert*, Münster: Aschendorff. *A study that ranges far beyond the title theme.*

Vones, L. (1993) *Geschichte der Iberischen Halbinsel im Mittelalter (711–1480): Reiche–Kronen–Regionen*, Sigmaringen: J. Thorbecke. *An absolutely reliable survey.*

The Baltic region

Benninghoven, F. (1965) *Der Orden der Schwertbrüder. Fratres Milicie Christi de Livonia*, Cologne/Graz: Böhlau. *A standard work that stays close to the sources.*

Christiansen, E. (1997) *The Northern Crusades: The Baltic and the Catholic Frontier, 1100–1525*, 2nd edn, London: Penguin. *A good, readable overview.*

Constable, G. (1999) "The Place of the Magdeburg Charter of 1107/08 in the History of Eastern Germany and of the Crusades," pp. 283–99 in F.J. Felten and N. Jaspert (eds) *Vita religiosa im Mittelalter. Festschrift für Kaspar Elm zum 70. Geburtstag* (Berliner Historische Studien 31 = Ordensstudien 13), Berlin.

Murray, A.V. (ed.) (2001) *Crusade and Conversion on the Baltic Frontier, 1150–1500*, Aldershot: Ashgate. *A collection of recent articles that gives proper credit to eastern European research.*

Paravicini, W. (1989–95) *Die Preußenreisen des europäischen Adels*, 2 vols, Sigmaringen: J. Thorbecke. *A fundamental and innovative study of the so-called "Prussia Reisen."*

Urban, W. (1994) *The Baltic Crusade*, 2nd edn, Chicago, Ill.: Lithuanian Research and Studies Center. *A reliable survey.*

Enemies within

Housley, N. (1985) "Crusades against Christians: Their Origins and Early Development, c. 1000–1216," pp. 17–36 in P.W. Edbury (ed.) *Crusade and Settlement*, Cardiff: University College Cardiff Press. *Examines the origins of the Sicilian crusades.*

—— (1986) *The Avignon Papacy and the Crusades, 1305–1378*, Oxford: Clarendon Press. *A good study of the Italian crusades and crusade negotiations from the papal perspective.*

Oberste, J. (2003) *Der "Kreuzzug" gegen die Albigenser. Ketzerei und Machtpolitik im Mittelalter*, Darmstadt: Primus. *The most recent study of the Albigensian crusades and Occitan society in this period.*

Šmahel, F. (2002) *Die Hussitische Revolution*, 3 vols, Hannover: Hahnsche Buchhandlung. *A broadly conceived examination of the context of late medieval religious movements.*

Wagner, K. (2000) *Debellare Albigenses: Darstellung und Deutung des Albigenserkreuzzuges in der europäischen Geschichtsschreibung von 1209 bis 1328*, Neuried: Ars Una. *A comparative study of the extant sources on the Albigensian crusade.*

Basis and beginnings of the military orders

Demurger, A. (2002) *Chevaliers du Christ. Les ordres religieux-militaires au Moyen Age (XIe–XVIe siècle)*, Paris: Seuil. *A current, broad, and readable survey.*

Favreau, M.-L. (1974) *Studien zur Frühgeschichte des Deutschen Ordens*, Stuttgart: E. Klett. *Detailed description of the beginnings of the Teutonic order in Palestine.*

Fleckenstein, J. and Hellmann, M. (eds) (1980) *Die geistlichen Ritterorden Europas*, Sigmaringen: Thorbecke. *Fundamental collection of essays.*

Forey, A. (1992) *The Military Orders from the Twelfth to the Early Fourteenth Centuries*, Toronto: University of Toronto Press. *A successful synthesis.*

Prutz, H. (1908; reprint 1977) *Die geistlichen Ritterorden. Ihre Stellung zur kirchlichen, politischen, gesellschaftlichen und wirschaftlichen Entwicklung des Mittelalters*, Berlin: E.S. Mittler und Sohn. *The standard work on the subject for almost a century.*

The military orders in Palestine, the Iberian Peninsula, and the Baltic

Ayala Martínez, C. de (2003) *Las Órdenes Militares hispánicas en la Edad Media: siglos XII–XV*, Madrid: Marcial Pons. *A very good overview of all the Spanish military orders.*

Barber, M. (ed.) (1994) *The Military Orders: Fighting for the Faith and Caring for the Sick*, Aldershot: Variorum. *A recent collection of articles on the caring side of the military orders, with a wide array of specific studies and recent bibliography.*

Biskup, M. and Labuda, G. (2000) *Die Geschichte des Deutschen Ordens in Preußen. Wirtschaft, Gesellschaft, Staat, Ideologie*, Osnabrück: Fibre. *A good overview from the Polish perspective.*

Boockmann, H. (1994) *Der Deutsche Orden. Zwölf Kapitel aus seiner Geschichte*, 4th edn, Munich: Beck. *Readable, compact, and reliable.*

Militzer, K. (2005) *Die Geschichte des Deutschen Ordens*, Stuttgart: Kohlhammer. *A new and successful synthesis from a mainly political history perspective.*

Nicholson, H. (ed.) (1998) *The Military Orders: Welfare and Warfare*, Aldershot: Ashgate. *An up-to-date collection of articles that go beyond the military aspects of the orders, with many case studies and recent bibliography.*

Ordines Militares (1983–　) Colloquia Torunensia Historica. Torun. *A good series, with collections of articles that deal above all with the history of the military orders in the Baltic.*

The consequences

Atiya, A. (1962) *Crusade, Commerce and Culture*, Bloomington: Indiana University Press. *On cultural contacts and economic exchange.*

Fischer, W. and Schneider, J. (eds) (1982) *Das Heilige Land im Mittelalter. Begegnungsraum zwischen Orient und Okzident*, Neustadt an der Aisch: Degener. *A good collection of articles.*

Goss, V.P. (ed.) (1986) *The Meeting of Two Worlds: Cultural Exchange between East and West during the Period of the Crusades*, Kalamazoo, Mich.: Medieval Institute Publications. *A methodologically excellent collection of articles.*

Jaspert, N. (2004) "Ein Polymythos: Die Kreuzzüge," pp. 202–35 in H. Altrichter *et al.*

(eds) *Mythen in der Geschichte*, Freiburg im Breisgau: Rombach. *On the long-term effects of the crusades in Christianity, Islam, and Judaism.*

Sivan, E. (1995) *Mythes politiques arabes*, Paris: Fayard. *A successful recent overview.*

Index

Routledge History

Western Warfare in the Age of the Crusades, 1000–1300

John France

'I am full of admiration for this excellent story of the practice of warfare in the Central Middle Ages. It is a work of both scholarship and synthesis, full of insight and communicated in an accessible and professional way' – *Norman Housley, University of Leicester*

Western Warfare in the Age of the Crusades, 1000–1300 examines war in the three hundred years between 1000 and 1300 and argues that it was primarily shaped by the people who conducted war – the landowners. John France illuminates the role of property concerns in producing the characteristic instruments of war: the castle and the knight. This authoritative study details the way in which war was fought and the reasons for it as well as reflecting on the society which produced the crusades.

ISBN10: 1–85728–466–6 (hbk)   ISBN10: 1–85728–467–4 (pbk)
ISBN13: 978–1–85728–466–9 (hbk)   ISBN13: 978–1–85728–467–6 (pbk)

The Medieval World

Edited by Peter Linehan and Janet L. Nelson

'The editors should be toasted for having distilled something of the lively spirit and substance of their subject into a single, concentrated product. Those with a taste, whether refined or modest, for the Middle Ages are urged to partake.' – *History Today*

This groundbreaking collection brings the Middle Ages to life and conveys the distinctiveness of this diverse, constantly changing period. From the contributions of 38 scholars, one medieval world, from Connacht to Constantinople and from Tynemouth to Timbuktu, emerges from many disparate worlds. This extraordinary set of reconstructions presents the reader with the future of the medieval past, offering fresh appraisals of the evidence and modern historical writing.

ISBN10: 0–415–18151–8 (hbk)   ISBN10: 0–415–30234–X (pbk)
ISBN13: 978–0–415–18151–8 (hbk)   ISBN13: 978–0–415–30234–0 (pbk)

Available at all good bookshops
For ordering and further information please visit:
www.routledge.com

Routledge History

The Two Cities: Medieval Europe, 1050–1320
Malcolm Barber

'Meets every conceivable need and effectively renders redundant all earlier textbooks on the high Middle Ages ... in short, the book is excellent in every respect.' – *History Today*

First published to wide critical acclaim in 1992, *The Two Cities* has become an essential text for students of medieval history. *The Two Cities* covers a colourful period from the schism between the eastern and western churches to the death of Dante. It encompasses the Crusades, the expansionist force of the Normans, major developments in the way kings, emperors and Popes exercised their powers, a great flourishing of art and architecture and the foundation of the very first universities. Running through it is the defining characteristic of the high Middle Ages – the delicate relationship between the spiritual and secular worlds, the two 'cities' of the title.

For the second edition, the author has thoroughly revised each chapter, bringing the material up to date and taking the historiography of the past decade into account.

ISBN10: 0–415–17414–7 (hbk)   ISBN10: 0–415–17415–5 (pbk)
ISBN13: 978–0–415–17414–5 (hbk)   ISBN13: 978–0–415–17415–2 (pbk)

The Routledge Companion
to Medieval Warfare
Jim Bradbury

'This work of reference in useful ... [it] has some very useful and well–set–out material ... [a] very good handbook.' – *History*

This comprehensive volume provides easily-accessible factual material on all major areas of warfare in the medieval west. The whole geographical area of medieval Europe, including eastern Europe, is covered, including essential elements from outside Europe such as Byzantine warfare, nomadic horde invasions and the Crusades.

Progressing chronologically, the work is presented in themed, illustrated sections, with a narrative outline offering a brief introduction to the area. Within each chronological section, Jim Bradbury presents clear and informative pieces on battles, sieges, and generals.

ISBN10: 0–415–22126–9 (hbk)   ISBN13: 978–0–415–22126–9 (hbk)

Available at all good bookshops
For ordering and further information please visit:
www.routledge.com